David Fahy

D1569164

THE LEGEND OF SEMIMARU
BLIND MUSICIAN OF JAPAN

Studies in Oriental Culture
Number 14
Columbia University

The Legend
of SEMIMARU
Blind Musician of Japan

Susan Matisoff

Columbia University Press

NEW YORK 1978

On the facing page: The Blind Poet Semimaru
Painting attributed to Iwasa Matabei [1578–1650]
Courtesy of the Smithsonian Institution, Freer Gallery of
Art, Washington, D.C.

*The Andrew W. Mellon Foundation, through a special grant,
has assisted the Press in publishing this volume*

Library of Congress Cataloging in Publication Data
Matisoff, Susan, 1940–
The legend of Semimaru, blind musician of Japan.
Revision of the author's thesis.
Bibliography: p.
Includes index.
1. Semimaru, 10th cent.?, in fiction, drama, poetry, etc.
2. Semimaru, 10th cent.?—Authorship.
3. Japanese literature—To 1868—History and criticism.   I. Title.
PL721.S46M37   895.6'09'351   77-24601
ISBN 0-231-03947-6

for Jim

CONTENTS

ACKNOWLEDGMENTS

Throughout the long years I have spent working on the subject of Semimaru I have benefited from the advice and support of many kind people. Only the most crucial are mentioned here, but all who have listened to my complaints and my enthusiasms deserve my thanks.

Research carried out in Japan in 1970 was made possible by a fellowship from the Foreign Area Fellowship Program. Though they bear no responsibility for my conclusions, their initial support is gratefully acknowledged. At that time I was fortunate to receive invaluable advice and assistance from Professors Hamada Keisuke, Iguchi Hiroshi, Yasuda Yukiko, and Yokoyama Tadashi.

A grant from the Japan Foundation took me again to Japan in 1976–77 and provided the opportunity to check remaining details and complete the final stages of the manuscript. I am grateful for the help received in this period from Miss Kawai Masumi and Professors Sakakura Atsuyoshi and Shinoda Jun'ichi.

Typing grants from the Center for East Asian Studies at Stanford University also eased my way and speeded completion of various stages of the manuscript.

The translation of the Nō Semimaru in Part II of this book is a slightly revised version of my original translation which appeared previously in Donald Keene, editor, *Twenty Plays of the Nō Theatre.*

Japanese proper names throughout the book are given in Japanese order, surname first. In a few cases my short form of reference for premodern authors or musicians follows traditional Japanese practice in that these men are commonly referred to by given names or pen names rather than surnames. Thus Akashi Kakuichi, for instance, is known as Kakuichi rather than as Akashi.

Acknowledgments

Several friends and colleagues have offered friendly criticisms and stimulating ideas. Sometimes a subject raised in casual conversation about Semimaru influenced my perceptions long afterward. I particularly want to thank Alton Becker, Karen Brazell, Frank Hoff, and Royall Tyler for their influence on my work, though all of course may disclaim any details they find disagreeable in the final product. In addition, the suggestions made by a reader for Columbia University Press helped me tremendously in transforming my Ph.D. thesis into its present, greatly revised, form as this book. I don't know whom I am thanking, but the thanks are no less sincere for that. Further I am grateful for the efficient assistance of all those at the Press involved in the editing and production of the book.

I can pinpoint my first interest in Japanese literature very precisely to the day during my high school years that I began browsing a secondhand copy of the *Anthology of Japanese Literature*. In that sense my continuing debt of gratitude to its author, Donald Keene, long predates our first meeting. It was he who initially suggested that I translate the Nō *Semimaru*, and as my thesis adviser he went far beyond the usual implications of that role in sustaining and supporting my interest in pursuing the topic.

As many before me have noted, it is those closest to the writer who bear the greatest burden. In my case my daughters Nadja and Alexandra have had the unique experience of growing up with half-comprehended conversations about Semimaru floating in the air. With unbelievable patience they have tolerated a sometimes rather preoccupied mother and have grown to the point of asking informed questions about my research.

Finally, above all, I thank my husband, Jim. When necessary he prodded me to continue. When essential he found time in his own very busy academic professional life to type for me.

Acknowledgments

He has understood and loved me through the work and in the realest sense has made it all possible.

Kyoto
February, 1977

THE LEGEND OF SEMIMARU
BLIND MUSICIAN OF JAPAN

Part I

THE LEGEND

ONE

Semimaru of Ausaka

The legend of Semimaru of Ausaka has endured in Japan for a thousand years. As with any legend of such prolonged vitality, the meaning associated with the name Semimaru has become richer and more complex with the passage of time. The answer to the question, "Who was Semimaru?" would have differed according to the time in history when the question was asked and depending on the social status and education of the respondent. Generally speaking, however, anyone describing Semimaru would have called him a lute player who lived in solitude in a simple straw hut at the place called Ausaka. All would say that he was a beggar, but many would claim that he had once been a prince. Most would add that Semimaru was blind.

These are the most basic general features of the legendary Semimaru. The details are the subject of this book. The growth of the legend is reflected in the body of literary works translated as Part II, ranging from a tenth-century poem attributed to Semimaru to a five-act puppet play from the late seventeenth century. Through this entire literary corpus, some features of Semimaru's identity remain constant while others are added or dropped. Changing historical realities affected the "meaning" of the blind beggar musician and inspired considerable variation in the mood of the many tales and plays concerning him.

The Semimaru legend reached the stage we might consider full maturity in the thirteenth century. It was at this point in history, due in part to the influence of a legend of Indian origin, that Semimaru began to be identified as a prince, born blind, and exiled to a life of poverty. The poignancy of a prince fallen to the level of a beggar has obvious worldwide parallels and was particularly affecting in Japan where society has nearly always shown strong hierarchical gradations.

Japanese emphasis on family lineage and the "genealogy" of schools of every kind of art and craft also played a part in the maturation of the legend. Semimaru was treated as an ancestor of several different types of itinerant performers of low social status. Like many another such figure in this ancestor-venerating society, Semimaru became, for some, the object of sincere adulation. At the high point of his prestige Semimaru was actually "deified," and for a time was revered as a local manifestation of a Bodhisattva.

In the later stages of the legend, a kind of neoclassicism combined with playful inventiveness led to the writing of plays where, in different acts to be sure, Semimaru had both his traditional tragic significance and, simultaneously, new, more lighthearted meanings at variance with the old. This process, whereby the old is preserved at the same time that the new is accepted and treasured in its turn, created a legend which in its sum is both deep and complex in meaning.

Japan has no dearth of literary and dramatic heroes. In comparison to the vast number of texts concerning the ill-starred martial hero Yoshitsune, for example, the total body of Semimaru literature is relatively small and manageable. It can safely be said that all the major literary sources of the Semimaru legend are translated in the second half of this book, yet the familiarity of the Semimaru legend was so great that there are many more texts which mention Semimaru, or Ausaka, in at least a single word or phrase of reference. There would be no point in trying to trace literally every allusion to Semimaru, for at least at the height of his legendary popularity, Semimaru was a name known to all.

If there was one and only one historical individual named

Semimaru of Ausaka

Semimaru, he lived at the latest in the first half of the tenth century, since his name is first recorded in 951. No reliable source from that time remains to reveal his true identity; though the lack of a surname is a clear indication that, whoever he may have been, he was not of high social status.[1]

His name has survived through legend and literature, and many different voices served to shape his "biography." Chapter 2 discusses the principal groups who had a hand in developing the legend of Semimaru. Each group fashioned its own Semimaru, shaping him to their own ends and in their own image. Each group saw Semimaru as its ancestor, and as a prince with the dignity of high social rank.

Clearly, the legendary Semimaru was not just one single historical individual. No one man could have been all that has been claimed for him. Much of the inconsistency, of course, develops gradually during the many overlaid stages of growth of his biography, but it is also possible that back in the tenth century there were, in fact, many Semimarus, that Semimaru was used as the group name of the beggar musicians of Ausaka as well as being the personal name of certain individuals. The name itself requires some consideration.

"Semimaru" consists of the characters 蟬 semi "cicada" and 丸, read maru or maro, which is used independently to indicate round or spherical objects but is also commonly used, from the Nara period, as a second element in male names. By Heian times -maru names were mere nicknames, probably having low-class overtones and sometimes also used for animals.[2] Most famous would be the unfortunate dog Okinamaro whose near-deadly beating is described in Sei Shōnagon's *Makura no sōshi*. In modern times -maru is best known as the final morpheme used in the names of ships.

---

[1] Yoshikawa, "Semimaru setsuwa," p. 200.
[2] Nakayama, *Nihon mōjinshi*, p. 58.

5

The *semi* element of Semimaru was used broadly in Heian Japan in the names of musical instruments and of various types of musical performance, the sound of the cicada being thought extremely beautiful. We know of a *koto* called *semikiyo* "cicada pure," flutes called *semiore* "surpassing the cicada" and *kosemi* "little cicada," and even of a flute called *semimaru*.[3] Moreover, it appears that *semiuta* "cicada song" was the tenth-century name of either a style of vocal performance or of koto music.[4]

Two features of the legend are absolutely fixed. In all cases Semimaru is known as a musician, nearly always a master of the lute. It is Semimaru's identity as a performer and entertainer that has given his legend its greatest sociological significance in Japan. The legendary Semimaru is an archetype of the performing artist in Japan, and, for some, was a virtual "patron saint." From the development of the Semimaru legend we can learn much about the history of the changing meaning and purpose of the performing arts—music, dance, and drama—in Japan. This complicated subject underlies every stage in the discussion of the growth of the legend.

The second fixed feature is the locale of the Semimaru legend: Ausaka. In the most literal sense, Ausaka is a slope about five miles east of the center of modern Kyoto. Its apex is a narrow pass through the eastern range of mountains separating Kyoto from the area of Lake Biwa and the city of Otsu on its southwestern shore. From ancient times Ausaka provided a natural barrier and stopping place on what once was the arduous journey eastward from the Kansai plain. In the rough geographical division of the main island of Honshu into Kanto and Kansai, "east of the barrier" and "west of the barrier," the

---

[3] Yoshikawa, "Semimaru setsuwa," p. 202. The last usage is reminiscent of a koto, also mentioned by Yoshikawa, known as Uda hōshi, "Uda priest."

[4] *Ibid.*, quoting a passage by Sugawara Michizane, in *Ruiju kokushi*, as found in Kokushi taikei, V, 397–400.

barrier in question was a check point at the summit of Ausaka.

The place name Ausaka is as old as the written history of Japan. The name occurs in the *Kojiki*, mentioned as the site of a battle between the forces of the Empress Jingū and certain rebel troops.[5] In the mid-seventh-century reign of the Emperor Kōtoku, before the establishment of the capital in Nara, the Ausaka Pass was the northernmost limit of the realm the emperor considered directly under his own control. In 646 the emperor established a formal, officially manned barrier, *Ausaka no seki*, to control the safety and security of his borders. The barrier fell into disuse in the latter part of the eighth century, was reestablished in the mid-ninth century, but later declined in military importance. Changing political realities affected the tightness or laxity of security at the barrier, but the strategic potential remained constant. Ausaka could always be manned as a means of guarding the Kyoto region. East-west traffic could be controlled and kept under careful observation through this pass. It delineated clearly the outer limit of the area of the capital and marked the beginning of the journey to the east.

The characters used to write the name Ausaka mean "meeting slope." Historical sound change has altered the spelling and pronunciation of this place name until it is now called Osaka. However, throughout this book I have deviated from the modern Japanese transcription for this one word and have retained the earlier spelling Ausaka. In this way the significance of the name of the slope is retained, since the verb *au* means "to meet." In addition, this old spelling serves to differentiate Ausaka from the modern city of Osaka, another place entirely (written with a different first character), where some of the Semimaru plays from the later stages of the legend were written and performed.

While its topography gave Ausaka its strategic significance,

---

[5] *Kojiki,* NKBT, I, 235.

the slope held deep-rooted religious associations as well. Like other remarkable features of the landscape—mountain summits and natural springs of water, for instance—mountain passes were generally viewed as inherently sacred places where men could easily contact the local deities. In the case of mountain passes, the deities in question were believed to guard the safety of travelers.

The word for mountain pass, *tōge* in modern Japanese, is derived from *tamuke* "prayer offerings," which in their original most specific sense were offerings to the gods of mountain passes.[6] Early Japanese poetry offers many examples where the word is used to indicate both the offering of prayers and the crossing of a mountain pass. One of the earliest is the following:

Suwa ni aru	On the day you cross
Iwakuni yama o	The mountains of the rocky land
Koemu hi wa	Of Iwakuni in Suwa,
Tamuke yoku seyo	Make your prayers well,
Arashi sono michi[7]	The way is rough!

Another such poem specifically concerns the Ausaka Pass. This poem, like the previous one, was included in Japan's earliest poetry collection, the *Man'yōshū*. The head note indicates that the poem was written by the Lady Ōtomo of Sakanoue when, "upon going to pray at the Kamo shrine, she crossed Mount Ausaka and looked out at the Lake of Omi."

Yuutatami	Crossing today
Tamuke no yama o	The manifold mountain passes
Kyō koete	Where I offer prayers,

---

[6] Two of the most authoritative modern dictionaries of old Japanese, *Kōjien* and the Iwanami *Kogo jiten,* are in agreement concerning this etymology.

[7] *Man'yōshū,* poem no. 567, NKBT, IV, 267.

Izure no nobe ni	In what field shall I
Iori semu ware[8]	Make my shelter hut?

Beginning, perhaps, with nothing more than a stone cairn, there must have been some simple "shrine" to the deity of Ausaka from the earliest days that travelers crossed the pass. Records from the ninth century refer to the deity of the pass simply as *sakagami,* meaning "slope deity."

At least by the tenth century—and probably much earlier in fact—there was a Shinto shrine building at Ausaka. The earliest history of the shrine is not reliably attested, but the question is academic since we are safe in assuming that the nature of the place had moved passers-by to prayer long before a formal shrine was established.[9] Sometime during or after the tenth century the name of Semimaru came to be associated with the shrine, and its present-day name remains the Semimaru *jinja.* In various records the shrine is associated with a pair of deities—one male and one female. In some cases they are identified otherwise, but after Semimaru's name was associated with the shrine the most common explanation made Semimaru the male deity and Sakagami the female.[10]

In many regions of Japan old stone statues of roadside deities sometimes represented an embracing couple. Particularly in the case of clearly marked boundaries between two areas, such as mountain passes like Ausaka, it was common to conceive of the area as a place of meeting between male and female gods.[11] In several different provinces there are pairs of

[8]*Man'yōshū,* poem no. 1017, NKBT, V, 175.

[9]*Jinja taikan,* p. 430, indicating that the record is imprecise, dates Semimaru's association with this shrine from 958. Yamagami Tadamaro in Hayashiya *et al.,* "Semimaru o megutte," p. 27, gives the year as 946 but does not ascribe a source for his information.

[10]*Jinja taikan,* p. 430.

[11]Yashiro, *Sakai no kamigami,* discusses the legends of the gods of numerous boundaries in the early Japanese landscape. See especially

9

mountain peaks known as Imoyama and Seyama—or jointly as Imoseyama. The term *imose* denotes a couple, understood as brother and sister or, more commonly, as lovers. In such cases of paired mountain peaks, the pass between the mountains was the place of meeting of the pair. In the case of Ausaka, slope of meeting, it is most likely that the name ultimately derives from the identification of the pass as a trysting place for mountain god lovers.

The gods met at Ausaka and there too man "met" the gods and offered prayers for safety in travel; but there was yet another sense in which Ausaka became the slope of meeting. A custom known as *sakamukae* "slope greetings" was commonly practiced at Ausaka for the benefit of travelers leaving and returning to the capital. Since Ausaka was the outermost boundary of the capital area, well-wishers would escort friends or family departing toward the east as far as this point, offering their prayers and wishes for safe travel. In cases where a newly appointed provincial governor was departing for his post, these send-offs may have reached major proportions. The slope of meeting was also deemed the appropriate place to greet homecoming travelers. Particularly for those returning from pilgrimages to the great shrine at Ise, the custom was carefully observed; but any traveler might properly be greeted, welcomed, and congratulated on his return to Ausaka.

Some believed that without a meeting party of sakamukae Sakagami, the god of the slope, might be angered and interfere with the traveler's safe return.[12] Formally or informally, in large groups or small, inhabitants of the capital must have had frequent occasion to walk out to Ausaka and offer greetings to their traveling friends and prayers to Sakagami. In times of di-

---

pp. 10 and 37 concerning these areas as the meeting place of male and female principles.

[12]Origuchi, *Origuchi Shinobu zenshū*, X, 289.

saster in the capital—plague for instance—purification rituals also were held at Ausaka and at the comparable boundaries in the other cardinal directions outside Kyoto, in the hopes of placating the anger of the gods causing the misfortune. In addition to Ise, the great temples Ishiyamadera and Miidera were also reached by journeying through Ausaka Pass; various sorts of religious outings and pilgrimages thus took Ausaka as their point of departure. All traffic to the east departed through this route, and immediately along the footroad itself, Ausaka was a busy, lively place.

The concept of Ausaka as a place of meeting very early became a poetic convention.[13] The name itself, as well as historical reality, suggested Ausaka as an appropriate spot at which to compose poems concerning meeting. Much of the art of composition of the classical Japanese verse form, the *waka*, lay in knowing the conventional associations of specific places and somehow using these set images in a fresh and interesting manner in writing a new poem.

It was considered proper to find inspiration from the same features of a place that had moved earlier poets. In the case of Ausaka, the meeting and parting of travelers, as immortalized in the first poem attributed to Semimaru, inspired countless later poetic efforts. Certain specific features of the landscape or

[13] In the *Man'yōshū*, the fixed epithet, or *makura kotoba*, regularly associated with Ausaka was *wagimoko ni [au/saka]*. *Imoko* had the ambiguous meaning of "little sister" or "beloved," and the underlying meaning of the makura kotoba is basically "Ausaka where I meet *with my beloved.*" Makura kotoba are different from the *utamakura* of *waka* in that their usage served a decorative function associated more with sound than with specific places. For instance, any mountain might be called *ashibiki no [yama]*, "foot-dragging" mountain, and any use of the sound *au* might inspire the makura kotoba *wagimoko ni*. In addition to Ausaka, this makura kotoba was linked to the place name Awaji or to the plant name *auchi* (modern *ōchi*), the Japanese bead tree.

11

characteristic plants found in a particular area might also become fixed poetic conventions known as *utamakura*, literally
"poem pillows." At Ausaka *seki no shimizu*, a spring of "pure
water by the barrier," was one persistent utamakura, and reference to Semimaru by name or to the Ausaka shrine could
also be counted on as ready-made "pillows."

Travel was an especially suitable occasion for poetic composition, and given the amount of traffic through Ausaka, the
large number of poems concerning the place is understandable. The repertoire includes both occasional poetry written upon passing Ausaka, and references to Ausaka included
in *michiyuki*—lyrical, though highly conventionalized songs of
travel included within longer literary forms, most notably
Nō plays and later puppet dramas.

This Ausaka poetry generally concerned the immediate area
of the barrier and the bustling traffic directly along the trail;
the surrounding slopes, however, were steep, and away from
the trail itself the area was evidently largely uninhabited, at
least through Heian times (794–1160). Not only in the case of
Semimaru, but also for the famous Heian woman poet Ono no
Komachi, the Ausaka area was considered a place of quiet,
desolate isolation. Legends of Komachi's last years, spent in
the Ausaka area, were in sharp contrast to the tales of her
younger life in Kyoto.[14] For both these legendary figures, Ausaka became a place of contemplation. For the wary traveler, as
well as for the solitary meditator, Ausaka could be a place of
meeting with the unknown, a location conducive to contacting
the gods, or, in Buddhist terms, a place well-suited to attaining enlightenment.

The evidence of poetry suggests that from very early times
the area of the Ausaka Pass was noted for the characteristic
music performed there. The following four poems are representative:

[14]See particularly the Nō *Sekidera Komachi*.

Semimaru of Ausaka

Ausaka no	Not having seen
Seki no anata mo	The far side of
Mada mineba	Ausaka barrier
Azuma no koto mo	They know not of
Shirarezarekeri [15]	The *koto* of the East.
Ausaka no	Even as I thought
Seki no iori to	"These are the huts
Omou ni mo	Of Ausaka barrier,"
Azuma no koto zo	The sound of an Eastern *koto*
Mi ni wa shimikeru [16]	Pierced my soul.
Ausaka no	*Koto* melodies
Seki no iori no	About the huts
Koto no ne wa	At Ausaka barrier
Fukaki kozue no	Deep among the branches
Matsukaze zo fuku	Pine winds blow.
Hikitomete	Drawn to a stop,
Ureshi to zo omou	How glad I was
Kimi ni kesa	To meet you yesterday
Ausaka yama no	At Mount Ausaka
Seki no shirabe wa [17]	Because of the barrier music.

The poems, particularly with their reference to the "huts" at Ausaka, point to a long-standing tradition of performance of

[15] This poem is by Ōe no Masahira (952–1012); poem no. 938, *Goshūiwakashū*, [Kochū] kokka taikei, III, 722.

[16] This poem is by the priest Jakuren (?–1202). It is included, along with the next poem given here, by Fujiwara Ietaka (1158–1237) in *Fuboku wakashō*, which was compiled in the late thirteenth century. [Kochū] kokka taikei, XXII, 479.

[17] By the priest Jien (1155–1225). *Shugyokushū*, [Kochū] kokka taikei, X, 816. In light of these four poems, Yoshikawa suggests that *Azuma no koto*, "the koto of the East," may in fact have referred to this music of the eastern pass rather than, as more commonly accepted, music from the eastern provinces. Yoshikawa, "Semimaru setsuwa," p. 208.

13

some kind of music at Ausaka by poor musicians who found shelter there in simple huts. Since the basic image of Semimaru is that of a beggar musician in a hut at Ausaka, it is clear that his legend is rooted in a broader historical reality. As the later chapters of this book will show, musicians and performers of various sorts have been, throughout the many centuries of growth of the Semimaru legend, associated with the shrine at Ausaka.

Semimaru's instrument, according to legend, was the *biwa*, the lute, rather than the *koto*, a term which in its most specific sense denotes a kind of horizontal harp. But since *koto* could also be used as a general term for "stringed instrument" in Japanese, these poems might also refer to musicians who, like the Semimaru of legend, played the lute at Ausaka. The legend of Semimaru as a specific individual doubtless developed out of many centuries' tradition of beggar musicians at Ausaka. Semimaru was, in effect, a composite individual, the literary personification of the many poor beggars to be found through the centuries at Ausaka.[18]

Why, then, should there have been beggar musicians at Ausaka? What was the significance of such performers and why were they associated with this specific place? Above all, why did such apparently insignificant characters have the potential to inspire an enduring, profoundly moving legend?

The answers to these questions are connected to the early meaning of musical performance in Japan. Arts which in later centuries were simply entertainment, oriented toward delighting an audience of ordinary, paying mortals, had their roots in performances which once served a religious function.

Evidence in various forms attests to the fact that music and dance were used from the earliest days in Japan as a means of

---

[18] Yoshikawa, "Semimaru setsuwa," p. 204. This was also the general conclusion reached by Nakayama Tarō in his *Nihon mōjinshi,* a study of the history of the blind in Japan.

summoning and communicating with the gods. The earliest
foreign account of Japan, a description written by a party of
Chinese who had visited its shores, remarks on the use of
song and dance as a part of a funeral ceremony. Performances
of entertaining songs and dances might serve to attract the notice of the gods and bring the deities' attention to bear on
questions or problems raised by the performers.

The *Kojiki* of 712, the earliest extant semihistorical Japanese
written record, includes instances of divination carried out by
mediums who attained their communication with the gods
through trances induced by the sound of the koto. In addition,
certain poetic passages in the *Kojiki* ending with a phrase
thought to mean "and this was the chant of the koto" were apparently the lyrics of performances combining words, music,
and dance which had the purpose of pleasing the gods. Such
songs are known as *kamugatari* "god chants," or *amagatari uta*
"songs chanted to heaven." While we can assume that the entertainment value of such offerings also pleased the bystanders
who witnessed the performance, support for the performance
could be understood as a means of deriving benefit from contact with the gods.

One of the best-known early Japanese myths reflects the use
of a kind of kamugatari entertainment to rouse the curiosity of
the sun goddess, to bring her out of hiding, and to return her
to the proper humor to favor her devotees.[19] The earliest performers were evidently shamanistic mediums who were capable of bringing themselves into a trance state through the use
of music and dance. The entranced shamanic performer summoned the god and became finally the visible embodiment of
the god, speaking or singing in trance with the voice of the
unseen deity.

[19] Yamagami, "Koto no katarigoto," discusses kamugatari and
amagatari uta, their musical accompaniment, and their similarity to
the mythological dance of entertainment for the sun goddess.

The oldest Shinto shrines in Japan often include a dance stage used historically for the performance of *Kagura,* a form of dance offered before the gods, which developed out of the shamanic tradition. Though these performances soon lost their shamanistic overtones, until the development of commercial theaters in the major cities in the seventeenth century shrine and temple compounds remained the most common stages for the performance of all sorts of music and dance.

Traces of the traditional power of music to summon the gods remain evident in various aspects of later performance. Plays concerning *monogurui*—deranged people who cannot keep themselves from dancing and ranting—seem to derive from the tradition of dances of ecstatic possession. Performers who chanted the medieval epic *Heike monogatari* were sometimes believed to be able to placate the spirits of dead martial heroes celebrated in their songs.[20] The principal role in many Nō plays turns out, as the play develops, to represent the visible embodiment of a god or a ghost.

One of the most striking phenomena of the history of Japanese folk performance is the frequency with which an actor dressed to represent a god is actually accepted as an embodiment of the god.[21] Perhaps precisely because of their assumed ability to communicate with powerful superhuman forces, many different types of folk performers seem to have been viewed by society with an attitude compounded of both awe and scorn. The performer capable of entering trance and speaking as a god was thrilling, but also threatening, possessed of a discomforting, awesome power.

Thoughout the early centuries of Japanese history, many different groups of musical performers, dancers, and actors—pos-

[20] As evidenced, for instance, by the folktale of Miminashi ("Earless") Hōichi who lost his ears to angry ghosts who wished to keep him constantly by their side playing his soothing lute.

[21] Hori, *Waga kuni minkan shinkō,* I, 709.

sessed in greater or lesser degree with these strange powers—
lived on the fringes of society. Many were treated as beggars
or outcasts, shunned except for the intermediary role they
could play on behalf of the patrons who supported them.

Many performers, especially prior to the Tokugawa period
(1600–1887), were at least seminomadic.[22] They might wander
from village to village, appearing as strangers who through
their performances impersonated or communicated with the
gods. From the seventeenth century such itinerants were
largely forced by the Tokugawa government to settle in fixed
villages, and their performances tended to become seasonal,
clustered particularly around the New Year. Their social standing evidently became ever lower, and the religious significance of the performances they offered became gradually
weaker and weaker.

Such folk performers may be seen as developing originally
out of the native Shinto religious tradition, wherein they were
necessary intermediaries between this world and the world of
the gods, but many kinds of performance, in fact, had Buddhist overtones as well. Among the complex variety of lowly
semireligious performers, some served to popularize basic
Buddhist teachings among the folk. A typical example might
be the *etoki* or "picture explainers," men and women who
created simple entertainment out of their comments on Buddhist pictures such as scenes of heavens or hells. In any case,
the syncretism of Japanese popular religion was such that it is
rarely meaningful to speak of the art of the performer as specifically "Shinto" or "Buddhist."

From the Kamakura through the Muromachi era, roughly

---

[22]The range of different arts having this characteristic of itinerancy
was quite broad, especially in the Muromachi period. The January,
1973, issue of the periodical *Kokubungaku kaishaku to kanshō* is a
special issue concerning this subject with a number of specialized articles.

speaking Japan's "Middle Ages," from the late twelfth to late sixteenth centuries, many types of itinerant, low-class entertainers were known by names which included the term *hōshi* "priest."[23] Thus a male etoki would be called an *etoki hōshi* "picture-explaining priest," and his female counterpart would be an *etoki bikuni* "picture-explaining nun." Performers of *sarugaku* and *dengaku*, two of the folk antecedents of Nō drama, were similarly known as *sarugaku hōshi* and *dengaku hōshi*, and the group whose history is most immediately connected with the early development of the Semimaru legend were known as *biwa hōshi* "lute priests." Inevitably, the term hōshi dropped out of usage as a designation for formally ordained priests, being replaced by other terminology, but its continued use in the names for these many types of simple folk performers reflects within a folk Buddhist context the underlying understanding of the semireligious function of the performing arts.

Beginning around the tenth century there was a noticeable influx of impoverished, overtaxed peasants into the protective domains of certain major Buddhist temples. It was evidently a fairly simple matter for those who left their lands to identify themselves at least symbolically as "priests." An eyewitness account from the year 914 still conveys the near-hysterical disapproval felt by an upperclass courtier who wrote concerning the phenomenon:

> In every province there are peasants who flee from taxation and conscripted labor; cutting off their own hair, without authority they wear priestly robes. There are crowds of people like this and with the passing years their numbers are gradually increasing. Two-thirds of the common people have become baldpates of this sort. They all have households and support wives and children. They eat raw, rotten animal flesh. In appearance they

[23] Hori, *Waga kuni minkan shinkō*, II, 376.

18

resemble monks, but in their hearts they are like butchers.[24]

The impoverished peasants described with such evident disgust by this observer likely included some who received food and lodging in exchange for taking care of such simple services as cleaning the temple grounds, but from among this pseudo-priestly group those whose lives had a bearing on the Semimaru legend were the many types of simple entertainers whose performances helped draw congregations to the temple grounds or helped carry elementary Buddhist teachings to the market places and crossroads where an audience might be gathered together. In chapter 2 some of these groups are discussed in greater detail.

Evidence from later ages suggests that the performers at Ausaka may have lived on lands belonging to Buddhist temples in Otsu and Kyoto, walking out to perform under simple temporary shelters at the Ausaka barrier where the abundance of travelers would always guarantee a good-sized audience. As we have seen, some of the travelers through Ausaka were departing or returning from religious pilgrimages. For the pilgrim, travel itself was a diversion from daily life. At wayside stops along the route, such as at Ausaka, the pilgrim was prepared to reward the priestly-attired entertainer who enlivened the journey. At Ausaka, as everywhere through the passing centuries, the role of the performer gradually changed from shamanic intermediary to folk proselytizer to secular entertainer. Much of the specific detail of the Semimaru legend is pure creative invention, but throughout there remains an undertone of the notion that Semimaru, the beggar lutenist, is blessed with extraordinary vision and understanding transcending that enjoyed by ordinary people.

This leads directly to the question of Semimaru's blindness.

[24]Miyoshi, "Iken jūni kajō," in *Gunsho ruijū,* XVII, 127.

THE LEGEND

The blind have played a key role in the history of Japanese shamanism. Most shamans were women, but blind men also served in this capacity. Even today in certain remote regions of northeastern Japan, a few old blind women still occasionally practice a sort of divination which is the modern remnant of shamanic tradition. In pre-Buddhist Japan, the blind were apparently understood to be particularly capable of communication with the gods. In more recent times as well, the congenitally blind in some areas have been trained from childhood to become shamanic intermediaries. This underlying belief in the spiritual "sight" of the blind also helps account for the large number of blind biwa hōshi and even the existence of blind "picture explainers."

However, the Buddhist world view judged blindness in a manner quite opposite to that of earlier native Japanese tradition. In the Buddhist view, blindness, like other congenital or incurable disabilities such as deafness or leprosy, was seen as a sort of divine retribution for misconduct in a previous incarnation. These illnesses, caused by the negative karma accrued in a former lifetime, dictated that the afflicted use this present incarnation as an opportunity to acquire merit, through austerities and faith, in the hopes of improvement in subsequent incarnations.

Compounded out of these different attitudes, society's feelings toward the blind naturally were quite ambivalent. The blind were apparently objects of pity, fear, ridicule, and awe in variously mixed proportions. Like Semimaru, the blind warrior Kagekiyo, for example, inspired a legend of considerable depth. Also reminiscent of certain aspects of the Semimaru legend are numerous folktales, some used to suggest a Buddhist moral, in which the blind, the deaf, and the incurably ill are rewarded for faith in the midst of their afflictions.[25]

[25] Such stories have considerable antiquity in Japan. Many are to be found in the early ninth-century text *Nihon ryōiki* as well as in later collections of Buddhist moral tales both in Chinese and in Japanese.

Semimaru of Ausaka

As the variety of themes touched upon in this introduction indicates, the Semimaru legend is neither simple nor totally constant in its import. Semimaru is without strong individual characterization and has different new associations with changing times. Herein, in fact, lies a good part of the interest of the legend, for its vitality, ironically, is reflected by the extent to which it could change and thereby acquire new layers of meaning.

TWO

The Background Affecting the Legend

Throughout the entire millennium of its existence, the legend of Semimaru has been affected by the activities and goals of a wide variety of singers, musicians, and other popular entertainers, both laymen and priests. Many of the men whose lives and livelihoods helped shape the Semimaru legend were themselves of very humble social status. History has taken little note of them. Yet to understand the various stages of the Semimaru legend, it is necessary to recreate, however tentatively, a picture of the historical developments underlying its growth.

Much of the history which follows in this chapter is necessarily speculative. Music is by its very nature ephemeral, and it is difficult to speak authoritatively of the possible influence of one form of music on another when the performance traditions in question are extinct and have left no clear notation. Many musicians who venerated Semimaru were blind, yet we can hardly hope to find reliable contemporary records written by the blind in a world without Braille.

At times low social status, too, affected the self-image that popular performers strove to present to the world at large. Their desire to create for themselves a socially acceptable, or even admirable, lineage of descent not only necessitated their invention of historical records, it radically affected the course of development of the Semimaru legend as well.

Semimaru's name in legend is almost always associated with the stringed instrument known in Japan as the biwa. Basically similar to the Western lute, the biwa has existed in Japan in several different forms.

The Gaku Biwa

The instrument antecedent to the first Japanese biwa originated in Persia or Central Asia, then was carried into China during the Han dynasty, at the latest by the end of the second century. It was utilized in China as an ensemble instrument, and the first record of a performance in Japan by both the biwa and its confederate instruments of the ensemble dates from 702. This was a court performance which celebrated the first full moon of the year. Such ensemble music is known in Japan as *gagaku*, and lutes of this variety as *gaku biwa*. Gagaku is preserved to this day as ceremonial music performed annually at court.[1]

The gaku biwa has four strings and four bridges. The upper section of the neck, including the area to which the pegs are affixed, is bent back at an oblique angle to the plane of the body of the biwa. In Heian Japanese performance style the lute was held with the strings horizontal. Sitting cross-legged and holding the instrument with its neck to the left, the performer pressed with the fingers of the left hand directly on the strings as they pass over the relatively low bridges. The musician's right hand held the *bachi*, or plectrum, with which he might strike the strings in several fashions. The most common attack was the arpeggio, several or all strings in one stroke. Strings could be struck individually, and there was also a technique which involved "scooping" a string with the corner of the bachi. Performance styles were complex and varied, and skill in playing gaku biwa was an admired pastime for both men

[1]Information on gaku biwa is based primarily on two works by Tanabe Hisao: *Nihon ongakushi*, pp. 125–31, and *Nihon no gakki*, pp. 76–83.

23

and women of the court. The usual gaku biwa was a bit over 100 centimeters in length, though slightly smaller and more portable versions called *ko-biwa* "small biwa" were also used.

Biwa were prized gifts from China to the Japanese court. The earliest examples of gaku biwa in Japan, preserved to this day, were received from China in 756.[2]

The Emperor Nimmyō (r. 833–50) was a great fancier of the biwa, and the time of his court marked a period of intense receptivity to this Chinese instrument. Fujiwara Sadatoshi (807–67), an adept performer, having taken up his family's tradition of lute playing, was sent to China as part of a great embassy commissioned in 835 by the emperor.[3] Sadatoshi and the others of his mission finally succeeded in reaching China in 838, returning the following year. In China Sadatoshi studied with a famous lute teacher, Liu Erh-lang, learning from him a repertoire of solo, as opposed to ensemble, pieces for lute performance. History records that the Emperor Nimmyō was "greatly pleased" by Sadatoshi's first concert before him shortly after his return to Japan.[4]

Individual instruments were often great works of art in their own right. On the most beautiful lutes a leather covering over the area struck by the plectrum was decorated with a painted design. The wooden surface of the body might be inlaid with mother-of-pearl. An instrument could be known by a "pet name" and passed down as a treasured family possession. For instance, one of the instruments which Sadatoshi himself brought back from China, a gift from his teacher, Liu, was called Seizan "Green Mountain." Modern music historians suggest realistically that the name derived from the painting on the leather surface,[5] but early Japanese tradition proposed a

---

[2] Yamagami, "Koto no katarigoto," p. 88.
[3] Reischauer, *Ennin's Travels*, p. 52 *et passim* describes the embassy.
[4] Tanabe, *Nihon ongakushi*, p. 78.
[5] Tanabe, *Nihon no gakki*, p. 76.

The Background

more exotic explanation. According to one account, as Sadatoshi was receiving instruction from his teacher, angels descended from the heavens, lit on the branches of the trees on
the green mountains near the lute master and his pupil, and
twirled the white sleeves of their celestial robes. Astonished
by this good omen, the master named the lute "Green Mountain," and presented it to Sadatoshi.[6]
   Sadatoshi acquired more than instruments alone from Liu
Erh-lang. Another important gift was instruction in three
tunes, called "Ryūsen," "Takuboku," and "Yōshinsō,"
which came to be known in Japan as the "secret melodies."[7]
Contemporary sources indicate that these three melodies were
a closely guarded mystery, and techniques of performance
were taught to only one disciple per master. Such secrecy has
been a common pattern in many fine arts of the upper strata of
traditional Japanese society.
   From Sadatoshi's time on, solo lute recitals assumed an importance in the Japanese court at least equal to and probably
surpassing the more formal performances of the gagaku orchestra. Many literary sources credit Semimaru with knowledge of the repertoire of secret melodies which were presumably familiar only in court circles and performed only by a
chosen few. However, Semimaru did not necessarily learn to
play the lute at court. The courtly tradition is but the first of
two distinct lines of development of the lute in Japan with
which the name of Semimaru has been associated.

Early Biwa Hōshi

   A second tradition of lute performance grew outside court
circles. The poems and diaries of literate aristocrats provide
the earliest glimpses of noncourtier lute players, and it is easy

[6]*Gempei seisuiki*, pp. 172–73.
[7]Tanabe, *Nihon ongakushi*, p. 168.

25

to see that biwa hōshi, or "lute priests," as such men were called, were alien, somewhat mysterious figures in the eyes of the courtiers who described them.

Taira Kanemori, sometime before his death in 990, collected in his personal poetry collection, the *Kanemori shū*, several of his poems describing various occupations of his day. One of these, entitled "Biwa no hōshi," presents the first picture of a lutenist from outside the courtly tradition. It depicts an itinerant stranger who supported himself by playing his biwa:

Yotsu no o ni	On the four strings
Omou kokoro o	He plays out
Shirabetsutsu	His feelings,
Hikiarikedomo	Wanders about
Shiru hito mo nashi[8]	Yet no one knows him.

Though Kanemori's poem may be an overstatement in saying "no one knows him," it does demonstrate that no one who mattered to Kanemori, that is to say, no one from his courtly environment, would be acquainted with a *biwa hōshi*, an unknown wanderer.

Another, later, poem by Minamoto Shunrai (?1057–1129), in his personal poetry collection, *Sambokuki Kashū*, conjures up the image of a biwa hōshi Shunrai saw while on a journey, performing by a remote river ferry in northern Kyushu. Shunrai notes: "At Ashiya I faintly heard the sounds of a biwa hōshi playing his lute, and it called to my mind memories of the past."

Nagarekuru	The strings of a *biwa*
Hodo no shizuku ni	Tuned to the flow
Biwa no o o	Of trickling water.
Hikiawasete mo	Drawn by the sound,
Nururu sode kana[9]	Tears soak my sleeves.

[8]Hayashiya, *Chūsei geinōshi no kenkyū*, p. 321.   [9]*Ibid.*

The Background

To the courtier's mind, the biwa hōshi apparently raised associations of journeying into remote isolation. In *Genji monogatari* when Genji is exiled to Akashi Bay, the aged ex-governor of the district entertains his visitor by playing his lute. The author's comment is that the old gentleman is making of himself a biwa hōshi.[10]

In the *Shin sarugakuki*, by Fujiwara Akihira, a document describing popular entertainments which dates from between 1058 and 1065, there occurs the intriguing phrase "tales of a biwa hōshi."[11] This has often been cited as evidence that at least by the mid-eleventh century, possibly much earlier, biwa hōshi were reciting some sort of oral narratives as well as singing with the lute. The later history of biwa hōshi is relatively well-documented, but the origins and early activities of the biwa hōshi have been the subject of much speculation.[12]

As the term "lute priest" suggests, biwa hōshi had shaved heads and wore the garb of Buddhist clergy. Evidently they were itinerant pilgrims who traveled from one community to the next finding shelter and sustenance at temples, traditional asylums for the lame, the ill, or the blind. As informal "priests," the biwa hōshi may have recited legends of the history of various temples and shrines and reported miracles attributed to the deities worshiped there.

These traveling musician storytellers also carried news and local legends. Most likely some were humorous raconteurs. They were important newsbearers, bringing word of developments in the outside world to remote villages in the course of their wanderings. News of the great battles of the Gempei

---

[10]*Genji monogatari,* NKBT, XV, 71.

[11]Tanabe, *Nihon ongakushi,* p. 129.

[12]A good overview of possible early biwa hōshi activity is found in a brief article by Tomikura Tokujirō, "Biwa hōshira no yakuwari," pp. 76–79.

27

war, signaling the end of the Heian period, developed into heroic battle tales sung by provincial biwa hōshi.[13]

It is clear that the biwa hōshi were not themselves courtiers, nor were they, in the Heian period at least, in close contact with those well-bred gentlemen who amused themselves by playing the lute. In fact, the instruments played by biwa hōshi were different from the gaku biwa of the Heian court. To find the ancestor of the biwa hōshi lute one must look back again to the lute's homeland in Persia and trace a separate line of historical development which led to the introduction of the biwa into the southern Japanese island of Kyushu.

The Mōsō Biwa

Sometime after the beginning of the Christian era, most likely in the second century, the Persian lute was carried into India.[14] There its evolution was affected by the native Indian *vina*. In India there was a traditional specialized use of this instrument of immediate relevance to the history of biwa hōshi. There the lute was played by blind men, described as priests, who traveled about chanting a sutra intended to placate violent local deities. According to Indian legend, this practice originated at the suggestion of Buddha himself. As the Buddha Shakyamuni sat preaching to a gathering of ardent disciples, he took note of the blindness of one of those in his audience. Out of pity for the blind man, known in Japan as Gankutsu Sonja, he presented him with a lute and taught him to perform the calming sutra. Blind itinerant Indian lute priests transmitted this story as the explanation of the origin of their profession. The lute, however, was not known in India

[13]Tomikura, "Akashi Kakuichi o megutte," pp. 37–41, discusses the later influence of these tales.

[14]Information on mōsō biwa derived from Tanabe, *Nihon onga-kushi*, pp. 125–30, and *Nihon no gakki*, pp. 83–88.

in the lifetime of the historical Buddha, and the legend seems, in fact, to postdate the development of the Indian lute. It has been suggested that this account was developed by blind Indian lute priests in an attempt to elevate their own social position. Indian lute priests apparently moved into China around A.D. 230–40. Very little is known of the history of these performers in China, but after the first of them brought the instrument into Kyushu, its use became widespread in southern Japan, where the performers were, according to their own later records, called simply *mōsō* "blind priests." Though there has been some disagreement among scholars concerning this point, it appears that the biwa hōshi referred to in the courtiers' poems and diaries cited above were the descendants of the mōsō of Kyushu.[15]

To distinguish it from the gaku biwa of the courtly tradition, the instrument carried by the mōsō is, appropriately, known as the *mōsō biwa*. Having resulted from the "marriage" of the Persian lute and the vina, it has a straight neck, four strings, and five bridges, considerably higher than the bridges of the gaku biwa.

The mōsō biwa was about four-fifths the size of the gaku biwa, while its plectrum was relatively larger. As with the vina, this lute was played by pressing, with the first three fingers of the left hand, between, rather than on, the bridges. The manner of performance involved striking the strings with

[15] Tanabe, *Nihon ongakushi*, pp. 129–30, insists that mōsō and biwa hōshi chanters of *Heike monogatari* were completely separate groups. Yet in writing of the origins of the Heike biwa, he suggests mōsō influence. Kikkawa, *Nihon ongaku no rekishi*, p. 60, differs with Tanabe, finding no other possible antecedents for the biwa hōshi if mōsō are ruled out. Tomikura, "Biwa hōshira no yakuwari," p. 77, states that he feels a "religious function," like that of mōsō, was common to all biwa hōshi.

the plectrum faster and more harshly than was the custom with the gaku biwa. In contrast to the arpeggios of gaku biwa performance, the strings of the mōsō biwa were commonly struck singly to produce a melodic line.[16]

Like their Indian antecedents, the mōsō of Kyushu used their biwa as accompaniment to the chanting of sutras for the purpose of placating and calming local deities of the earth. Their principal text, called *Jishinkyō*, was the ninth chapter of the Konkomyo sutra. Recitation of this text was believed to help ensure the fertility of the soil and an abundant harvest.

The services of mōsō were believed necessary to ensure successful harvests and as a means of satisfying the hearth god of each local farmhouse. So basic were the gods served or rather subdued by mōsō that a performance by lute priests seems to have been desired by every household in the areas in which they were active. They offered assurances, if not insurance, against fire and disaster.

Since early Japanese traditionally used song to contact and placate the native gods, the *kami*, it is not at all surprising that this simple Buddhist ceremonial to ensure the benevolence of the gods of hearth and harvest was deemed necessary and welcome by the Japanese peasantry. The blind, too, would have seemed the natural candidates to perform such rites since they were credited in Japan with extraordinary ability in communicating with invisible, yet very powerful, natural forces.

Though much etiolated and now preserved as a matter of antiquarian interest rather than active religious faith, mōsō biwa is still performed today in two areas of Kyushu. The tradition as preserved in the northern areas of the island is known as Chikuzen mōsō, centered in modern Fukuoka province. The southern tradition, called Satsuma mōsō, is based in Kumamoto. There are certain dif-

---

[16]Kikkawa, *Nihon ongaku no rekishi,* p. 108. His descriptions of performance style are based on modern practices of Kyushu mōsō.

ferences in the lutes and characteristic performance styles of
the two areas, but the general practice is identical: recitation
with lute accompaniment of *Jishinkyō,* the sutra for pacification of the deities of the land.

Each of these two long-standing schools has its own written
record explaining the history and development of its arts. Both
texts date from the mid-Tokugawa period and purport to document events from as far back as the sixth century. Though
not strictly reliable as historical sources, they are of great interest. While some of the details must be rejected as self-glorify-
ing invention on the part of the mōsō, the general outlines
of their history, presented in both texts, are accepted as accurate by music historians.[17]

Both sources avow that Chinese blind lute priests introduced the chanting of Jishinkyō to Kyushu during the
reign of Emperor Kimmei (539–71). They describe the first Japanese who learned this art from one of the Chinese priests as a
youngster, son of a local official, who had become blind and
was living in a cave in Udo in Hyuga (modern Myiazaki prefecture). Later, on the occasion of building the imperial palace
at the beginning of the Nara era, several mōsō, according
to these accounts, were summoned to Nara to practice their
rites in order to ensure the safety of the ground on which the
palace would be built. Similarly, when the Enryakuji, the Tendai monastic complex on Mount Hiei, east of Kyoto, was founded, mōsō were summoned from Kyushu to pacify the
spirits of the mountain and to ensure the propitious begin-
nings of the monastery.

Later in the Nara period a famous mōsō from the Hakata area, Gensei, traveled up to the capital, presumably accompanied by a number of his fellow mōsō. There Gensei
founded a tradition of mōsō under the control of the Ten-

[17]Tanabe, *Nihon ongakushi,* pp. 127–29, presents an outline of the
features common to both traditional accounts.

31

dai sect known as the Tendai Bussetsushū, the "Tendai Buddha-expounding sect." Gensei thereafter returned to Hakata and established the headquarters of the Chikuzen mōsō line.

On Gensei's return to Kyushu, a number of his followers remained in the region of the capital, continuing his work in establishing mōsō activity in the area. The center of the school was at Mount Ausaka, at a small temple founded by one of Gensei's followers and known as the Myōon-den. According to the Satsuma mōsō text, Semimaru was the fourth head of the Myōon-den.

The center of mōsō control, around the time of this mysterious Semimaru, was moved from Mount Ausaka to an area called Shinobi, central to the Mount Hiei monastery complex. At the beginning of the Kamakura period, when Minamoto Yoritomo dispatched Shimazu Tadahisa to control southern Kyushu, the nineteenth head of the *myōon mōsō* tradition from Shinobi accompanied Tadahisa to pray for his peaceful success in the south. This mōsō, called in the Satsuma text Hōzan-kengyō, was considered the founder of the Satsuma school of mōsō biwa.

It is in the very nature of such documents—their purpose of securing some social status and prestige—that they claim in the ancestry of the group close personal connections with eminent historical individuals. We need not give much credence to the idea that the first Japanese student mōsō was necessarily the son of an important official, nor that the emperor himself invited mōsō to Nara, nor that it was Saichō, founder of the Tendai sect, who requested the assistance of mōsō. But stripped of the details of precise individuals and events, the general outlines of mōsō history as discernible through this account are accepted by music historians.

That is to say, mōsō are believed to have been active in

The Background

Kyushu shortly before the Nara period and to have become established in the area of the capital and Mount Hiei around the early ninth century. When first active in this area, the mōsō were under the control and protection of the powerful Tendai sect, but that control weakened or was totally severed after the return of mōsō leaders to Kyushu around the end of the Heian or early Kamakura period.

Then there is the vexing question of Semimaru. The Satsuma mōsō text which mentions him dates from Tokugawa times when Semimaru was a well-known name, popular among new urban audiences through several successful puppet plays and works for the Kabuki theater. It is possible that the Satsuma mōsō record seized on Semimaru as a famous name from the right place at the right time. But it is also possible that Semimaru was, in fact, the fourth leader of a mōsō tradition based in Ausaka. The timing is exactly right if we believe that the Ausaka mōsō tradition was founded in the early ninth century and Semimaru was a man of the early tenth.

There simply is not adequate evidence by which to determine whether or not Semimaru was truly the fourth head of the mōsō at Ausaka. It is possible, but not provable. It is not difficult to accept the notion of mōsō activity at Ausaka, however.[18] The original, primary function of mōsō was the pacification of local deities. Through the recitation of simple sutras, they were understood to calm the resident spirits of a given locale. At Ausaka, the local deity was Sakagami, spirit of the slope. Since Ausaka was the departure point for journeys away from the safety of the capital, a service of propitiation of Sakagami would help the traveler depart

[18] Kadokawa, "Katarimono to Jishin mōsō," pp. 110–13, accepts the tradition that mōsō were active at Ausaka, and believes they were supported by several major religious institutions in the Kyoto area.

secure in the knowledge that his journey was not offensive to the gods. The mōsō of Ausaka could intercede with the local god on the traveler's behalf.

Despite the feelings of malaise some historians have felt over accepting the Kyushu mōsō sect records, no Japanese scholar has unearthed any concrete evidence concerning the origins of biwa hōshi that would prove a history radically different from the general picture shown by the Tokugawa mōsō documents. If the biwa hōshi are accepted as the descendants of the mōsō, we are dealing with one continuous tradition of low-class blind men, loosely connected with the Tendai sect, whose art as sutra chanters, storytellers, and oral poets spread gradually from Kyushu throughout Japan.

In their role as pacifiers of local deities they might chant tales which emphasized the efficacy of those deities. There is some indication, for instance, that biwa hōshi around Kumano served the gods of Kumano in this way.[19] However nominal their shrine or temple connections may have become, the biwa hōshi were, loosely speaking, "priests," and the listeners who supported them could consider their donations as an act of religious merit. The audience of a biwa hōshi might be amused, diverted, or excited by the performance it witnessed, while simultaneously acquiring a sense of security from the belief that the biwa hōshi could, by virtue of his performance, intercede with the local deities on his listeners' behalf.

It is helpful to imagine local variation in the fare offered by biwa hōshi, with some groups continuing the recitation of Jishinkyō as their major occupation, while others tended more to develop the recitation of local tales, stories glorifying specific local deities, metered oral delivery of the latest news, and finally, accounts of the battles which raged across the country at the end of the Heian period.

[19]Tomikura, "Biwa hōshira no yakuwari," p. 76.

One way in which biwa hōshi could assure their audience of their importance and efficacy was by singing of their illustrious ancestry. One such tale, of course, was the Indian legend of the blind disciple of Buddha discussed above. In addition, another, somewhat similar Indian legend, preserved in Japan among the tales of Indian origin collected in *Konjaku monogatari,* may originally have been brought from China to Japan by the early immigrant mōsō. This is the legend of Prince Kuṇāla, blinded son of the famous Buddhist king Aśoka, discussed further in chapter 3.

The tales recited by the early biwa hōshi have been all but totally overshadowed by *Heike Monogatari,* the great epic narrative account of the rise and fall of the Taira clan, ending in the defeat of the Taira by the Minamoto. The genesis and growth of this epic constitute a complex tale. Its effect on the life and art of the biwa hōshi was overwhelming. Questions both of textual development and of musical accompaniment are relevant not only to the later centuries of the biwa hōshi's activity but also to the growth of the Semimaru legend itself.

We will discuss the texts later. First let us look at the lute that accompanied the chanter's voice.

The Heike Biwa.

Though the biwa hōshi of earlier centuries played the instrument I have already described (the mōsō biwa), a new variety of lute known as *Heike biwa* developed in the early Kamakura period as the musical vehicle used to accompany recitation of the *Heike monogatari.* The mōsō biwa continued in use only in Kyushu, perpetuated by those lute priests who had left the capital area a few decades before the composition of *Heike monogatari.*

The Heike biwa may be understood, both in form and in manner of performance, as a cross between the two earlier forms of Japanese lute, the gaku biwa and the mōsō biwa.[20] Like the latter, the Heike biwa has five bridges, while the gaku biwa has four, all grouped relatively close together high on the neck of the instrument. The position of the bridges of the Heike biwa is very close to the mathematical average of the distances of the bridges from the bottom of the strings of the two older types of lute. In overall form the instrument resembles the pear shape of a gaku biwa rather than the more narrow, rather clublike shape of the mōsō instrument. So far as size goes, the Heike biwa is the smallest of the three varieties: about two-thirds as big as the average gaku biwa, and three-fourths the size of a mōsō biwa. On the other hand, the plectrum of the Heike biwa is larger and wider than that used with the gaku biwa.

In traditional style the Heike biwa was played in flat horizontal position, like the gaku biwa; but the bridges were high, and (as with the mōsō biwa) pressure was applied to the strings between the bridges rather than directly above them. Plectrum technique was basically similar to the style of mōsō biwa performance.

In short, the Heike biwa appears to be a product of the conscious collaboration of adherents of the two earlier, distinctly separate lute traditions.

Shōmyō

Heikyoku, the music played on Heike biwa as accompaniment for the recitation of *Heike monogatari*, is derived from vocal music known as *shōmyō*, the traditional singing of Buddhist sutras. From the earliest days of Indian Buddhism, shōmyō served an important function in making the sutras appealing to congregations who might have found their

[20]Tanabe, *Nihon ongakushi*, pp. 135–39, and *Nihon no gakki*, pp. 89–92.

content too difficult to appreciate in simple nonmusical recitation.

From at least the early eighth century, shōmyō was avidly studied by Japanese Buddhist priests. The same mission of the year 835 which took Fujiwara Sadatoshi to China, making it possible for him to learn secret lute melodies, also carried the Tendai priest Ennin (793–864), later to become abbot of the Enryakuji on Mount Hiei. One of the aspects of Buddhist scholarship which he eagerly absorbed during his nine-year sojourn in China was the art of shōmyō. Ennin was not the first to introduce shōmyō to Japan, but he was extremely influential in ensuring for it a place of importance in the history of Japanese music.

Until the end of the Heian period the shōmyō of the Tendai and Shingon sects continued to be the most important Buddhist musical tradition of the capital area. Of all the great names in the history of shōmyō, Fujiwara Moronaga (1137–92) is important to consider here because his activities in the last decade of his life may foreshadow the union of vocal shōmyō and biwa accompaniment which led, a generation or two after Moronaga's death, to the development of *heikyoku*.

Moronaga's fame was both political and musical.[21] An aristocrat of high rank, he served for a time as prime minister in the latter days of the Heike regime. Twice suspected of complicity in overthrowing Heike rule, he spent altogether some ten years in exile though he was finally pardoned in 1181 and returned to the capital, having taken orders as a priest during his second period of exile. Perhaps Moronaga whiled away his hours in exile by practicing the lute, for his biographers report his great fame as a lutenist. His instrument was, of course, the gaku biwa.

[21] Tanabe, *Nihon ongakushi*, pp. 133–34; *Daijimmei jiten*, V, 440–41.

There is one anecdote from the life of Moronaga which shows him engaging in an activity rather similar to a mōsō. Just as they recited prayers and sutras to pacify local deities into granting a good harvest, Moronaga, too, used his music to sway the will of the gods. Moronaga's skill on the biwa, it would appear, granted him the gift of rainmaking. During a severe drought which plagued the Kyoto area, Moronaga went to the Hiyoshi shrine at Sakamoto, the eastern foot of Mount Hiei, there played his lute, and prayed for rain. His recorded success brought him, no doubt, the thanks of the people of the capital as well as the additional nickname of Ame Daijin, "the Rain Minister."

Moronaga was the author of two important musical treatises, one concerning koto music, one pertaining to the biwa. Evidently a scholarly sort, once Moronaga conceived an interest in shōmyō, he made a comparative study of the several shōmyō traditions actively practiced at the time. His principal teacher was the Tendai priest Genchō, but Moronaga's mature style differed from that of his master sufficiently to justify considering it the beginning of a new tradition. Moronaga was known as Myōon-in, a title of respect derived from the name of the Bodhisattva Myōon, the subject of the twenty-fourth chapter of the Lotus sutra. The name, appropriately, means "Wonder Sound." The style of shōmyō created by Moronaga was known as the Myōon-in school, and though this tradition is no longer extant, it lasted into the Tokugawa period.

Since Moronaga was already a lutenist of great fame at the time he took up the study of shōmyō, it seems reasonable to suppose that he may have experimented with using the biwa as accompaniment for shōmyō, and this possibility makes Moronaga's title Myōon-in extremely intriguing. For, it will be recalled, the Kyushu mōsō records refer to the center of mōsō activity at Ausaka as the Myōon-den or

"Myōon hall," and call Semimaru the fourth leader of mōsō activity there. The mōsō of the Myōon-den performed a shōmyō recitation of one sutra chapter, the *Jishinkyō*, to the accompaniment of the mōsō biwa. As with so many fine points in the early history of music, there simply is not enough evidence to allow certainty, but it is possible that Moronaga's title Myōon-in indicates a connection between him and the Myōon-den tradition of mōsō recitation. Such an environment of contact between gaku biwa and mōsō biwa performers was necessary for the development of the instrument which came to be known as the Heike biwa. It is quite possible that the first steps toward development of the new instrument, and experiments in using it to perform shōmyō-derived music, preceded the composition of *Heike monogatari*.

Heike Monogatari

The talents of men with a courtier's mastery of gaku biwa, a blind priest's knowledge of mōsō biwa, and a Tendai priest's ability at shōmyō are all reflected in the music of *Heike monogatari;* and the earliest account of the circumstances of its composition credits the creation of *Heike monogatari* to cooperation among representatives of exactly these three traditions.[22]

The account is given in *Tsurezuregusa,* a miscellany of recollections and personal opinions of the priest Yoshida Kenkō, dating from around 1350.[23] According to Kenkō, a former provincial governor whom he calls the lay priest Yukinaga suffered embarrassment at court over an incident which to twentieth-century ears sounds distinctly trivial. Yukinaga, a man of high repute as a scholar of Chinese, suffered a lapse of mem-

[22]Tanabe, *Nihon ongakushi,* pp. 135–37.
[23]*Hōjōki, Tsurezuregusa,* NKBT, XXX, 271–72.

ory during a public disquisition on a well-known Chinese poem. Becoming as a consequence the object of teasing ridicule at court, Yukinaga renounced the life of a court scholar, took Buddhist orders, and went to live on Mount Hiei. He was taken in and supported by the Abbot Jichin, better known as Jien (1155–1225). While resident on Mount Hiei under Jien's sponsorship, Yukinaga wrote the original manuscript of *Heike monogatari*. Kenkō dates these events to the time of the Retired Emperor Go-Toba, that is, between 1218 and 1221.

By the mid-fourteenth century when Kenkō wrote, the *Heike monogatari* had become extremely well-known as a recited text chanted episodically by biwa hōshi.[24] It had far outstripped in popularity any other material presented by blind lutenists. Kenkō believed that Yukinaga had intended his own text as a recitation libretto, and *Tsurezuregusa* states that Yukinaga taught the *Heike monogatari* to a blind man named Shōbutsu and had him recite it. Further, Kenkō tells us that the biwa hōshi of his own day studied the natural voice of Shōbutsu.

Until recently scholarly interpretation tended to accept Kenkō's view that *Heike monogatari* was originally composed expressly for recitation, although no contemporary evidence concerning the identity of the chanter Shōbutsu has ever been found. Among biwa hōshi themselves there existed the belief that *Heike monogatari* was first written to be read and only later revised for recitation with musical accompaniment.[25] Recent textual analysis of extant early manuscripts has led to support for the beliefs of the biwa hōshi.

[24] Butler, "The Textual Evolution of the *Heike Monogatari*," pp. 17–18. Butler's interesting article is the basis for much of my analysis of *Heike monogatari*. My comparison of the Semimaru passages from several *Heike* textual variants tends to confirm Butler's suggestions about the order and relationship of several texts.

[25] *Heike monogatari*, NKBT, XXXII, 46.

The Background

Yukinaga, it seems, as one might expect of a scholar learned in Chinese, wrote in Kambun, the Japanese version of Chinese; later texts of *Heike*—there are over a hundred—include both revised versions written to be read in Kambun, as well as the interesting series of revisions by different chanters aimed at producing texts for memorization and oral recitation. Oral recitation of *Heike monogatari* was the apotheosis of the biwa hōshi art. *Heike monogatari* continued the traditions of biwa hōshi war tale recitation while tremendously enriching their scope and historical detail. In *Heike monogatari* references to events at court include precise, accurate information acquired through Yukinaga's use of the diary of Kujō Kanezane (1147–1207), prime minister, imperial regent, and the elder brother of the Abbot Jien, Yukinaga's benefactor.

In the 150-year period following Yukinaga's composition of *Heike monogatari,* various groups of biwa hōshi amended and elaborated the original text to create versions more suited to memorization and oral recitation. Detailed battle descriptions—among them the most exciting, intense passages in the later texts—have been shown to be dramatic fictions based on the orally composed battle tales of a group of biwa hōshi from Harima province, for instance.[26]

The *Heike monogatari* thus evolved some oral versions which combined accurate historical information about events in Kyoto with gripping heroic fictional accounts of the finest details of individual hand-to-hand, sword-to-sword, combat among warriors on distant battlefields.

The culmination of this initial century and a half of major revisions was the version known as the Kakuichi text, of 1371. This text was dictated, probably gradually over a period of some years, by a blind chanter named Akashi Kakuichi. Kakuichi had apparently entered the Buddhist priesthood in his

---

[26] Butler, "Textual Evolution," p. 37.

41

youth and turned to biwa recitation in mid-life after losing his eyesight. Originally a native of Harima, Kakuichi there was involved in the creation of a text including the stirring battle descriptions I have mentioned. With that text in hand or mind, Kakuichi moved to Kyoto where he collaborated with biwa hōshi of the area in creating a definitive recitation text combining textual developments from Harima with the texts developed by Kyoto biwa hōshi. Kakuichi completed the dictation of his final text only a few months before his death, around the age of seventy, in 1371. The Kakuichi text was the last major revision of *Heike monogatari;* revisions following it, though numerous, represent only minor variations of practice among different schools. The Kakuichi text has become the scholarly and popular standard.[27]

During the period of development of the oral recitation of *Heike monogatari,* certain subtle changes took place in the social status of some biwa hōshi.[28] At shrines and temples, performances of *Heike monogatari* before public audiences of varied social backgrounds continued, but Heike biwa hōshi were also welcomed as performers in the banquet halls of the governing military families of the day. The diary of the retired emperor Hanazono, in the year 1321, mentions summoning blind performers to entertain the emperor and his ladies with recitations from *Heike monogatari.* The diary makes it clear that the emperor was charmed by the music and found it quite different from the gaku biwa music with which he was already familiar.[29]

Many biwa hōshi came to specialize in the recitation of *Heike monogatari* to the exclusion of all earlier material. Those who performed at noble households sought for themselves

[27]See *Heike monogatari,* NKBT, XXXII, 44–51, concerning Kakuichi and textual variants. The Kakuichi text is the basis for the NKBT text.
[28]Gōtō, *Senki monogatari no kenkyū* 2, pp. 104–12.
[29]*Ibid.,* p. 106.

status equal to their hosts', and medieval diaries indicate that some biwa hōshi traveled about the country with letters of introduction from their aristocratic patrons.[30] Upwardly mobile biwa hōshi, welcomed as entertainers and associates by men of wealth and power, sought to dissociate themselves from the beggarly status of their mōsō antecedents. Recitation of *Heike monogatari*, rather than the *Jishinkyō*, was the road to preferment.

Tōdōza

By Kakuichi's lifetime, the biwa hōshi was more entertainer than priest. The powerful guild of blind *Heike* chanters which Kakuichi founded was known as *Tōdōza*[31] the "proper path guild," and the name may reflect the specialization of its members in *Heike monogatari* recitation exclusively as their "proper path."

Recognized by the Ashikaga government as a regulatory agency, the Tōdōza had supervisory control over those blind lutenists who practiced recitation of *Heike monogatari*. Members of the Tōdōza were classified according to a system of four graded titles, divided into sixteen ranks. Though originally the guild of Heike reciters only, by the Tokugawa period the Tōdōza had extended its control to include all blind lute performers in Japan. They became, in effect, a country of the blind, controlled by their own system of regulations outside direct government management.

Tōdō yōshū was the official guild record.[32] The document as it is currently known was brought into final shape in

[30]Mushakoji, *Heike monogatari to biwa hōshi*, p. 221.

[31]Nakayama, *Nihon mōjinshi*, pp. 166–74, offers an extensive discussion of Tōdōza.

[32]Kondō, "Heike biwa izen," p. 69. My discussion of *Tōdō yōshū* is based on sections exerpted by Kondō in this article.

1635 by a later guild leader called Koike, though original authorship is attributed to Akashi Kakuichi himself.

According to *Tōdō yōshū*, the guild's founder and ancestor deity was called Amayo. It identified Amayo, whose name means "Heaven Night," as Prince Saneyasu, the fourth son of Emperor Nimmyō. According to this record, the prince lost his eyesight at the age of twenty-eight as the result of illness. The following year he entered the priesthood. Embarrassed over his blindness, he fled the capital and called together blind men of good lineage to keep him company at his villa outside the city. He then taught them to play various stringed instruments and flutes and instructed them in several styles of song as well as the secret biwa melodies. After his death in 872, *Tōdō yōshū* continues, his brother, Emperor Kōkō, in 885 established a shrine at Shinomiya, the site of his villa, and gave Saneyasu the posthumous title of Amayo.

The dates in *Tōdō yōshū* jibe with solid historical information, making it difficult to draw a firm line between the realities and the inventions of the text. Reliable imperial genealogies confirm that the fourth son of Emperor Nimmyō was, indeed, Saneyasu.[33] Though blindness is never mentioned, historical sources indicate that, because of an unspecified illness, Saneyasu took Buddhist orders in the fifth month of 859, then retired to a villa near Anjō temple in Yamashina (in an area of modern Higashiyama district, Kyoto, where a small local train stop still bears the name Shinomiya).[34]

It has been suggested that Saneyasu in retirement at his villa carried on family tradition by presiding over a literary and musical salon.[35] Ono no Komachi commemorated Saneyasu's death in 872 with a touching poem in which she used the

[33]*Seishi kakei daijiten*, I, 64.
[34]"Sandai jitsuroku", *Rikkokushi*, IX, 50.
[35]Tashiro, "Yōkyoku *Semimaru*," XXIII, 137.

phrase *kanashi no miya* "sad prince." The phrase is interpretable as a pun on *shi no miya* "fourth prince," confirming that this was, in his own lifetime, a common term of reference for Prince Saneyasu and the probable source of the place name.

That Saneyasu actually trained "blind men of good lineage" is rather doubtful. In claiming Saneyasu as Amayo, their sacred founder, those biwa hōshi who formed the Tō-dōza were sanitizing their origins, cloaking themselves in the reflected majesty of a true imperial prince.

The veneration of Amayo began long before the formation of the Tōdōza, in fact, in the first half of the thirteenth century. Elevation of Amayo to the status of deified founding father of the biwa hōshi tradition did not mean, however, that all biwa hōshi turned their backs on Semimaru. The literary evidence, as presented in chapter 3, indicates that bands of blind reciters faithful to the memory of Semimaru reacted against the followers of Amayo. In effect fighting fire with fire, they associated Semimaru with the Shinomiya area and called Semimaru himself "fourth prince," inventing for him spurious descent from the ninth-century emperor Daigo.[36]

The legend of Semimaru did not die when the predecessors of the Tōdōza abandoned him; rather it gained both complexity and vitality at this turn. Semimaru continued to be venerated as ancestor-deity, but not by the Tōdōza biwa hōshi specialists. In their stead, lower class biwa hōshi, particularly those who continued to perform for alms at the Semimaru shrine at Ausaka, persisted in identifying Semimaru as their ancestor.

The biwa hōshi of the Semimaru shrine were familiar with the legend of the Indian prince musician Kuṇāla, a tale which their mōsō ancestors had carried to Japan from the Asian continent. Once the influence of Amayo biwa hōshi

[36] Kondō, "Heike biwa izen," p. 70; Kōsai, "Semimaru," p. 21.

had precipitated Semimaru's "retaliatory rebirth" as a prince, The Kuṇāla legend fused with that of Semimaru.

The Semimaru biwa hōshi of Ausaka sang of Semimaru as a prince, but one who had fallen from grace to become, like themselves, a beggar. The Amayo biwa hōshi and the Tōdōza which descended from them strove to mingle with their socially acceptable, powerful audience, and dissociated themselves from Semimaru.

Meanwhile, the Semimaru biwa hōshi perpetuated his legend, and his name remained associated with Ausaka, the spot at which he, as outcast prince, was believed to have been abandoned. There Semimaru was revered both as patron god of those biwa hōshi who remained faithful to him and as the local deity, "god of the slope," the protector of travelers passing by.

Sekkyō Proselytizing and Semimaru as a God

Those who set out on journeys eastward from the capital traversed the Ausaka Pass and there offered up a prayer to Semimaru as the god of the pass. His name appears in the medieval travel diaries of pilgrims who passed Ausaka, and the earliest such reference sets the tone by telling us that "the tutelary spirit of Ausaka Pass was Semimaru of old."

There was nothing exceptional about Semimaru being revered as a local deity whose legend was recited by local priest entertainers. Countless local deities throughout Japan were similarly served, each providing the focus of religious veneration of a local clan or village in the Shinto tradition.

To understand the last great step in the development of the Semimaru legend, where Semimaru becomes, on top of all his earlier identities, a Bodhisattva, we must again take one step back in time and consider the development of popular Buddhist proselytizing in Japan, beginning in the latter days of the Heian period.

Buddhism had long been active in Japan as a monastic religion with many prosperous institutions thriving in Nara and
Kyoto, as well as in the great monastic complexes of Mount
Hiei and Mount Kōya. The major revolution which took place
in Japanese Buddhism of the late Heian period brought many
clergy out of their monasteries and into the community where,
by means of vigorous proselytizing, Buddhism was spread
throughout a wider spectrum of society.

Two terms used to describe popular teaching of Buddhism,
sekkyō and *shōdō,* seem to have been roughly synony-
mous.[37] The former means literally "sutra explanation"; the
latter, "chant leading." Whereas these terms were originally
used to designate religious training for laymen, there was apparently always an element of humor and drama in the activities of the *sekkyōshi* and *shōdōshi,* the preachers of sekkyō and shōdō. In later days, sekkyō became, in fact,
largely a form of popular entertainment.

At its inception, Heian sekkyō was nonmusical, pure and
simple preaching enlivened somewhat by the use of interesting parables or folktales from which an appropriate moral
might be drawn. The comment of the Heian court lady Sei
Shōnagon, to the effect that only a handsome preacher could
hold her attention,[38] serves as a clear reminder that a sekkyō
preacher did not enjoy the luxury of a fervent and committed
audience. He had to work to capture their attention and would
use whatever means were available to make the teachings of
Buddhism interesting and reasonably accessible.

The Heian sekkyō audience included men and women of
the court aristocracy, and the preachers who addressed these
audiences were often full-fledged ordained priests, themselves
of aristocratic social status. Perhaps as early as the Heian

[37]The terms are used interchangeably by Kikuchi throughout his
article "Shōdō bungei." Much of the information on early *sekkyō* presented here is based on this article.
[38]*Makura no sōshi, Murasaki Shikibu nikki,* NKBT, XIX, 73–76.

47

period, musical elements of shōmyō sutra chanting were adopted by sekkyō preachers to enrich the attractiveness of their texts. Though Japanese music historians cite shōmyō influence on the development of sekkyō,[39] the absence of musical notation for the earliest sekkyō texts makes it impossible to judge just how musical they may have been. However, it appears that sekkyō soon included some sung passages as well as nonmusical discourses on the meaning of sutras and the moral lessons derivable from familiar folktales and that this music contributed greatly to the popular appeal of sekkyō.

The religious environment of Mount Hiei nurtured the early development of sekkyō, and a priest from Hiei, Chōken (1125–1203), led the first group of sekkyōshi who moved out actively into the community. The members of this group were known as the *Agui shōdō* school. While they were not the only priests to practice sekkyō, their activities are the best documented.

The Agui shōdō founder, Chōken, was the son of Fujiwara Michinori, better known as Shinzei, an active court politician and partisan of Taira Kiyomori. Shinzei was beheaded by his political enemies in the course of the Heiji uprising of 1159–60, and his son Chōken thereafter eschewed politics and spent his later years actively involved in Buddhist teaching. Chōken was the author of a number of prompt-books for sekkyō preachers, works written in ornate literary Kambun from which the priests extemporized orally.[40]

On Chōken's death, his son Seikaku (1166–1235) succeeded him as head of the Agui school. Seikaku was an early disciple of Hōnen, founder of the Jōdo sect, and it was during Seikaku's lifetime that the Agui school became as-

[39]Tanabe, *Nihon ongakushi*, p. 220.
[40]Kikuchi, "*Shōdō bungei*," p. 50, lists the texts authored by Chōken and Seikaku.

sociated with this sect and its new endeavors to circulate Buddhist teachings.

Agui was the name of a monastic residence, a branch temple used by Hiei priests when living in the capital. Though the name Agui suggests that this monastery may originally have been intended for use in short-term religious retreats, it was Chōken and Seikaku's regular residence. It would seem that even at this early stage, sekkyō preachers did not necessarily observe all the precepts of monastic Buddhism. In 1120 a courtier's diary spoke of a famous, successful old sekkyō priest who did not observe Buddhist clerical discipline but had a wife and children and lived "in the capital."[41]

Though Chōken led a monastic life for some years, he married in middle age and fathered several children, including the son who succeeded him. Within the Agui, hereditary leadership became the rule rather than the exception; by Muromachi times sekkyōshi were thoroughly secularized, commonly dressed as laymen, and left their heads unshaven. Though still retaining access to the priestly community, most sekkyōshi in later days were laymen who lived outside the monastery. Many apparently led an itinerant life, moving about from temple to temple, preaching as they went.

The sekkyōshi who, during the Kamakura and Muromachi periods, traveled about Japan carrying the world view and teachings of Buddhism to ever more remote areas developed a style of preaching which was livelier and more colloquial than that of the earliest sekkyōshi of the capital. Much of their preaching was aimed at creating a harmonious accomodation between the native beliefs of common villagers and the new message of salvation and rebirth in the Pure Land as promised to those who embraced true faith in Buddha.

Toward this end, sekkyōshi borrowed and adapted many

[41]*Ibid.*, p. 48.

local legends, reinterpreting and elaborating them for their own purposes. In this sense sekkyō can best be understood as a function or purpose toward which many sorts of stories might be used rather than as an independent story style.

The opening lines of *Heike monogatari*, a passage from the Nirvana sutra, had already become familiar to sekkyō audiences through Chōken's explications and were included in a text of his authorship which preceded *Heike monogatari*.[42] Furthermore, *Heike monogatari* itself may have been used for sekkyō purposes. It has been suggested that the very first revision of the original Kambun text was made by Seikaku for the purpose of using this exciting tale as an extraordinary promptbook for sekkyōshi furthering the teachings of the Jōdo sect.[43] Whether it was Seikaku himself or one of his immediate disciples who wrote the revision known as the Hiramatsuke text of the *Heike monogatari*, the case in point is an early example of the freedom with which sekkyōshi might use a popular story for didactic purposes.

Sekkyō preaching became a lively, impromptu art. Extemporizing from promptbooks rather than reading a carefully prepared text, sekkyōshi created an exciting ambiance. We read diary accounts of sekkyōshi who could "laugh or cry at will" and envision performances of emotional intensity and effective audience appeal.

Sekkyō has a long history, lasting down into the Tokugawa period, by which time it became a form of popular entertainment with the tales of the sekkyō chanter dramatically enacted by puppets. The many stages of evolution of sekkyō are rather elusive, but generally speaking, medieval sekkyō performers seem often to have recited folktales beloved by the faithful believers of a local Shinto deity and to have given those tales a new, deeper meaning through the process of

[42]*Ibid.*, p. 50.   [43]Butler, "Textual Evolution," p. 35.

amalgamation of Shinto and Buddhist belief.[44] The common pattern in many of these tales is to recount the terrible sufferings of a mortal human who after death becomes the local deity, a power to be placated and revered, the common object of fear and veneration by the local residents who know the god's painful history.

The sekkyōshi, rather than undercutting entrenched faith in local deities, developed tales in which they praised the gods as manifestations of various Buddhas and Bodhisattvas. The notion of equating gods with Buddhas is known in Japan as *honji-suijaku,* which literally means "the original land" and "the remaining trace." Though most honji-suijaku stories date from the Kamakura-Muromachi period, the theory was not invented by the sekkyōshi of these eras; rather, it was expounded in Japan as early as the ninth century and was consistent with the generally accommodating spirit in which Buddhism was easily accepted in Japan and harmonious relations established between the two religious systems.[45]

When a honji-suijaku element was added to a tale of a Shinto deity, or kami, the deity acquired richer significance. Faith in the local deity, now understood to have been in his lifetime a human manifestation of a Buddha or Bodhisattva, implied that the kami-Bodhisattva would aid in the salvation and rebirth in paradise of those who held faith in him. In this sense the tales chanted by sekkyōshi helped spread the belief that no matter how much suffering one's present life entailed, the common simple man or woman might be assured, through faith, of rebirth into a blissful incarnation.

Just listening to a sekkyō tale might itself be an act of merit, aiding salvation. When an itinerant sekkyōshi gath-

[44]Kikuchi, "Shōdō bungei," pp. 74–80.
[45]Matsunaga, *The Buddhist Philosophy of Assimilation,* discusses the history of *honji-suijaku* theory in Japan. Pp. 264–70 trace literary applications of the theory.

ered an audience and chanted his tale of the kami of Kumano, for instance, he would conclude by assuring all who heard him blessings equal to those of pilgrims who had journeyed as far as the Kumano shrine.[46]

Sekkyōshi carried honji-suijaku tales along their circuits, creating and recreating, with song and dance, to the rasping whine of a bamboo scraper, and the beat of a drum, marvelous tales of the gods and Buddhas. Some forty tales of suijaku and of their shrines and temples are collected in a work called *Shintōshū*, a collection totaling fifty tales gathered in written form in the late 1350s.[47] Nine *Shintōshū* tales, including the first, which suggests the title, deal with matters which might be considered, strictly speaking, Shinto—the origins of Shinto, the reason for the *torii* shrine gateway, taboos concerning menstruation, for example—but the bulk of the collection consists of the suijaku tales. Some are little more than basic formulas, a few lines in length, minimal promptings for the chanter. They needed extensive elaboration on the part of the sekkyōshi.

Some twenty temple histories, or *engi*, and the honji-suijaku tales are relatively rich narratives. It is these which are the finest record of the art of the fourteenth-century sekkyōshi. Each tale includes at its head the notation "Agui composition." The deities honored in the tales come from a broad range of locations, several tales showing accurate knowledge of the geography of the northeastern provinces, for example. Apparently, itinerant sekkyōshi brought these tales back in oral form from the provinces to Kyoto where they were written up and collected at the Agui center.[48]

[46]Kishi, *Shintōshū*, p. 293.

[47]*Ibid.*, p. 298, dates the text between 1354 and 1358. Kikuchi, "Shōdō bungei," places it between 1356 and 1361.

[48]Kikuchi, "Shōdō bungei," lists the relevant provinces. Kishi, *Shintōshū*, pp. 300–301, summarizes several scholars' tentative

The Background

Sekkyō at Ausaka

In addition to the Agui school, there was another sekkyō school, founded around 1240 by a priest from Miidera. Miidera, a Tendai temple on the shores of Lake Biwa, had since the ninth century been engaged in fierce rivalry, even outright warfare, with the Tendai establishment on Mount Hiei. The Monk Jōen from Miidera founded a school of sekkyōshi which, bearing his name, was known as the Jōen tradition. Though not so well-documented as the Agui, Jōen's followers were apparently quite popular, successfully entertaining, and widely accepted.[49]

During Jōen's lifetime his home temple was engaged in such violence that Jōen may have been burned out of Miidera by Hiei forces or he may have fled, simply seeking quiet elsewhere; or possibly one of Jōen's successors led the move, but at some uncertain date the center of activity of the Jōen sekkyō tradition shifted from Miidera to the Kinshōji, a branch temple of Miidera at Ausaka Pass.

In early Tokugawa times sekkyōshi active in central Japan all carried licenses issued by the Kinshōji and the Semimaru shrine at Ausaka, the shrine and temple being jointly administered. The Tokugawa government-established licensing system formalized with official sanction a bond between sekkyōshi, the Kinshōji, and the Semimaru shrine which had existed for centuries. The licensing system is discussed further in chapter 5.

Each licensed Tokugawa sekkyōshi carried a document which told the history of Semimaru. The first extant text from this tradition dates from the early seventeenth century, but its

views on authorship, including some suggestions that the collection was compiled in the northeast rather than in Kyoto.
[49] Kanai, *Nō no kenkyū*, pp. 547–52.

53

intellectual atmosphere seems more typical of the Muromachi period. It is basically similar to the honji-suijaku narratives included in the *Shintōshū*. It tells first of the sufferings undergone by Semimaru in his lifetime, then of his veneration after death at the Semimaru shrine, and finally reveals that Semimaru was an avatar of the Bodhisattva Myōon. Though he made himself manifest as a beggar, praying at Ausaka for the benefit of others, his soul was inferior to none.

This Semimaru honji-suijaku tale is rather artless, lacking in style and possibly slightly garbled. It shows certain points in common with two Nō plays which long predate the license text itself, and the most reasonable conclusion seems to be that both the Nō Semimaru and the Tokugawa license document were based on an oral tale about the beggar prince which was current at Ausaka before the composition of the Nō.[50]

A close reading of the text of the license (translated as section P in Part II) shows that it claims a companion of Semimaru rather than Semimaru himself as the ancestor of Tokugawa sekkyō performers; however, the license also served to associate sekkyō performers with the dignity of Semimaru. They were by Tokugawa times, at least, little more than beggars, but by implication they too might claim souls inferior to none. Though the text says Semimaru's companion was the first sekkyōshi, other evidence indicates that the Tokugawa sekkyōshi revered Semimaru himself as their ancestor deity.[51] Traces of sekkyō uses of the Semimaru legend—and of the equating of Semimaru with sekkyō performers—are evident in the two Semimaru Nō plays which are analyzed in chapter 4.

[50] Muroki, *Katarimono*, p. 215.

[51] Nakayama, *Nihon mōjinshi*, p. 54, quotes a Tokugawa commentary on the Tōdōza which makes this assertion.

 THREE

The Literature of the Legend

Seven poems in the classic thirty-one syllable waka form have been attributed to Semimaru. Of these seven, four appear in imperial anthologies with Semimaru given as author. The other three appear in the *Kokinshū* of 905, the first imperially commissioned anthology, and are there considered anonymous, gaining ascription to Semimaru some three hundred years later in the writings of the highly respected court poet Fujiwara Teika (1162–1241).

The completion dates of the various imperial anthologies are known, but the individual poems appearing in those anthologies are generally not dated. The compilers included old poems as well as recent ones in creating their collections for the court; and the date of an anthology tells us only that the poems it contains were written no later than the time of presentation of the collection. For example, a Semimaru poem in *Shokukokinshū*, an anthology of 1265, also appears in *Konjaku monogatari*, a collection of tales from some 150 years earlier.

We cannot analyze Semimaru's poems in chronological order, nor can we be certain that all the poems attributed to Semimaru are, in fact, by the same hand. In point of historical fact, as we have noted, there may well have been more than one Semimaru, but the Semimaru of legend is understood to be a single individual. Since we are here tracing the literary sources of a supposed individual, it is pointless to worry over the impossible task of checking, at this late date, the accuracy of court anthologists' ascriptions. Dating and authorship aside, the seven Semimaru poems show striking thematic con-

 55

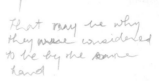
That may be why they were considered to be by the same hand.

sistency. Taken together they form the first general literary image of Semimaru.

Of the seven Semimaru poems, one—poem A in Part II of this book[1]—stands out both for its unusual structure and for its remarkable persistency. Appearing in the *Gosenshū* of 951, it is the earliest poem officially attributed to Semimaru in an imperial anthology. It reappears again and again, quoted in full or in part, in much of the later Semimaru literature:

Kore ya kono	This, now this!
Yuku mo kaeru mo	Where people come and people go
Wakaretsutsu	Exchanging farewells
Shiru mo shiranu mo	For friends and strangers alike
Ausaka no seki	This is meeting barrier.[2]

The first line of the poem, *kore ya kono*, is a strong exclamation and an unusual line, grammatically set apart from the rest of the poem. The distinguished Japanese folklorist Origuchi Shinobu, one of the rare scholars ever to concern himself with the earliest traditions of the area of Ausaka and Omi province, conjectured that this line may have been a phrase of invocation intended to summon Sakagami, the god of the Ausaka Pass, to hear supplicant travelers' pleas for safe passage.[3] Two other non-Semimaru poems, one from a tale in *Ise monogatari*,[4]

[1] Throughout Part I capital letters are used to designate translations included in Part II in "Poems and Prose Selections"; bibliographical references to the sources translated are given in the footnotes to Part II.

[2] This translation is based on one by Donald Keene in *Anthology of Japanese Literature*, p. 92. Though Keene's translation is more graceful, I have changed the first line for purposes of comparison with translations of other poems which share the line.

[3] Origuchi, *Origuchi Shinobu zenshū*, X, 284.

[4] *Ise monogatari* consists of 209 poems arranged in 125 sections which provide contexts for the poems. The contexts range from single-line introductions to well-developed short prose narratives.

the other from a story in *Konjaku monogatari*, show the same striking opening line. Both poems share with Semimaru's poem wordplay in which the verb *au* "to meet" puns with the place names Ausaka or Omi (Aumi). The poems are embedded in tales concerning the unsuccessful reunion of a couple, in Omi province, who had been long separated from each other and met again by chance.

The two "meeting" poems cited by Origuchi are:

Kore ya kono	This, now this!
Ware ni aumi o	While you've continued
Nogaretsutsu	To avoid our meeting,
Toshitsuki furedo	Though years have passed,
Masarigao naki[5]	You seem no better off.

and

Kore zo kono	This, now this!
Tsui ni aumi o	Meeting at last,
Itoitsutsu	You still despise me.
Yo ni wa furedomo	I go on day by day
Ikeru kai nashi[6]	But there's no point in living.

These poems share with the Semimaru poems more than just the opening invocatory line and the puns on "meeting." Each has for its third line a verb in the continuative *-tsutsu* form. Though waka was a highly constrained literary form, the limits of grammatical structure in these poems were not so rigid as to make these similarities insignificant.

---

[5]*Ise monogatari*, NKBT, IX, 144. See McCulloughh, *Tales of Ise*, 109–10, for a complete translation of the tale which includes this poem.

[6]*Konjaku monogatari*, NKBT, XXVI, 233. Origuchi considered this first line identical to *kore ya kono*, not pausing to comment on any difference between the two exclamatory particles *ya* and *zo*. Any subtle difference is beyond my poetic sensibilities and, inevitably, untranslatable.

If Origuchi's speculations are correct, it may be that the common features of these three poems are remnants of a regional song style associated with the Ausaka-Omi area. If so, the Semimaru poem in *Gosenshū* would, in its day, have been immediately identifiable from the opening line as a song from the Ausaka area.

Another grammatical feature that gives the first Semimaru poem its strikingly unusual structural quality is the fourfold repetition of the particle *mo*. The second line, *yuku mo kaeru mo*, is echoed by the fourth line *shiru mo shiranu mo*. Such repetition was frowned upon in the canons of courtly poetics of the day, and its appearance in another Semimaru poem adds credence to the notion that this was a distinctive element of "local color."

Finally, we are struck by the insistent repetition of the *k* sounds running through the first three lines: *kore ya kono/yuku mo kaeru mo/wakaretsutsu*. Unusual in its own time, the hypnotic rhythm of this little poem has kept it alive and interesting for a full millennium after its composition. The modern poet Hagiwara Sakutarō (1886–1942) found it effectively symbolic, saying, "This should clearly be called a sound-symbolism poem. The content finds expression by melting into the rhythm. This poem should be valued as extraordinarily superior in terms of its poetic rhetoric."[7]

Throughout the centuries-long history of Japanese court poetry, it was Fujiwara Teika and the other compilers of the *Shinkokinshū* (1206) who most highly valued sound symbolism,[8] and Teika appears responsible for having contributed more than any other individual to keeping alive the fame of Semimaru as poet. As mentioned above, Teika attributed to Semimaru three poems (D, E, F) considered anonymous in the

[7] Hagiwara, *Hagiwara Sakutarō zenshū*, III, 319–20.
[8] Tashiro, "Yōkyoku *Semimaru*," p. 131.

The Literature

Kokinshū.[9] He and his colleagues included two Semimaru poems (B, G) in the *Shinkokinshū*. This must be seen as significant homage to a relatively unknown poet, dead some three hundred years.

Teika included the *kore ya kono* poem of Semimaru in three collections in which he assembled his favorite waka. The most important of these for Semimaru's long-term fame was the *Ogura hyakunin isshu* compiled in 1235 when Teika was an old man of seventy-three. This collection, containing one poem each by 100 poets of the seventh through early thirteenth centuries, was understood to embody in its examples Teika's principles of poetic excellence. The collection was widely circulated and much emulated. Numerous other *hyakunin isshu* appeared thereafter, following its model. Teika's collection was the subject of at least two dozen premodern critcal works and became nearly universally known in Japan because of its use as a copybook for calligraphic practice.

Sometime in the mid-Tokugawa period the collection became the basis for a popular card game. The game utilizes pairs of cards, each bearing half a poem; the object of play is to be first to "cap" a poem with its closing lines when the card showing the first part of the poem is turned up. Adept players soon memorized the hundred poems. In an ironic twist of history, thanks to this game of cards, the name Semimaru for many people even today summons up first and foremost the earliest poem ever associated with him.

While no other Semimaru poem received quite the same kind of attention as the first one, one of the two selected for the *Skinkokinshū,* poem B, has also had wide circulation. Prior to its inclusion in the *Shinkokinshū,* it appeared in four

[9]The three *Kokinshū* poems are nos. 987–89. They are included in *Hekianshō,* a collection of Teika's notes and criticisms on poems from *Kokinshū, Gosenshū,* and *Shuishū. Hekianshō, Gunsho ruijū,* X, 600.

59

other sources: in the *Wakan rōeishū*, compiled by Fujiwara Kintō (966–1041), a collection in which Chinese and Japanese poems were paired on the basis of thematic similarities; in *Konjaku monogatari* (I) and the related story in *Gō-danshō*, and in *Toshiyori zuinō* (C). The third line of this poem was particularly unstable; three variants are known, strongly suggesting the probability that the poem was spread principally through oral recitation rather than learned through reading. None of the variants affects the meaning of the poem significantly.

This second early Semimaru poem shares the unusual four-fold repetition of the particle *mo*. Here the second line is *tote mo kakute mo* "this way or that," and the fourth line strengthens the contrast: *miya mo waraya mo* "palace or hovel." From these early poems we have already seen established two of the most basic elements of the Semimaru legend, the location at Ausaka and the contrast—and similarity—between life in a palace and life in a beggar's shelter.

Many poems in the *Gosenshū* have brief headnotes indicating the circumstances of their composition. Semimaru is there said to have written poem A, "On seeing the passers-by when living in a hut at Ausaka Barrier." The earliest evaluative comment on poem B is consistent with this headnote in *Gosenshū* and adds a little more substantive information on the first phases of the Semimaru legend. In his *Toshiyori zuinō* (C), a collection of poems and critical evaluation which dates from 1114 or 1115, Minamoto Shunrai comments on the reasons prompting Semimaru to compose poem B. Shunrai believed Semimaru to be a beggar who lived in a straw hut at Ausaka, played the koto, and sustained himself on the charity of passing travelers. He saw in Semimaru's poem a defensive posture taken in response to travelers' mockery of his simple hut. Shunrai made no suggestion that he or the men of his time believed Semimaru himself had ever lived in a palace. Neither is Semimaru specifically called blind. He is just a beggar whose poem points out the impermanence of all mens' lives, however favored. Shunrai's view of Semimaru was not unique. A passage very similar to Shunrai's comments appears in a collection of tales dating from around 1130.[10]

A consistent air of impermanence, uncertainty, and suffering permeates all seven Semimaru poems. We have no headnotes, critical comments, or other extraneous information on poems D through G, but their imagery is noticeably unified. D, E, and F all evoke Semimaru's sense of homelessness: "What home can I/ Point to as my own?"; "Knowing no future destination"; "One with no known future." The literary legacy of Semimaru begins grounded on an imagistic sense of nothingness—no home, no future, no possessions, no comfort or security, no rest. The cold reality behind the poems—the life of a miserable beggar—finds expression in frequent mention of the wind. "At Ausaka/ The storm winds/ Blow chill." The poet is "A speck of dust/ Tossed aimlessly on the winds," his life as fragile as "Dew drops trembling/ In uncertainty/ On every reed-tip/ In the autumn wind." Through poems A, E, and H Semimaru is associated with Ausaka. He lives there, just barely, day to day, but has no true home. The image of Semimaru thus far is cold, lonely, and profoundly negative.

Poem H sums up the pathetic uncertainty of Semimaru's life as seen in the early poems. It also introduces a fourth major element of Semimaru's legendary identity. We have already come to recognize Semimaru as an Ausaka beggar, and we have had one indication that he played a musical instrument—the koto mentioned by Shunrai. Now here is the first hint of his blindness. I have translated the poem "In the violence/ Of the storms/ at Ausaka Barrier/ I plan, somehow, in blindness/ To pass my days." The phrase "somehow, in blindness,"

[10]*Kohon setsuwashū sōsakuhin*, pp. 67–68.

61

translates two senses for the single word *shiite* of the original. *Shiite* here first has its usual meaning of "perforce," "of necessity," "willy-nilly." The notion, then, is that Semimaru has little or no idea how to get by, day by day, at Ausaka, and remains there only for lack of choice in the matter. This is the range of meaning lying behind the perhaps excessively innocuous translation, "somehow."

The second sense of *shiite* depends upon the word's being interpreted as a loose pun on *meshii,* an old Japanese word for "blind." The use of pivot words, double in meaning, to enrich texture and deepen significance was standard practice in the waka form.[11] It becomes a matter of critical judgment to decide whether a particular word is meant to serve as one of these serious puns. In the case of poems set within prose works, extrapolation from context will also affect interpretation. The pun, or pivot word, in poem H is not obvious. Looking at the poem alone, one might sensibly argue that the diction is simply straightforward. But the double meaning becomes convincing in the context of the story surrounding the poem, a tale in *Konjaku monogatari* which is the earliest extant narrative to mention Semimaru. In *Konjaku monogatari* blindness becomes an unequivocal feature of Semimaru's literary identity; and it is to this tale that we now must turn.

Tales of Two Blind Men

In *Konjaku monogatari* Semimaru's literary legend shifts from first person to third person. Unlike the poems which were attributed to Semimaru himself, the *Konjaku* tale takes the narrative viewpoint of an outside observer. In part the tale explains the circumstances underlying two of Semimaru's poetic compositions, but this is more than a simple poem tale, more than

[11]Brower and Miner, *Japanese Court Poetry,* pp. 13, 205–8.

a sketchily expanded headnote explaining the poems. The poems are not the principal focus of the story, nor is Semimaru the only important character.

As its cumbersome title, typical for *Konjaku monogatari*, indicates, this is "The Story of How Lord Minamoto no Hiromasa Went to the Blind Man's Place at Ausaka" (I). The blind man of Ausaka was Semimaru, but who was Minamoto no Hiromasa? Though a small body of later legend has grown up around his name, it is possible to identify Hiromasa as an historical individual. The most reliable genealogy of the major Heian courtier families identifies him as the eldest son of Prince Katsuakira who was, in turn, the eldest son of Emperor Daigo.[12] His dates are given as 918–80, and his mother, though herself unnamed, is identified as the daughter of Fujiwara Tokihira.

Hiromasa is better known by the alternate reading of his name, Hakuga; in the later stages of the Semimaru legend he is identified most commonly as Hakuga no Sammi, "Hakuga of the Third Rank." It is possible that Hakuga's reputation in his own lifetime was not too high. A passing reference to him in a courtier's diary entry in 1016, thirty-six years after his death, says only, "Hakuga was a calligrapher and musician, but he was lazy and foolish."[13]

As the Semimaru legend itself bears ample witness, reputations can easily change. By the late eleventh to early twelfth centuries Hakuga had escaped his negative image, threafter moving upward to acquire an ever more illustrious name.[14] By 1254 one source records that the heavens rang with music at
∟ KKCMJ 244

[12] *Sompi bummyaku,* a genealogical record which in its present form dates from the Muromachi period. The entry on Hiromasa is quoted in Tashiro, "Yōkyoku *Semimaru,*" p. 131.

[13] From *Shōyūki,* the diary of Fujiwara Sanesuke (957–1046). Quoted in Tashiro, "Yōkyoku *Semimaru,*" p. 131.

[14] Discussed in Tashiro, "Yōkyoku *Semimaru,*" p. 132.

the birth of Hakuga no Sammi and that thieves underwent a total change of heart upon hearing him play his flageolet. Hakuga no Sammi's name even appears in the short story "The Mother of Captain Shigemoto," by the modern novelist Tanizaki Jun'ichirō. There he is mentioned as possessing the epitome of courtly musical talent.[15]

Though there are intresting parallels to the case of Semimaru, it is not my purpose here to trace in detail the facts and fantasies surrounding Hakuga no Sammi. One such character at a time is sufficient, and the focus remains Semimaru. We need simply realize that Hakuga (or Hiromasa) existed both in reality and in legend independently of Semimaru.

A story very similar to the Hiromasa-Semimaru tale in *Konjaku* appears in the *Gōdanshō*, a collection of tales edited by the scholar Ōe no Masafusa (1041–1111) between 1104 and 1106, the same decade during which *Konjaku monogatari* is now commonly thought to have been completed. *Gōdanshō* and *Konjaku monogatari* contain many sections which are nearly identical in content. Though the style of *Gōdanshō* is more unwieldy and more Chinese-influenced than that of *Konjaku*, whole sentences and paragraphs are at times identical, word for word, in the two texts. Such is definitely the case with the two Hiromasa tales.

Konjaku monogatari scholarship is a complicated subject best left to the experts, but a brief summary of a few currently accepted facts may help explain the relationship between the two collections we are here considering. *Konjaku monogatari* is a vast work containing over twelve hundred tales. Of its original thirty-one volumes, ten consisted of tales of foreign origin, Indian and Chinese. Obviously, this monumental collection was not created all at once in a brief span of time. While some of the tales were possibly transmitted only orally up to the

[15]Tanizaki, *Tanizaki Jun'ichirō zenshū*, XVI, 191, 230.

time of their inclusion in *Konjaku,* certain earlier written collections, including some now no longer extant, were, we believe, sources for some of the tales now known only from *Konjaku.*

In the case of the Semimaru-Hiromasa story, it seems likeliest that both the *Gōdanshō* and the *Konjaku* versions were derived from a common, but no longer extant, written source. The other, less likely possibility is that the *Konjaku* version derives directly from that in *Gōdanshō.* The phraseology in some parts of the two stories is completely identical, so textual copying rather than oral transmission is definitely indicated.

Semimaru's name does not appear in the *Gōdanshō* story.[16] There the story is titled "Hakuga no Sammi Studies the Lute," and Hakuga travels back and forth to Ausaka for three years to the hut of an unnamed blind musician. The subject of interest is definitely Hakuga rather than the blind man. The story ends when Hakuga has learned his desired melodies from the nameless teacher. Unlike the *Konjaku* ending, there is no mention of the blind man as first in a tradition of blind lute players. Otherwise the *Gōdanshō* story shows no significant differences from the *Konjaku* version.

In yet another source Hakuga is described as having learned secret lute melodies from "some blind priest in, perhaps, Kohata."[17] The legend of how Hakuga no Sammi learned three secret melodies for the lute existed, at first, independently of the legend of Semimaru. And the legend of Semimaru existed independently of Hakuga no Sammi. Even around the time of the completion of *Konjaku,* Shunrai, in writing his *Toshiyori zuinō,* thought of Semimaru as a laughable beggar who played the koto, not as an accomplished lutenist possessing secret knowledge.

---

[16]*Gōdanshō, Gunsho ruijū,* XVII, 592–93.
[17]*Yotsugi monogatari* in *Zoku gunsho ruijū,* XXXII, pt. 2, 164.

Konjaku names the "blind man of Ausaka" as Semimaru. Whether accurate—as with Hiromasa—or invented—as may be the case with Semimaru—the identifications of characters peopling the tales in Konjaku are usually quite specific. Semimaru here becomes a former "servant of Prince Atsuzane." He is called a zōshiki, a term designating commoner servants who were used to perform a variety of menial tasks about court. The story indicates that Semimaru had learned from his former master, the prince, the secret melodies which he transmitted to Hiromasa.

It is interesting to note that the Konjaku story does not include the famous kore ya kono poem (A). Apparently it was only later, after Fujiwara Teika's time, that that particular poem became so widely known that any reference to Semimaru summoned the poem to mind almost automatically.

The Konjaku tale does include two other Semimaru poems B and H. Poem B is here said to have been written not because of the laughter of passers-by but in response to a request from an emissary of Hiromasa's who was urging Semimaru to return to life in the capital. When this poem had first appeared, in 1013 in the Wakan rōeishū, it was labeled "anonymous," yet clearly by the eleventh century there existed some notion that this was Semimaru's poem. Shunrai and the unknown author of the Konjaku story had different ideas about Semimaru's identity and different explanations for the circumstances of composition, but both called the poem Semimaru's.

Since the Konjaku identification of Semimaru as a servant of a prince allows for the possibility that Semimaru had once lived in or around a palace, the lines "Whether in a palace or a hovel/ We cannot live forever" take on new overtones. Perhaps Semimaru lived at court during the liftime of Prince Atsuzane, moving to Ausaka upon the death of his prince in 967. The Konjaku tale implies that Semimaru was an old man, older than Hiromasa, who died in 980 at the age of sixty-two.

The Literature

Though these "facts" fit together nicely, they may fit because they were invented to do so. By the time of *Konjaku,* the creation of a legendary Semimaru was well under way, though his legendary identity was not yet fully unified. One major importance of *Konjaku monogatari* to the development of the legend is that Semimaru is here, for the first time, loosely linked with the imperial court and life in the capital.

Semimaru's blindness, too, is first established in this story. His blindness adds an affecting element to the legend, an element which remains dominant in later Semimaru literature. Because of his blindness Semimaru does not know that Hiromasa is nearby watching him and waiting for him to play. The blind Semimaru plays his lute for solace in his loneliness, only then to learn that he is not alone. This motif—the sad and lonely blind man watched by a silent observer—reappears in several Semimaru plays and proves to have strong dramatic possibilities.

The Semimaru of *Konjaku monogatari* is no longer pitiful. True, he lives in a simple hut at Ausaka, but he lives there by his own choice. He is the sole master of secret melodies for the lute, and he is therefore sought after by a great musician from the court who subjects himself to a three-year-long ordeal in order to learn those melodies.

Semimaru's blindness is more than a simple physiological condition, more than a poignant literary motif. *Konjaku* tells us that "since his time it has been said that he was the first of the blind lute players." Semimaru now becomes the ancestor or forerunner of a tradition of blind lute players. We can easily imagine an itinerant, mendicant blind man chanting this story of Semimaru to the accompaniment of his own lute. The blind storyteller would gladly speak of this man as the ancestor of his art, for this is a positive image of Semimaru, something to counteract the miserable figure called to the minds of Shunrai and others who, like him, found Semimaru pitiful. *Konjaku*

67

monogatari records a tale which we can imagine to have been told by blind, lute-playing beggars to elevate their own level of dignity.

The Legend of Kuṇāla

There is yet another tale in *Konjaku monogatari* which served to dignify the image of blind musicians. This tale, found in one of the *Konjaku* volumes of tales of Indian origin, is also preserved in several Indian and Chinese sources. As suggested in chapter 2, one tradition of blind lutenists in Japan, the mōsō, had, ultimately, Indian origins. It was apparently in connection with this tradition that the *Konjaku* story in question, the tale of Prince Kuṇāla (J), first made its way from India through China to Japan. There it coalesced in part with the legend of Semimaru, adding rich new dimensions to Semimaru's name. Though the amalgamation of the Kuṇāla legend with the Semimaru legend only finally becomes obvious in the Nō plays *Semimaru* and *Ausaka Madman* (translated in Part II) three centuries later, Kuṇāla was long known in Japan. We can only imagine the process whereby blind storytellers ascribed to their "ancestor" Semimaru some of the attributes of the Indian Prince Kuṇāla. The coexistence of Semimaru and Kuṇāla legends in *Konjaku monogatari* dictates a digression here to examine the basic themes and history of the Kuṇāla legend with the understanding that its full effect will only come later, in the Nō.

   The legend of Prince Kuṇāla has been of remarkably far-reaching influence both east and west of its homeland in India.[18] It was originally part of the Sanskrit Buddhist canon, appearing in the *Divya Avadana;* and the first Chinese translation dates from the third century, sometime before the death

[18]See Keene, "The Hippolytus Triangle, East and West."

of the translator, Sêng Hui, in A.D. 280. Whereas several Chinese versions of the story of the blind prince take on strongly Confucian coloration, the version which made its way into *Konjaku monogatari* is very close, in almost every detail, to the account of Kuṇāla which the Chinese Buddhist pilgrim Hsüan Tsang recorded in his pilgrimage diary, *Records of Western Countries (Hsi Yü Chi)*. Hsüan Tsang undertook his pilgrimage to the homeland of Buddhism in 629, returning to China in 645. He recorded an account of Prince Kuṇāla when he visited a stupa, outside the city of Taxila, which marked the spot where the unfortunate prince's eyes were gouged out.[19]

Here, in brief, are the principal features of this rather grisly story as it became known in Japan. In format it is clearly meant to inspire faith in the power of the law of Buddha, for as its long *Konjaku* title tells us, this is "The Tale of How Prince Kuṇāla's Eyes Were Plucked Out and Then Regained Through Reliance on the Power of the Law" (J).

Kuṇāla was the son of King Aśoka, the first Buddhist ruler of India. According to this legend, Kuṇāla resisted the romantic attentions of his stepmother, the king's second wife, and she, in her rage at being rejected, manipulated the king into sending his son away to govern the distant province of Taxila. Thereafter, through a clever stratagem, the queen sent a counterfeit royal order commanding that the young man's eyes be plucked out and that he be driven beyond the borders of the country. Despite the doubts of those around him, Kuṇāla insisted on obeying this order, not doubting its authenticity. Later the prince restrained his father from punishing his stepmother, and though the *Konjaku* version lacks this particular line, in Hsüan Tsang's account Kuṇāla even calls

---

[19]Hsüan Tsang is translated by Samuel Beale, *Buddhist Records of the Western World*, I, 139–43.

the woman's scheme a "loving order." After he had been blinded Kuṇāla was reduced to wandering about as a beggar musician. Ultimately he was reunited with his father when the emperor recognized his son's unique style of music. The story ends on a positive note with the miraculous restoration of Kuṇāla's eyesight.

In the *Konjaku* version of the story Kuṇāla plays an instrument called in Japanese a koto, but the term was apparently used to translate the name of any unfamiliar stringed instrument, in this case the Indian vina. Because of its vagueness of reference I have taken the liberty in my translation of calling the instrument a lute. For it certainly was not a Japanese koto and was more closely related historically to the Japanese biwa or lute.

In Kuṇāla we find a prince who because of his blindness becomes a poor wandering musician. He is a prince who has been sent away from court, yet interprets his exile as an act of compassion. When reunited with a relative, his identity becomes clear because of the uniqueness of his music. Three centuries after the compilation of *Konjaku monogatari*, all these motifs reappear in the Nō *Semimaru*.

The process whereby Semimaru took on many features of Kuṇāla's identity cannot be traced in any great detail, developing gradually in the interval between *Konjaku* and the Nō. It would seem that the blind lutenists of the twelfth through fourteenth centuries, in venerating their "ancestor" Semimaru, first made him a prince and then gave him some of the qualities of his exotic foreign counterpart. In foreshadowing this reidentification of Semimaru, however, I have jumped ahead in the chronology of events. We are still in the early twelfth century, when Semimaru was to some people a simple beggar and to some a court servant and supreme musician. There remain several references to Semimaru in purely native Japanese literary sources which we must trace before turning to the fifteenth century Nō plays where the Kuṇāla themes find new life in Japan, blending easily with other developments in the ever-growing Semimaru legend.

Princes and Supernatural Beings

I have suggested that it was during the third decade of the 1200s that Semimaru's name began to gain greatly in prominence through the attention paid him by Fujiwara Teika. Prior to Teika's interest it appears clear that Semimaru was not a well-known name in court circles. The eminent poet, critic, and philosopher Kamo no Chōmei (1153–1216) held a view of Semimaru quite at variance with any other we have seen so far. In 1211 Chōmei comments on Semimaru in his *Mumyōshō* (K), in a little four-line note, tucked among the major sections of this work, recording Chōmei's own training as a poet and his critical evaluations of the work of other poets.

Semimaru's name is important to Chōmei as a man from Ausaka who instructed a courtier in a musical art. But Chōmei thought Semimaru's instrument to be the *wagon*, the Japanese koto, and his pupil to be Yoshimine no Munesada (816–90), one of the "six poetic geniuses" mentioned by name in the preface to the *Kokinshū*. Whether he had read the story in *Konjaku monogatari* and then forgotten most of the details, or whether he had heard someone telling the story with garbled characters, Chōmei's "facts" about Semimaru were an idiosyncratic confusion recorded nowhere else.

This, however, is not the most interesting aspect of Chōmei's remarks. More intriguing is his opening comment: "The tutelary spirit of Ausaka Pass was Semimaru of old." From this one line we know that already in Chōmei's time passers-by were treating Semimaru as the deity of the pass. In the Japanese view, divinity was not inconsistent with

prior historical reality. The gods often took human form. Semimaru was a "man of old," by now transformed into a minor
deity, a god protecting the spot on which the crumbling remains of his hut, says Chōmei, still stood.[20]

We know from other sources that Semimaru became more
than the local deity of Ausaka; he became, as well, the ancestor deity of several types of itinerant musicians and entertainers. As ancestor deity, it seems, Semimaru needed a more
glorious identity for his this-worldy incarnation than mere
"beggar" or "court servant." Our first glimpse of Semimaru's
new identity comes from a travel diary of disputed authorship,
Tōkan kikō (L), which records a journey from Kyoto to
Kamakura and back in the year 1242.

The opening lines of the diary reference to Semimaru are
completely consistent with, and probably based on, Konjaku
monogatari. Then comes the great shift. According to the diary,
"it is said that because Semimaru was the fourth son of Emperor Daigo the area near this barrier is called Shinomiya-
kawara." Semimaru has become a prince, and the meaning of
the name here given for the area near the pass is "dry riverbed
of the fourth prince."

From the point of view of historical fact it is known that
Semimaru without question was not the fourth son of Emperor
Daigo. The emperor's fourth son is identified in genealogies of
the imperial family as Prince Saneakira, who died in 954.[21]
The compilers of Gosenshū, who in 951 identified Semimaru
as a beggar, were the contemporaries of the fourth son of the
Emperor Daigo and knew the prince's true identity.

The place name Shinomiya-kawara puts us on the trail of
another, true "fourth prince" who once lived in the area and
in whose memory the name of the area developed: Saneyasu

[20]Hōjōki, Tsurezuregusa, NKBT, XXX, 39.
[21]Seishi kakei daijiten, I, 73.

The Literature

(831–72), fourth son of the Emperor Nimmyō, as confirmed by the same imperial genealogies that are mute on the name Semimaru.[22]

As shown in chapter 2, Saneyasu, under the name Amayo "Heaven night," was claimed as ancestor by the powerful Tōdōza, the guild of blind reciters, organized in mid-fourteenth century, who specialized in *Heike monogatari* recitation.

As *Konjaku monogatari* is first to suggest, some blind biwa players claimed Semimaru rather than Amayo as their ancestor deity. These musicians must have been a different group from the antecedents of the Tōdōza. The most reasonable explanation for Semimaru's sudden elevation to fictitious princedom is to suppose that it results from rivalry between what may be called the Amayo faction and the Semimaru faction of blind biwa players, sometime prior to the writing of *Tōkan kikō*. Not to be outdone by the Amayo-identified performers, the Semimaru faction reidentified their own ancestor as the "fourth prince." The leap in lineage would not have been too difficult to make credible since Semimaru was already vaguely associated with the court in his *Konjaku* identity as minor servant. Hiromasa of the *Konjaku* tale was Emperor Daigo's grandson, thus suggesting a good emperor from whom to claim paternity; and since Daigo's reign was looked back on as a golden age, he was the finest emperor one might wish to choose as fictive father.

The genealogical legerdemain of the Semimaru-venerating biwa hōshi is further evidenced by early texts of *Heike monogatari*, dating from around the time of *Tōkan kikō*.

The *Shibu kassenjō bon* text of *Heike monogatari*, a Kambun text written to be read rather than recited, may be the original text of *Heike monogatari*. It apparently dates from between 1218 and 1221 and contains no reference to Semimaru. The earliest

[22]*Ibid.*, p. 64.

73

extant *Heike* revision intended for oral recitation is the *Hiramatsuke* text, which is thought to have been developed at the Kyoto center of the Agui shōdō. This text, dating from about 1235, mentions Semimaru briefly, and accepts him as a prince.

Only those versions of the Semimaru legend which call him prince make any mention of the place name Shinomiya-kawara, and all the recitation texts of *Heike monogatari* with which we are here concerned incorporate this telltale confusion about the exact spot where Semimaru lived.

Describing the first stages of a journey to Kamakura from the capital the Hiramatsuke *Heike monogatari* states: "They came to Shinomiya-kawara. This is the place where, long ago, Semimaru, the fourth son of Emperor Daigo, calmed his feelings in the storms at the barrier by playing his lute." It then goes on to recount briefly Hakuga's three years' of patient travel and his final reward, instruction in the three secret melodies. Since the barrier referred to here is Ausaka Barrier, the text has Semimaru, in a sense, in two places at once, though the two spots were within easy walking distance of each other.

The *Yashiro-bon Heike monogatari,* another recitation revision which dates from the mid-thirteenth century,[23] likewise refers to Semimaru as the fourth prince. Though two or three phrases of this text are worded differently from the Hiramatsuke text, the import of the passage is exactly the same. The authorship and circumstances of composition of these two texts are not precisely known, but the similarity between them in the Semimaru passages is typical of a general similarity throughout, suggesting influence from the Hiramatsuke version in the Yashiro text.

The compilers of the Hiramatsuke text may have been taking

[23] See Butler, "Textual Evolution," pp. 10, 25, and 33–38 on the dating and significance of the Hiramatsuke and Yashiro texts.

a conscious, factional position in identifying Semimaru as a prince, through the very brevity of the Semimaru passage indicates relatively little emphasis on the veneration of the "prince." If factional rivalries lay behind Semimaru's elevation to royal status, they had been quickly forgotten, as those responsible for later textual revisions continued to accept and sustain this passage.

Akashi Kakuichi, founder of the Tōdōza and author of the 1371 Kakuichi text of *Heike monogatari*, venerated Amayo, not Semimaru, as ancestor of his guild. Ironically unaware of the process whereby Semimaru became known as prince, Kakuichi accepted both Semimaru and Amayo as princes and master lute soloists, praising Amayo at great length in the guild records while incorporating Semimaru as prince in his version of the *Heike monogatari*.

Kakuichi's version of the Semimaru passage (M) is identical with the Hiramatsuke text with the addition of a single phrase. In producing his textual revision, Kakuichi drew on both the Hiramatsuke and Yashiro texts or their respective later recensions. In this passage he chose the slightly longer, richer version from the Hiramatsuke text.

Gikeiki, a later text in the *Heike monogatari* tradition, of unknown authorship and uncertain date, probably reached its final form in the first half of the fifteenth century. It shows the same double location for Semimaru as does the Kakuichi text of *Heike monogatari*. "They passed Shinomiya-kawara where Semimaru of Ausaka lived," it says in one passage, and in another, "They came and saw the floor of the straw hut where Semimaru of Ausaka lived." [24] Despite the importance of Shinomiya-kawara in making Semimaru a prince, his name was inextricably bound with Ausaka as well.

[24]*Gikeiki*, NKBT, XXXVII, pp. 265, 311. See also the complete English translation of *Gikeiki*: McCullough, *Yoshitsune*, 214, 244.

Gempei seisuiki (N) is the last important pre-Nō source of the Semimaru legend. It is a variant text and considerable expansion of *Heike monogatari* and is approximately contemporaneous with the 1371 Kakuichi text. The interest of the *Gempei seisuiki* passages concerning Semimaru is twofold. On the one hand, they give the most complete information available concerning the popular understanding of the secret melodies of which Semimaru was considered master. On the other hand, *Gempei seisuiki* is important because it tied together several disparate elements of the Semimaru legend as they had developed up to that point.

Konjaku monogatari suggests that Semimaru learned his secret melodies from his former master, a prince. Historical sources indicate that the melodies were first imported to Japan from China by the fully mortal courtier Fujiwara Sadatoshi, thereby becoming known in ninth-century court circles. *Gempei seisuiki* also itself mentions Sadatoshi's learning the secret melodies from a Chinese master, but it credits a "heavenly being"—no mere prince—as having been Semimaru's teacher.

Gempei seisuiki describes two of the three secret melodies in a section entitled "Concerning the Lute Seizan, Ryūsen and Takuboku."[25] "Ryūsen" is described as a favorite melody of the Bodhisattva Miroku, one which he played to awaken the spiritual consciousness of mankind. It is said to have been played for the Chinese emperor Han Wu-ti, on the occasion of his visit to a certain hermit, by celestial beings who descended to earth from the abode of the Bodhisattva. Its name, meaning "flowing stream," derives from a spring bubbling in the garden at the time of the emperor's divinely favored visit to the hermit.

"Takuboku" is also called celestial music. To hear it puts the listener's mind in the right state of awareness to escape from

[25]*Gempei seisuiki*, 172–74.

the eternal cycle of rebirth. The passage states that numerous ascetics gathered on Mount Shang (Shō) in China and secretly played this tune. The spirits of the mountain were transformed into bugs which bored into the trees. The name of the melody means "pecked trees." In these colorful passages *Gempei seisuiki* reflects the medieval Japanese understanding of the power of music to open the mind to the realm of gods and Buddhas.

There are two passages in *Gempei seisuiki* concerning Semimaru. Both passages refer to Semimaru as a prince and as the teacher of Hakuga no Sammi. Of these the one given as translation N2 is the more interesting in tracing the development of the legend. It repeats the Semimaru-Hakuga connection while at the same time linking this Semimaru with the Semimaru of the *Gosenshū* poem A where the legend first began. Skipping only the first invocatory line *kore ya kono*, *Gempei seisuiki* weaves the last four lines of the poem into a metered section following the prose description of Semimaru's instruction of Hakuga. Moreover, in its reference to Prince Semimaru at Au-saka, *Gempei seisuiki* speaks of the prince as having been "abandoned." Not only is Semimaru accepted as a prince, we also glimpse the influence of the Kunāla tale, the story of a prince abandoned.

After this step-by-step development, discernible primarily from minor sources and passing references, the Semimaru legend in the fifteenth century inspired two major plays for the newly important world of Nō theater. With these plays we move into a new chapter of the legend. Before proceeding to analysis of the Nō, however, it is interesting to note evidence of one last-ditch, futile effort to stop the spread of Semimaru's legendary identification as prince.

Ichijō Kanera (1402–81) was one of the leading political and intellectual figures of medieval Japan. A major force in court politics, he thrice served as imperial regent. He was an eclectic, traditional scholar, noted for his thirty-volume study of *Genji monogatari* as well as for his writings on poetry, Buddhism, and government. In his *Tōzai zuihitsu* (O), Kanera recorded miscellaneous comments under eleven general subject headings: plants, animals, Buddhism, Shinto, and so forth. The first subject was music, and in that connection he turned his attention to Semimaru.

As a member of the inner court circles, Kanera was probably familiar with the imperial genealogies which served as evidence that Semimaru was, in fact, not a prince. Writing at some time in the fifteenth century, Kanera accepted the accuracy of *Konjaku monogatari*, repeating the basic outline of the *Konjaku* Semimaru story and reaffirming Semimaru's identity as a servant of Prince Atsuzane. "Mere facts," however, are often powerless in the face of captivating legend. This is the case with Semimaru. The appeal of the legend of a beggar prince was too broad and powerful to be stopped by a courtier scholar bent on keeping the facts—as he understood them—straight. By this time the legend of the blind outcast prince had acquired the power to inspire major works of drama which, in turn, spread the fame of the musician-beggar-prince to a still wider audience.

The Nō *Semimaru* and
Ausaka Madman

Changing tastes on the part of Nō audiences through the centuries have dealt different fates to the two Nō plays based on the material of the Semimaru legend. *Semimaru* is still performed today by all the principal schools of Nō actors, though it seems to have undergone a period of eclipsed popularity in the centuries immediately following its composition. *Ausaka Madman* is now never performed. In the company of some two or three thousand other Nō, it has dropped from the performance repertoire. The height of its popularity occurred in the lifetime of its author, the playwright Zeami (1363–1443), but it was probably last performed in the sixteenth century.

As is invariably the case with Nō, the dates of composition of these plays are unknown. Both date from the lifetime of Zeami, who is universally accepted as the author of *Ausaka Madman*. Most critics have also considered *Semimaru* the work of Zeami, and on the basis of stylistic criteria as well as certain passages in Zeami's critical writings, I too am convinced that this is the case. In discussing *Semimaru* I shall refer to it as Zeami's work, later in the chapter presenting the reasoning to support this assumption.

Ausaka Madman

Ausaka Madman was composed before 1423. It is mentioned in Zeami's text concerning the composition of Nō which he completed in that year, his sixtieth.[1] In 1430 Zeami's son recorded, in a collection of Zeami's "conversations" concerning Nō, a list of twenty-two titles of Zeami plays which includes *Ausaka Madman*.[2] The same work briefly discusses a play called *Sakagami*, seemingly referring to the play now known as *Semimaru*.

Zeami wrote that as the playwright opens the ears of the audience, the principal actor opens their eyes.[3] The critic of Nō in turn must attempt to elucidate the entire concept of a play. Nō appealed both to the ears and to the eyes, both intellectually and emotionally, and criticism must, so far as possible, take account of both the literary value of a Nō text when read now and the totality of its impact at the time of performance as music drama.

Modern performances can be helpful guides, but one cannot rely entirely on current performances owing to changes in style since the time of composition and also, obviously, because many plays worth evaluation are no longer performed. Textual analysis of *Semimaru* and *Ausaka Madman* can demonstrate the themes and predominantly literary values of the texts, but the reader of a Nō play, in the original or in translation, must through an effort of creative imagination seek to perceive the performance born from the text.

As music dramas Nō are compositions more than literary texts. Zeami first chose his materials, then wrote his words, setting his texts to music; but even on the printed page the

[1] *Sandō (Nōsakusho)* in NKBT, LXV, 480.

[2] *Sarugaku dangi* in NKBT, LXV, 520. In both cases the play is referred to as *Ausaka. Ausaka, Ausaka monogurui, Ausaka mekura* (the blind man of Ausaka), and *Waraya mekura* (the blind man in the straw hut) have all at one time or another been used as alternate titles of the play I have translated as *Ausaka Madman*. See Tanaka, "Ōsaka monogurui," p. 253.

[3] *Sandō*, NKBT, LXV, 478.

musical aspects of performance can be at least partially de-
duced from the syllable patterns and degree of lyricism of the
songs and speeches of the actors. Given musical-textual patterns recur from play to play and have standard labels: "opening song," "naming-speech," "arrival speech," and so on. The
total composition is the summation of these constituent parts.

Certain sequences of patterns are common, and Zeami's critical writings reveal much, though not a complete picture, concerning ideal structural patterns for whole plays. Both structural and thematic analysis of a Nō play are necessary and
are mutually complementary as the presentation of an idea in a
play in an unusual or structurally marked position may force-
fully affect the prominence and importance of that idea within
the context of its play.

Thematically, there are certain points of great similarity between *Semimaru* and *Ausaka Madman,* and some of the lines of
the two texts are identical. Structurally, the two plays are very
different. *Ausaka Madman* is simpler and more ordinary in
structure than *Semimaru*. Both plays are set at Ausaka and both
show the amalgamation of the legends of Kuṇāla and Semimaru, as discussed in previous chapters, yet each play emphasizes somewhat different aspects of its source material.

As might easily be assumed from its title alone, *Semimaru*
contributes more directly than *Ausaka Madman* to the further
development of the Semimaru legend. Zeami and his audiences accepted Semimaru as a prince, and the royal status of
this man is the basis of much of the pathos of the play.

Semimaru

In *Semimaru* a young man, blind from birth, is abandoned
on a mountainside on his father's orders. A beautiful young
woman suffers episodes of inexplicable madness which com-
pel her to wander the countryside aimlessly. The two sufferers

are sister and brother; and were this not sufficiently moving, the family so afflicted is the royal house. The wandering sister by chance finds her deserted brother, yet, in her madness she wanders off, leaving him again alone. Many have found this the single most tragic Nō performed today.[4]

Semimaru begins with the formal *shidai* "opening song" pattern characteristic of about half the plays of the current Nō repertoire.[5] Always in high melodic style, sung to fixed rhythm in a simple manner without ornamentation,[6] the opening song is most commonly recited by the *waki*, the secondary character, sometimes, as here, accompanied by attendants. Typically, as in *Semimaru*, the opening song has a certain mysteriously prophetic, oracular quality. It comes to have specific meaning as the play progresses, and different developments being possible, several opening songs occur in more than one play. The shidai of *Semimaru* also opens the play *Yoshino Shizuka:*[7]

[4]Sanari Kentarō, editor of the massive compendium *Yōkyoku taikan*, was of this opinion: III, 1673. See also the comments of Roy Teele concerning a recent performance of the play in "The Structure of the Japanese Noh Play," p. 204.

[5]Yasuda, "The Structure of *Hagoromo*," p. 36. Yasuda has made frequency counts for the occurrence of several set patterns in the plays of the modern Nō repertoire. Several of my comments on frequency follow his findings. In my discussion of *Semimaru* I am basing my comments on a theoretical performance following the stage directions of the Kanze school as recorded in *Yōkyoku taikan*. There are no significant differences in lines among modern published editions of *Semimaru*, but there are variations in staging among the five different schools of Nō.

[6]The reader interested in pursuing further in English matters pertaining to musical and metrical structural patterns in Nō is referred to the above-mentioned articles by Yasuda and Teele as well as the long article by Hoff and Flindt, "The Life Structure of Noh," *Concerned Theatre Japan*, Spring, 1973, pp. 209–56.

[7]Exclusively in Komparu school texts.

> The world is so unsure, unknowable
> The world is so unsure, unknowable,
> Who knows—our griefs may hold our greatest hopes.

The opening song suggests the possibility of joy in grief. Developing this apparent paradox, *Semimaru* unfolds as a play of opposites through the elaboration of two characters, Semimaru, the beggar prince (*tsure* the "companion" role) and Sakagami, the mad princess (*shite,* the principal role).

The waki continues speaking, shifting from the high melodic style of the opening song to a recitative style in lower tones (*sashi*). The language is arrhythmic but poetic. The lines immediately following the opening song in most Nō serve as a self-introduction of the character speaking. In *Semimaru,* however, the waki introduces not himself but the tsure, thus quickly and strongly establishing Semimaru as a focal character. Semimaru alone remains silent. We learn more of him through the continuing recitative of the waki, a character as yet unidentified and of unclear relationship to Semimaru, who speaks in unison with two attendants. Semimaru's silent entry seems to mark his passivity, a striking feature of his character throughout the play. His silent passivity serves dramatically to emphasize his blindness, as does the tentative style of walking some actors employ in performing Semimaru's stage entrance.

The waki begins developing the theme of the opening song by reminding the audience that the events of a person's life are fated, determined by karma, and that it was Semimaru's karma to have been born a prince, yet blind. The actor in the waki role attempts to convey a mood of restrained sadness, presenting the lines less briskly than in the usual sashi.[8]

The waki's mission begins to emerge. He reveals that he has

[8] My comments on the actor's presentation of lines, throughout the account of *Semimaru,* are derived from an article by the actor Miyake Noboru, "Utaikata kōza *Semimaru,*" pp. 34–37.

been ordered by the emperor to abandon Semimaru secretly at Ausaka. The ruler responsible for this apparently heartless decision is the Emperor Daigo. This emperor was usually held as a model for later generations, as the ideal ruler of a golden age. As one Japanese critic has suggested, Semimaru is a "Buddhist morality play."[9] The inflexibility of karma is powerfully symbolized by the inability of the most perfect emperor to affect its course.

Just as his sovereign is powerless in the face of karma, the imperial escort is powerless to go against the will of the emperor. The journey of abandonment begins with a few lines in low-pitch, fixed rhythm, the *sageuta:*

> Like lame-wheeled carriages
> We creep forth reluctantly
> On the journey from the capital.

Though the tsure Semimaru has not yet spoken, we imagine all four characters on stage as reluctant travelers; the image of the lame-wheeled carriage is associated especially with Semimaru, crippled by his blindness.

The low-pitched *sageuta* is followed by a relatively long *ageuta*, a song in fixed rhythm in high-pitched melodic style. Beginning with the line "How hard it is to say farewell," the song serves as a *michiyuki*, a song of travel, which ends with the arrival of the group at Mount Ausaka. The images of sadness introduced in the opening theme continue to develop. His escorts sing of Semimaru as friendless, afflicted, having only the most fragile chance of ever returning to the life of the court. Semimaru's "path is in darkness." Accordingly in this michiyuki there occur no scenes glimpsed in travel, nor even the place names that are typical of most travel passages. Rather, the michiyuki conveys the difficulty of wandering in

---

[9] Kōsai, "Semimaru," pp. 20–22.

the darkness of the blind. The only place named is their final destination, Ausaka.

In a great many Nō, the waki's arrival at the end of the travel song, at the locale of the main action of the play, is followed by the entrance on stage of the principal character, his or her self-description, and a dialogue between the waki and the shite. Semimaru is different, having no encounter at all between the waki and the shite. The dialogue (*mondo*) follows immediately upon the michiyuki with the waki conversing with the tsure, Semimaru, rather than with the shite. In *Semimaru* the entry of the shite comes late, only in the second half of the play, and the tsure, accordingly, becomes an important role. The actors performing the mondo attempt to convey a mood of sadness, the waki striving to evoke sympathy for Semimaru. Semimaru's first speech is a single word; he calls out the name of his escort, the waki who has thus far been the main voice of the play, "Kiyotsura!"

The mondo is largely in prose, with some poetic, melodic passages interspersed. However, the melodic range through this exchange of lines is very limited, and the actors deliver their lines in a restrained manner, with care to avoid any sense of gaiety.

In the mondo there is a further elaboration of the imagery of the imperial line's magnificence as well as Kiyotsura's continuing complaint of his inability to resist the emperor's unwelcome decree. Semimaru realizes, confirms, and accepts the fact that his father has ordered him abandoned, though the motivation behind the emperor's order is unclear. The theme of a prince sent into blind exile by his father came to *Semimaru* from the Kuṇāla legend, but the motivation of the Kuṇāla legend—meddling by a vicious stepmother—is absent.[10]

---

[10]The same may be said of *Yoroboshi* by Motomasa, another Nō which shows the influence of the Kuṇāla legend. Its shite is a youth

Like Kuṇāla, Semimaru accepts his father's order as pro-
voked by compassion. The play has established dramatic sympathy for Semimaru. But Semimaru is not sorry for himself.
Paradoxically, the blind prince accepts his fate. "Our griefs
may hold our greatest hopes" he reminds himself in acknowl-
edging his father's orders as a plan to purge him of the karmic
causation of his suffering.

The dialogue between Kiyotsura and Semimaru continues,
attended with considerable stage action and use of props. The
exchange between actors is calm throughout, the lines being
delivered with particular precision. While remaining onstage,
Semimaru is dressed in a priest's headgear and his outer robe
is changed. The on-stage recostuming is highly effective vi-
sually, transforming Semimaru from prince to beggar before
the very eyes of the audience. But the actors strive to make the
import of the scene comprehensible from the lines alone. Recostumed with a straw rainhat, and the wanderer's staff of a
blind beggar, Semimaru has undergone a complete visible
transformation. The pace is leisurely up to the emphatic final
line, delivered with great emphasis by Semimaru, a single
word: "Abandoned."

Both through his recostuming and because of other conventions of his stage treatment, Semimaru looks more like a blind
beggar than a prince though the impression is relative, all
Nō costumes being beautiful. In plays which emphasize the
extraordinary quality of an emperor or member of the imperial
family, *kokata*, child actors, appear in the role of the imperial

---

who has been driven out of his family home because of another's
slander. The intensity of his grief has caused him to go blind. The
boy's contemplative existence as a beggar on the grounds of the Shitennōji and his eventual reunion with his father form the substance
of the play. The "slander" is unspecified and mentioned only briefly.
There is no hint of the Hippolytus theme of the Kuṇāla legend, the
love of stepmother for stepson.

adults. Such special coloration of the role is not called for in the case of Semimaru.

Lines delivered by the chorus, speaking first for Semimaru then for Kiyotsura, conclude the first segment of the play. The tone, again, is one of grief.

In its lines spoken for Semimaru, the chorus cries, "Behold—this is how a prince, Daigo's son, has reached the last extremity of grief."

The line of the chorus translated "you who know me, you who know me not" is in Japanese the fourth line of the first and most famous poem (A) attributed to the "historical" Semimaru. There the line is translated "for friends and strangers alike," but the different context of the line in the Nō necessitates a different translation in this case. And the chorus, for Kiyotsura, goes on to sing of travelers to and from the capital such as first inspired that poem. The entire first half of *Semimaru* provides the dramatic setting of the poem, familiar from allusion alone.

Kiyotsura departs at daybreak, but for Semimaru, in blindness, there can be no dawn. With its last line the chorus subsides to a very quiet tone as Semimaru is finally abandoned, alone, weeping and clutching his lute. (The actual stage prop is a fan, used symbolically as the lute.) Though the lute will figure significantly in the latter half of the play, it had not been mentioned up until this time, perhaps because the legendary Semimaru was so inextricably associated with the lute that Zeami could take it for granted that the audience would simply assure Semimaru to be carrying the instrument.[11]

Kiyotsura exits from the stage, leaving Semimaru momentarily alone, seated and weeping. Hereupon the tension of the play is broken by an interlude featuring a *kyōgen* character; such characters are commonly low-class rustics, typically an

[11]Tashiro, "Yōkyoku *Semimaru*," No. 23, p. 127.

unnamed "local." In this play, the kyōgen identifies himself as Hakuga no Sammi, the courtier lutenist who received musical instruction from Semimaru in earlier versions of his legend.

Here, however, an inversion has taken place. In *Konjaku monogatari* (I) Hakuga is a courtier and Semimaru a servant. Now Semimaru has become a prince and Hakuga, a humble peasant serving him. Hakuga leads Semimaru into the straw hut he has built, then leaves the prince with an offer of continued service.[12]

The texts of the kyōgen interludes were not fixed in Zeami's day but were blocked out only roughly, then improvised in performance by the kyōgen actors. It is possible that the part of Hakuga no Sammi in *Semimaru* was originally longer, with Hakuga, as in earlier stages of the legend, receiving lute instruction from Semimaru. *Semimaru* was apparently a relatively unpopular play for some time during the late Muromachi and early Tokugawa periods,[13] and when it was revived in mid-Tokugawa, Hakuga's legend was moribund and his significance to the Semimaru story minimal. In the interlude as presently constituted, Hakuga simply serves the purpose of guiding the blind prince into shelter. During the kyōgen break, though the actual stage time is brief, dramatic time is long enough for Semimaru to regain his composure. At the conclusion of the first half of the play Semimaru was weep-

---

[12] Amano Fumio, "*Semimaru no tanjō*," p. 59, mentions that there also existed another earlier version of the Semimaru-Hakuga legend similar to the tale in *Konjaku monogatari* except for the fact that, as here in the Nō, Hakuga comes to Ausaka to console Semimaru rather than to learn secret melodies from him. Amano's interesting article, which appeared as this book was in the middle of the final editing process, confirms many of the points in my discussion of the Nō *Semimaru* and in the comparison of *Semimaru* and *Ausaka Madman*.

[13] Tashiro, "Yōkyoku *Semimaru*," No. 23, p. 129. See also Nose, *Nōgaku genryū kō*, p. 1316.

ing in distress, but when he commences speaking in the second half, he has reached a state of calm.

The shite, the principal character, in *Semimaru* is not the prince himself, but his elder sister, Sakagami. The most unusual structural feature of this play is the delayed entry of the shite, who first appears only in the latter half. While it is not unusual for the shite to make a formal stage entrance at the start of the second half, this is normally the second entrance of the character, now possibly recostumed and reidentified. The delayed entry of Sakagami in *Semimaru,* coupled with the preceding unusual naming passage, puts very heavy emphasis on Semimaru, the tsure. Zeami himself called this play *Sakagami,* its original title, yet fairly quickly the importance of Semimaru caused a change to the present title.[14]

The music presaging and accompanying Sakagami's entrance is the *issei,* a pattern typically associated with the shite. It is a lively pattern in the high range. In this case the shite does not sing the song form itself, also known as *issei,* but rather begins with a *sashi,* poetic recitative.[15] Zeami's one extant comment on the play concerns the costuming of Sakagami and the impression created at her entrance.

"In the Nō *Sakagami* a princess becomes mad. Since her appearance is very important, if she is costumed in a *mizugoromo,*[16] it pleases the audience."[17] Zeami's comment may have

[14]Within the Kanze school there exists a traditional variant style of performance (*kogaki*) in which the lines are unchanged but a few lines normally spoken by the chorus are taken by Semimaru. In this kogaki both Semimaru and Sakagami are considered to be shite.

[15]Yasuda, "The Structure of *Hagoromo,*" p. 42, lists seventeen plays having issei music followed by a sashi or other unidentified verse. He also mentions (p. 44) the prominent use of issei music for second-half entrances by the shite.

[16]*Mizugoromo* is a short, thin, silk overrobe worn as a cloak over the kimono. In current performances this costuming is *not* used for Sakagami.

[17]*Sarugaku dangi,* NKBT, LXV, 525.

been meant to remind the actor that, as a princess, Sakagami is not the usual madwoman found in many other Nō. Concerning the interpretation of this role a modern actor has commented that he strives to convey in Sakagami a sense of a strong-hearted woman. Her lines are delivered with greater emotional strength than is customary in other madwoman roles, where the woman has been unbalanced by the loss of her child or husband. Throughout his performance the actor strives to make Sakagami appear to be under mental strain. He achieves this effect in part through the hypnotic, yet tense, fluttering of the branch of bamboo grass Sakagami carries.

In her opening sashi Sakagami identifies herself as "the third child of the Emperor Daigo, the one called Sakagami, Upturned Hair," then explains her own emotional state. Bad karma, the result of unknown evil in some former life, has caused her madness. Her strange hair is the tangible symbol of her distress. In a sense Sakagami is both Semimaru's sister and his double, both being socially estranged because of karmic forces beyond their control. Where Semimaru is quiet and resigned, Sakagami is a vivacious, vocal character of truly extraordinary dimensions. The very embodiment of paradox, she rejects normal social values and espouses their opposites. Zeami may have found the idea of a sister for Semimaru, named Sakagami, in oral legend popular around the Ausaka area, but he was apparently the first to develop her character. Her lines have been called the most philosophical in all Zeami's Nō.[18]

Delivered with strong emotion and a brilliant tone, her lines are also somewhat broken and jerky as she turns from side to side and looks up and down, responding to the supposed taunts of children who laugh at her strange standing hair.

----

[18] Umehara, *Jigoku no shisō*, pp. 158–62. Umehara analyzes *Semimaru* as a play about social outcasts.

Perhaps the teasing itself exists only in her tortured mind. Her response is conveyed entirely by monologue; no other actors appear with her as she speaks while progressing along the bridgeway leading to the stage proper. Semimaru is seated on stage within the prop straw hut, but he is dramatically not in the action and does not react to her presence.

The increasing intensity of her madness is signaled by the musicians at the back of the stage who begin playing *kakeri,* music typical of many madwoman plays.[19] Holding her peculiar hair, Sakagami begins to dance in a deranged manner. The lines leading up to her dance are delivered strongly; her madness is different from most portrayed in Nō in that she suggests no weakness. Her madness is, in fact, particularly tragic precisely because it is so strong and because it remains unrelieved to the end of the play.

The last line of Sakagami's at this point is, "What's this—the hair-tearing dance? How demeaning!" Hereupon the shite begins to dance with the chorus speaking for the dancer. The change in tone is markedly dramatic. The opening lines of the chorus are from *Azuma kudari.* A dance piece which will be discussed further below, it was very popular in Zeami's day and quite familiar to the Nō audience. In contrast to the free rhythm of the preceding sashi the chorus sings an ageuta in fixed rhythm, high register. The song narrates the journey of the shite and is in effect a michiyuki, a song of travel which, like Semimaru's michiyuki earlier, culminates in arrival at Ausaka.

Unlike the michiyuki of the blind Semimaru, Sakagami's song describes a scene or two along the way and features several place names. Because of its two travel songs, the locale of *Semimaru* is very strongly emphasized. This ageuta is the most

[19] Kakeri also are used in some warrior plays. See Nogami, *Nōgaku zensho,* I, 133, 143–44.

famous song in the play, and contemporary actors consider it the high point. The *shimai*, Sakagami's dance, is a difficult challenge for the actor who must show Sakagami's madness through the mimetic dance while simultaneously preserving a tranquil mood. There is a danger, if the actor is insufficiently delicate and restrained, of dancing too roughly and ruining the mood. The challenge is to present Sakagami as gentle, yet strong, and increasingly deranged.

The ageuta of the chorus is broken by three lines sung by the shite, known as *ageha*, following which the chorus resumes, now quickening the pace. In great concentration and distress, Sakagami examines her own reflection in the stream at Ausaka. With increasing derangement she becomes less philosophical; now seeing her reflection quite as others see it, she says, "Though my own face, it horrifies me." The dance concluded, the shite sits down, indicating that she has arrived at Ausaka, and Semimaru begins to speak.

Semimaru opens his fan, understood by stage convention to be his lute. His speech is again a sashi, delivered in lowered tones to convey a sense of resignation. The actor seeks to portray Semimaru with inner strength and outer calm, and his voice is relatively strong and emphatic in reciting, as the closing lines of this passage, the Semimaru poem B: "Our lives,/ This way or that,/ Pass just the same./ Whether in a palace or a hovel/ We cannot live forever." Semimaru approaches acceptance of his fate.

Semimaru plays his lute as solace for his loneliness. A modern commentator on the play sees in Semimaru's lute playing an example of the notion of salvation through music or through beauty, citing as a modern equivalent Tanizaki's short story "Shunkinsho."[20] His solitary lute playing has increased Semimaru's inner calm and enhanced his inner vision. He

[20]Tashiro, "Yōkyoku *Semimaru*," No. 24 p. 52.

shows none of the tearful distress of the first half of the play.

Semimaru's music draws Sakagami to him. Before he is aware of her presence, she stands, listening and watching his hut. In this respect the scene is straight out of *Konjaku monogatari* (I) with Sakagami instead of Hakuga in the role of the silent onlooker. In fact, Semimaru at first imagines Sakagami to be Hakuga. With Sakagami speaking first, here begins a section of alternating speeches shifting between the shite and tsure. As the two characters reach a state of shared perception, recognizing each other, the lines become progressively shorter and faster and are delivered with increasing intensity until the chorus picks up the lines in place of the two actors saying, "They speak each other's names as in one voice."[21] The moment of meeting is the emotional high point of the action. At Ausaka, the barrier of meeting, they are reunited and both are moved to tears.

Here begins a complex of patterns, recited principally by the chorus, called *kuri, sashi, kuse*. In terms of the development of narrative in a play, the kuri, sashi, kuse sequence is extremely important. The weight of plot development is balanced toward that half of a play which contains this sequence, a very common feature of Nō found in over two thirds of the works in the modern repertoire.[22]

In this segment of the play comes a major elaboration of the theme which has been implicit since the opening lines: the mysterious work of karma. In the kuri the chorus sings of the memories shared by the royal brother and sister. The shite's sashi follows with Sakagami mentioning other royal siblings who bear unfamiliar, euphonious names with an exotic appeal to the audience.

[21]Yasuda, "The Structure of *Hagoromo*," pp. 59–60, describes a similar passage in *Hagoromo* and its effect in showing the psychological closeness of the two characters sharing the lines.

[22]*Ibid.*, pp. 45, 63–65.

The kuse of Semimaru is a "seated-kuse" (*iguse*) in which the actor remains seated, rather than dancing, as the chorus chants his lines. Again, like Semimaru's silence during the opening passages, his immobility here emphasizes his blindness.[23] The more usual pattern in Nō would be for the shite to perform the kuse, both as dancer and as speaker of the line or two called ageha, an interpolation in the midst of the kuse recitation of the chorus. The kuse of *Semimaru* is unusual in that in the first segment, preceding the ageha, the chorus speaks for Sakagami, switching with Semimaru's ageha to become, instead, his voice. The effect of this format is to strengthen the impression of the extreme psychological closeness of the two characters, an impression first conveyed by their shared lines leading into the kuri.

The imagery now concerns change and loss. Contrasting the luxury of the court with the deprivations of the outcast Semimaru, the kuse expands the contrast between "a palace or a hovel" introduced earlier by Semimaru's poem. In contrast to *Konjaku monogatari*, for instance, Semimaru is clearly an exile rather than a hermit. Semimaru's ageha is gloomy, tinged with pathos: "My only visitors—how rarely they come—." The chorus then picks up for Semimaru, continuing the lonely mood, as it narrates Semimaru's emotional search for relief in his terrible blindness by playing his lute. Throughout the play we are shown Semimaru's struggle to accept with grace his unfelicitous karma. The kuse ends with a poignant line indicating how incomplete that acceptance remains as, speaking for Semimaru, the chorus concludes, "How painful to contemplate life in this hut!"

The intense power of the play derives from its unresolved ending. Sakagami's urge to wander is unrelieved. Semimaru's

[23]Miyake, "Utaikata," p. 37, mentions that there is a variant performance style in which Semimaru dances, but that the dance itself is then slow and gentle.

loneliness and suffering are still acute. The rapid conclusion is particularly affecting as Semimaru and Sakagami again exchange a series of speeches which grow shorter and shorter, leading into a few final lines by the chorus. The emotional closeness indicated by the shared lines gives heightened emphasis to the pain both feel at parting. Sakagami moves across the stage and outward onto the *hashigakari*, the bridgeway, acting out their parting. In *Semimaru* the use of the hashigakari is particularly effective, not only in the entrances, but also in this painfully dramatic exit. The actors project their lines toward each other as from a distance, as if Semimaru remains at the foot of the slope and Sakagami is passing far off, almost out of hearing, over the ridge at Ausaka. As indication of the impossible distance now separating them, the chorus resumes, concluding the play:[24]

> She turns a final time to look at him.
> Weeping, weeping they have parted,
> Weeping, weeping they have parted.

This is a highly unusual ending for Nō and one which is particularly moving. Other plays show the parting between, for instance, a priest and the spirit of one long dead who has, for a time, become visible to the priest. Other plays show the happy reunion between previously separated relatives.[25] It is not the meeting between Semimaru and Sakagami which is remarkable, it is their parting. In this sense the play as a whole dramatizes the Buddhist premise that human attachments

[24]The actor Kanze Motomasa in a discussion of this play comments that in earlier days Kanze school performances had the chorus deliver all the final lines now shared by the shite and tsure. He indicates that he and his fellow actors find the effect better with alternating lines. "Zeami no nō 4," p. 53.

[25]Zeami comments on *hōka* plays, specifically mentioning that they should conclude with the reunion of previously separated relatives. *Sandō*, NKBT, LXV, 476–77.

inevitably bring pain, that "meeting initiates the pain of parting."[26]

Semimaru is a difficult play, presenting problems both in theme and structure. Modern critics of the theater see in *Semimaru* the qualities of an allegory[27] or, as mentioned, those of a Buddhist equivalent to a Western morality play, one illustrating the awesome power of karma and the absolute necessity of acceptance. Sakagami, in particular, is a mysterious character who with the clarity of vision which ordinary mortals can only interpret as "madness" sees embodied in the natural world around her the essential unity of apparent opposites.[28] Meeting and parting, up and down, palace or hovel, it is all the same. The play seems to have as its theme—as represented by Sakagami, the shite—a Zen puzzle.

Many aspects of the structure are extraordinary. Zeami wrote, concerning the structure of Nō, that a play divides into five sections: one introductory (*jo*), three elaborative (*ha*), and one fast conclusion (*kyū*). Trying to discern this five-part division in *Semimaru*, the Nō critic Nogami Toyoichirō considered the entire first half of the play up to the kyōgen interlude to be the introductory section. As such it is very long. Conversely, the finale is very short, consisting only of the final dialogue between shite and tsure and lacking the dance typical of closure in most Nō.

The jo-ha-kyū principle in Nō is somewhat variable, and it is not always easy to apply in detail in structural analysis of any given play,[29] but we are safe in assuming striking deviations to be significant. In the case of *Semimaru*, the ex-

---

[26]*Aibetsurikū* is the Japanese phrase used to express this principle.

[27]Tashiro, "Yōkyoku *Semimaru*," No. 23, p. 118.

[28]*Jungyaku funi* is the phrase denoting this principle in many Buddhist texts.

[29]Teele, "The Structure of the Japanese Noh Play," pp. 204–5, discusses the structure of *Semimaru* in comparison with *Nishikigi*.

panded introduction allows for the development of the tsure as
a major second character offsetting the shite. This development facilitates the most moving presentation of the final parting, a parting between two characters of equal importance.
Likewise, the brief finale, because of the absence of dance, has
a heightened starkness, evocative of the weak and helpless
state of the blind Semimaru.

Ausaka Madman

Several Muromachi and Tokugawa lists of plays and authors
call *Semimaru* Zeami's play,[30] and though these lists are not
fully reliable, their unanimity on this subject is reassuring.
Most modern critics, while hesitating slightly, consider *Semimaru* almost certainly Zeami's composition.[31] The lesser-
known work *Ausaka Madman* raises no authorship problems. It
is without question Zeami's play, being explicitly so listed in
Zeami's own critical writings.

Referring to the popularity of this play, Zeami included it in
a list of thirty plays he recommended as ideal models for the
composition of further successes.[32] Zeami classed his recommended model plays in several categories, grouping *Ausaka
Madman* with three other titles[33] as a type he calls *yūkyō*
"entertainer ecstatic." All four of these plays have as shite men
who sing and dance and perform as lay preachers while accompanying themselves on drums and *sasara*, a simple bamboo instrument we might call a "scraper."[34]

[30] Nose, *Nōgaku genryū kō*, p. 1383.
[31] Kōsai, "Semimaru," p. 20; Omote Akira and Yokomichi Mario
in "Zeami no nō 4," pp. 52–54. However, Yokomichi expresses
some slight reservations based on the fact that, unlike most critics, he
finds the ending of *Semimaru* unsatisfying.
[32] *Sandō*, NKBT, LXV, 480.
[33] *Tango monogurui, Jinen koji,* and *Kōya.*
[34] The sasara is a simple bamboo instrument consisting of two parts
which are rubbed together. One part is made from the end of a length

Plays about such popular entertainer priests hold an important place in Zeami's writings concerning the composition of Nō. After describing three basic role types underlying Nō composition—the old man, the woman, and the warrior—Zeami next discusses several further subsidiary role types, the first of which are roles he calls *hōka*.[35] Having the literal meaning "to cast down," hōka was originally a term used in the Zen sect to refer to a monk, one who had cast off worldly things. By extension it came to refer, rather, to entertainers who wore the dress of monks—specifically the sekkyōshi described in chapter 2.[36] And in Zeami's writings hōka is also used as a synonym for *yūkyō*.[37]

In his specific comments concerning the structure of hōka plays, Zeami mentions only two by title: *Jinen koji* and *Kagetsu*. In addition he includes madman and madwoman plays in this category. Though he does not at this point cite *Ausaka Madman* specifically, he elsewhere likened it to *Jinen koji*, and the details of structure which he here suggests do in fact fit the pattern of *Ausaka Madman*. A detailed comparison with the pattern suggested by Zeami is outside the scope of this book,[38] but generally speaking *Ausaka Madman* is as close to the ideal form as *Semimaru* is aberrant.

Ausaka Madman opens with the most typical introduction, the shidai "opening song" of the waki, followed by the common self-introduction of the waki. The shidai is less enigmatic than most, including that of *Semimaru*. The waki recites:

―――――

of bamboo cut into a "whisk" of thin prongs. Against this a notched stick is rubbed to produce the scraping sound.

[35] *Sandō*, NKBT, LXV, 472–77.

[36] In the introductory kyōgen passage of *Jinen koji*, Jinen koji is specifically called a sekkyōshi, a sekkyō performer.

[37] *Sandō*, NKBT, LXV, 471: "Among hōka are the yūkyō Jinen koji, Kagetsu, Togan koji and Saigan koji."

[38] The model structure is given in *Sandō*, NKBT, LXV, 476–77.

> Moon of the Eastern Road brings with it autumn
> Moon of the Eastern Road brings with it autumn
> To the moon-lit capital I shall return,

then describes himself as a "man from a western province" now returning to the capital after journeying to the east in search of his son who had been stolen by slave traders.

In the sashi which follows, the waki's speech develops the intensity of his longing for his son and, in rapid retrospective, reviews the three long years of his journey. A sageuta song in the low register briefly describes the beginning of that journey, and the shift up in register to ageuta reinforces, through the change in music, the reversal of his direction of travel as he describes turning back westward. The sageuta-ageuta sequence serves as his song of travel, bringing him finally to the Omi Road, east of Kyoto, just beyond the Ausaka Barrier. This is a michiyuki of average length and complexity, including the names of five places passed in travel. The image of the moon from the opening shidai is continued here, the moon serving as the traveler's constant companion on his journey.

Following the *tsuki-zerifu*, a few prose lines establishing the arrival of the waki at his destination, comes a mondo, dialogue, between the waki and the kyōgen character, as usual a man of the locale. In this case the kyōgen is an innkeeper from whom the traveler obtains lodgings. The innkeeper provides certain information concerning the shite before the shite enters the action. He informs the traveler that there is a blind madman at Ausaka who performs all sorts of strange antics while playing the drum and sasara.

Because *Ausaka Madman* has not been performed for several centuries, we have no texts indicating the stage action attendant on the lines. However, since the following sequence of rhythmic patterns is the classic formal pattern accompanying the first stage entry of the shite,[39] we can assume that the

[39] Yasuda, "The Structure of *Hagoromo*," p. 56.

sequence begins with the entrance of the shite through the curtain at the far end of the hashigakari. He is accompanied by a child, played by a kokata, a child actor. The two together chant the issei, formal entrance song of the shite, which continues the theme of the passage of time.

As is often the case, the recitative sashi following the issei here serves to amplify the nature of the shite. In this case it is the shite's blindness which is emphasized, and he specifically likens himself to Kuṇāla and Semimaru, both princes and both blind. The image of a helplessly floating blind turtle, found in *Semimaru*, appears here as well, and the following lines contrast moonlight, the prevalent image thus far, with the darkness of the blind.

The subsequent sageuta and ageuta each contain a famous classic poem which continue the moon imagery. The sageuta quotes a tanka by the Heian poet Izumi Shikibu concerning the moon as an inspirational light leading her at the hour of her death, whereas in the ageuta the poem concerns the moon reflected in the waters at Ausaka barrier. This is the same poem that appears in *Semimaru*, also there recited by the shite:

When in the clear water
At Ausaka Barrier
It sees its reflection
The tribute horse from Mochizuki
Will surely shy away.

The blind shite, by painful contrast, sees nothing; but as in *Semimaru*, his acute hearing informs him that someone has arrived outside his straw hut. It seems probable, judging from this line, that like Semimaru, the madman of Ausaka was seated on stage inside a prop straw hut. (In stage presentation the two plays may have had greater similarity than the lines alone suggest.)

A dialogue (mondo) ensues between the blind man and the traveler. When the traveler asks the blind man about himself, he says he has lived by the pass for so long that anyone who does not know him must be a fool. As is the case in several hōka plays, his dialogue is tinged with humor.[40] An air of mystery also permeates the blind man's words: "Even among people living in other places, some certainly know me. Yet surely some who associate with me do not know me." Despite his blindness, the old man's "vision" is superior to the sight of those who fail to recognize him. He is known to some, unknown to others, and this place is "For known and unknown, Meeting Slope." The shite here is reciting the line which, above all others, is poetically associated with Semimaru.

The response of the waki includes a further allusion to the Semimaru poem (A), for as in the poem, he speaks of Ausaka as the famous place "where people come and go." In fact, the whole passage seemingly alludes to the Semimaru legend. The shite speaks of Ausaka as a place "true to its name," a place of meeting. Like Semimaru himself the blind man here describes the storm winds at the barrier as in the Semimaru poems (E and H).

The ensuing ageuta recited by the blind madman shifts from visual to auditory imagery, principally the cries of fowl heard at dawn at the Ausaka Barrier. As dawn breaks, ushered in by the cries of cocks, the blind man seems to become increasingly distressed. The kyōgen innkeeper asks the blind man why, since travelers have come to see him, he is not performing, playing the sasara and drum. Here, as in a great many madman and madwoman plays in Nō, we have a performance of "madness" by request.[41]

---

[40]*Ibid.*, p. 14.
[41]Two well-known examples of this occur in the plays *Hanjo* and *Sumidagawa*.

> Meeting slope mountain wind
> Rattles the leaves of trees, dancing
> Drums the waves of Shinomiya-kawara
> Here—there—blind reeling madness
> Passionless pity—feel for me.

Here the traveler first becomes aware of the sensitivity and acuity of the blind man, finding the mysterious man quite fascinating. The blind man chides the traveler for considering him insensitive and calls the traveler madder than a madman. The blind man has clearer vision than those who see him. The madman is saner than those who laugh at him. The conception here is very similar to Sakagami's speech in *Semimaru* where she tells onlookers laughing at her that it is they, not she, who are out of order.

The thematic similarity between *Ausaka Madman* and *Semimaru* now becomes fully explicit. The shite and kokata exchange several lines in which they compare themselves to Semimaru, first explaining the meaning of the place name Shinomiya-kawara as a reference to Semimaru, the fourth son of Emperor Daigo. The older man likens himself to Semimaru because of his blindness, while the child says he, like Semimaru, has been separated from his father and reduced to begging. Clearly, in writing *Ausaka Madman*, Zeami already bore in mind the legend of Semimaru in the form that appears in the Nō *Semimaru*, minus the element of Sakagami.

The shite next quotes with minor variation poem B, also recited in *Semimaru*, ending "Whether in a palace or a hovel/ We cannot live forever." Two further lines are shared with *Semimaru*, lines concerning the four strings of the biwa, which here lead by association to the blind madman's instruments, the drum and sasara. In a state of increasing agitation, the shite prepares to dance, and the innkeeper specifically requests the blind man to perform "that famous *kusemai*, 'Descending the Eastern Sea Road.' "

The shite's acceptance of this request is followed by a shidai, introducing the kuse section of the play. It has the characteristic opaque quality of most shidai:

Even on a withered branch in snow
Even on a withered branch in snow
Flowers may bloom once again.

In many Nō, kusemai, which originally existed as independent narrative dance pieces, are integrated into the narative structure of the play and lack the character of independent dance per se. However, in a few plays the kuse section represents an actual performance of kusemai. Like *Hyakuman, Yamamba,* and *Jinen koji, Ausaka Madman* is an example of this latter sort.

The kusemai of *Ausaka Madman* has several alternate titles. In the innkeeper's request in the play, the dance is called *Kaidō kudari,* "Descending the Eastern Sea Road." It was also known as either *Tōgoku kudari* or *Azuma kudari:* "Descent to the Eastern Provinces." Independently of its incorporation into *Ausaka Madman* this narrative dance song had already achieved great popular success. It was an example from fairly late in the tradition of kusemai having been written in the last quarter of the fourteenth century at a time when the modification of kusemai for adoption into Nō had already gotten under way.[42]

Azuma kudari had an important place in Zeami's own personal history, and when in old age he dictated to his son the reminiscences which are the basis for *Sarugaku dangi,* he discussed the circumstances in which *Azuma kudari* was com-

[42] O'Neill, *Early Nō Drama,* p. 55.

103

posed. When Zeami was yet in his early teens, an old col-
league of his father Kan'ami had somehow fallen into disfavor
with the Shogun Yoshimitsu (r. 1368–1408), the great patron of
Nō actors. The unfortunate object of Yoshimitsu's wrath was
the *renga* poet Tamarin, also known as Rin'ami, who was a
member of the *dōbōshū*, a select band of master artists
and craftsmen who served in close attendance upon the
Shogun and were honored with titles ending in the syllables
-*ami*.[43] Rin'ami was sent in exile to the east where he wrote
Azuma kudari, then sent it back to the capital where another
member of the dōbōshū, Nan'ami, set it to music and
choreographed it as dance. Nan'ami, perhaps banking on the
strength of Yoshimitsu's affection for the young Zeami, asked
Zeami to perform the dance for the Shogun. Yoshimitsu in-
quired about the author of this new piece, and, on learning
that it had been written by the exiled Rin'ami, pardoned him
and permitted him to return to the capital.[44] The narrative
describes the journey of Taira Morihisa, a captive of the Minamoto in the Gempei war, as he was sent eastward, under
guard, for judgment by the Shogun Yoritomo at Kamakura. Of
course, the painful journey of the song was as much Rin'ami's
as Morihisa's. And when incorporated into *Ausaka Madman* it
became an appropriate narrative both of the journey of the boy
stolen by slave traders and the journey undertaken by his father.

[43] The syllables -*ami*, abbreviated from Amidabutsu (Amida Buddha), formed the suffix of names of priests of the Ji sect, an offshoot
of Amidism founded in the thirteenth century. In the case of artists
and craftsmen under shogunal patronage, the title was an honorary
one, granted by the shogun to elevate (or at least obscure) the social
status of his companions. Zeami took orders as a Zen monk late in his
life, but while holding the title of an apparent Ji sect priest, had led
the life of a layman. See Hayashiya, *Chūsei geinōshi*, p. 502.

[44] *Sarugaku dangi*, NKBT, LXV, 504–5.

The lines of the shidai opening the kuse section of the play were the closing lines of the independent kusemai. In addition to this reordering, nearly half of the independent kusemai was eliminated from the version included in *Ausaka Madman.* Yet the remaining half alone makes an uncommonly long kuse. Moreover, much of it is in regular seven-five meter leading to the danger of monotony. Zeami generally avoided such regular meter in the kuse of his mature works.[45]

Like the travel song of Sakagami in the second half of *Semimaru,* this kusemai, having a journey as its subject, has something of the effect of a second michiyuki within a single play. The similarity is even closer, as several lines of *Azuma kudari* are quoted as the opening strains of Sakagami's song of travel.

The notation of the only printed text of *Ausaka Madman* is not entirely clear, but suggests that at the conclusion of the kusemai itself the madman of Ausaka performs a dance of the type known in Nō as *chū no mai.* With this dance begin the kyū section, the fast close of the play, though this is not the fastest of Nō dances. Through his song and dance the madman reaches an exalted, ecstatic state in which he chides his onlookers, revealing his own identity by saying, "Do you not know I am a god? Fools!"

The finale of the play is a last dialogue between the waki and shite in which the shite, now identified as the god of the pass, reunites the waki with his long-lost child, the child who had been accompanying the old madman. This reunion accomplished, the god disappears, stepping back into the shrine at Ausaka dedicated to his glory. Though no stage directions are extant, it seems likely that the shite would have moved off along the hashigakari so that he exited through the curtain at the far end of the hashigakari just following the final repeated line: "He vanishes—miraculous."

[45] Konishi, "New Approaches," p. 7.

This ending, which is poetically quite beautiful, was probably very effective on stage. Zeami wrote that the conclusion of a hōka play should feature the reunion between separated relatives and their exit from the stage. In this case the reunion and presumed exit of the waki and the child fit the description, but the exit of the shite following the revelation of his true form is the emotional focus of the final lines.

The Relationship between the Plays

Several factors lead to the suggestion that *Ausaka Madman* was a relatively early work of Zeami's, showing the playwright at less than full creative power. One rather glaring weakness of this play is its overly long, verbose kuse section. Considering how little the kusemai serves to advance the narrative action of the play, it is quoted at quite extraordinary length. Later in life Zeami came to find *Azuma kudari* a potentially boring piece of music,[46] and it seems highly unlikely that he would then have borrowed from it so extensively; yet, in his younger days, remembering the success he had had through dancing this piece, in obtaining a pardon for its author, he might well have thought it auspicious to include it in a composition of his own.

Secondly, though there is much beautiful writing in *Ausaka Madman*, the total conception of the play is rather flawed. After the long kusemai, the reunion between father and son seems inadequately developed. Zeami's own critical comments call for a dialogue between the reunited relatives in the finale of hōka plays, but here that dialogue is lacking. Zeami's interest focused, rather, on the blind beggar musician at Ausaka, the manifestation of the god of the pass.

Thirdly, *Ausaka Madman* resembles the work of Zeami's pre-

[46] O'Neill, *Early Nō Drama*, p. 50.

decessors,[47] and we may here see Zeami trying his wings with a relatively familiar type of play.

It is similar in content to the three other entertainer ecstatic plays with which Zeami groups it. The other plays—*Jinen koji, Kōya monogurui,* and *Tango monogurui*—are all thought to have been reworked by Zeami's revising earlier compositions by Kan'ami (in the case of *Jinen koji* and *Kōya monogurui*) and Iami (*Tango monogurui*).[48] All three of these plays have as their shite a performer who by playing on the sasara and drum is transported into an ecstatic, sometimes trancelike state in which he brings about the felicitous resolution of the play, the reunion of a lost child with his parents. In the case of *Jinen koji,* the most persistently popular of the four plays, the parents of the lost child are, in fact, already dead, but the girl is rescued from slave traders and returned to society, and the auspicious miraculous effect of the sekkyōshi performer's dancing is thus basically similar to the other plays of the group.

The most noteworthy difference between *Ausaka Madman* and the other yūkyō plays is the cause of the shite's madness. The plot of *Ausaka Madman* concerns search and reunion, but the searcher father is not the mad character. The madness of the blind man of Ausaka is a mark of his godliness. While all sekkyōshi in Nō show a certain "divine madness" through their dancing which leads to the miraculous reunion of separated relatives, in no other yūkyō play is the shite in fact revealed as himself an earthly manifestation of a god. In

[47]Jinen koji, for instance, was the subject of *Ennen furyū* (an ancestral dramatic form preceding Nō) written as early as twenty years before the birth of Zeami's father, Kan'ami. Kanai, *Nō no kenkyū,* p. 534. Further, Kan'ami was the first to incorporate *kusemai* into Nō and it seems likely that the young Zeami might have been less than fully adept at doing so.

[48]Nose, *Nōgaku genryū kō,* pp. 1309, 1352–54, 1393.

THE LEGEND

Ausaka Madman Zeami dramatizes the belief expressed in the *sekkyō* license document (P) and shows us the god of the Ausaka Barrier temporarily made manifest as a poor "crazy" beggar dependent on the charity of passing travelers.

Whatever weaknesses *Ausaka Madman* may have, it was, as we have seen, popular in Zeami's own lifetime. Having suggested it as a model to be emulated in creating future successful plays, Zeami apparently took his own advice. He wrote *Semimaru*, basing it on the same thematic material of the legend of the blind musician of Ausaka. But using old material in a new way, he elaborated the character of Semimaru as an ordinary mortal man and balanced against him a great new creation, the character of the madwoman Sakagami, after whom, orginally, his play was named.

One difficulty with *Ausaka Madman* was that the role of the beggar musician was presumably, as with other madman roles, performed unmasked. Zeami indicated in his own critical writings that unmasked madman roles were particularly difficult. He wrote:

> In the case of unmasked madman plays the performance will not be fully satisfactory unless the actor is of absolutely ultimate ability. If his facial expression is not exactly accurate, he will not resemble a disturbed man. If he fails in some particular and the facial expression varies, it will not appear right.

Zeami then went on to call all madness parts, but particularly those of unmasked men, the most demanding of roles, requiring special talent and practice.[49]

Though several madman plays are attributed to Kan'ami and Zeami, madwoman plays supplanted them in popularity, apparently within Zeami's own lifetime.[50] *Semimaru* (*Sakagami*) was probably written in an attempt to use the Semimaru

[49] *Fūshi kaden*, NKBT, LXV, 351–53.   [50] "Zeami no nō 4," p. 54.

legend in a form that would answer to the rising taste for
madwoman roles on the Nō stage.

Zeami was a practical man, a successful playwright, and an
adept manager. He fully approved of the idea of revising old
plays to make new, more appealing versions and in his critical
writings often identified plays which had undergone such re-
working. Immediately after suggesting *Ausaka Madman* and
the other yūkyō plays as possible models for further revisions, he listed several contemporary successes which had resulted from the updating of earlier plays. *Semimaru* is not included in this list, which appeared in 1423,[51] but it may well
have been written between 1423 and 1430 when the title *Sakagami* first appeared in Zeami's writings.

The great new innovation in the play is the madwoman
Sakagami. A figure of extraordinary dramatic power, she is a
madwoman of more profound significance than most Nō
madwomen, from whom she is subtly different. The cause of
her madness is neither obsession nor possession, the usual
causes cited by Zeami in his writings concerning madness
plays.[52] Rather, like the blind sekkyōshi in *Ausaka Madman*,
Sakagami is mad because she is, at one level of the playwright's awareness, a manifestation of the god of the slope.
Her very name, Sakagami, reveals this. For, written with different characters, the name means precisely "god of the slope"
and was, since the earliest written records, the name used to
refer to the indigenous deity of Ausaka.[53]

Sakagami is never in the Nō play specifically revealed as
the god of the slope at Ausaka. Through the pun on her name
she is transformed into an apparently ordinary, yet somehow
peculiar, mortal madwoman. Yet in her madness, like the

[51]*Sandō*, NKBT, LXV, 480.
[52]*Fūshi kaden*, NKBT, LXV, 351–53.
[53]*Sandai jitsuroku*, entry date corresponding to January 5, 876,
records Sakagami as the god of the pass. *Sandai jitsuroku*, p. 36.

blind man of Ausaka, she preaches higher truths. She affirms the necessity of achieving understanding which can cut through apparent opposites and see the essential unity of all. She reconfirms the truths Semimaru seeks to accept, the oneness of all life, the sameness of a palace or a hovel. An enlightened being, she wanders off, leaving Semimaru to continue his search for salvation through discipline. Depending on the sophistication of the audience, *Semimaru* can be understood as a play about the pathos of the truth that all who meet must part, or as a play revealing the wild appearance, enigmatic behavior, and superior wisdom of a mortal manifestation of a god.

As the original title *Sakagami* indicates, this play puts Semimaru in a secondary, albeit important role. For the audience of Zeami's day Sakagami was doubtless the more interesting character, yet she evidently did not suit the tastes of Tokugawa audiences. As we shall see in chapter 5, she plays only a very minor part in the Tokugawa period plays based on the Semimaru legend. When, at some time in the Tokugawa period, *Semimaru* was revived, it was most likely his character rather than Sakagami's which most interested the audience.

If, as I have been suggesting, *Semimaru* was a relatively late Zeami play, written some time after 1423 when Zeami was past sixty, it may reflect in part his own experience. Beginning with the death of his patron Yoshimitsu in May, 1408, Zeami suffered a gradual estrangement from shogunal and court circles. Perhaps as a result of his own loss of favor, Zeami was especially moved by the situation of one who has known comforts, fame, and power only to lose these advantages and face the necessity of living in poverty and isolation. He returned to this subject often. It is the predicament of the principal characters in several of his most beautiful and affecting plays.

Ono no Komachi in *Sekidera Komachi* has grown old and ugly, an "old woman who has built her hut at the foot of the mountain."[54] Like Semimaru she lives in a straw hut at Au-saka. She describes the contrast between this hut and the lux-uries of her youth in imagery very close to that with which Sakagami laments the loss of Semimaru's comforts:

> Long ago, wherever I spent a single night
> My room would be bright with tortoise shell,
> Golden flowers hung from the walls,
> And in the door were strings of crystal beads.
> Brilliant as the Emperor's chair in grand procession
> The jewellike gowns I wore, a hundred colors.
> I lay on bright brocaded quilts
> Within a pillowed bridal chamber.
> Look at it now, my mud-daubed hut!
> Can this be my resplendent room?[55]

As the play closes, she returns alone to her miserable hut, still lamenting the loss of youth and luxury.

The famous warrior Kagekiyo suffers in Zeami's writing the same difficult fate as the prince and the beautiful poet.[56] "Kagekiyo went blind in both his eyes, and finding himself helpless, shaved his head and called himself the beggar of Hyūga."[57] Like Semimaru he is both blind and banished. He looks back not on luxury and comfort but on the power and glory he enjoyed as a Taira warrior, and relives this memory in narrative dance when his daughter succeeds in finding him in exile. Not yet freed of the torment of memory, he must, again like Semimaru, remain alone. The daughter leaves, obedient to his command.

[54]*Komachi at Sekidera,* trans. Karen Brazell, in Keene, *Twenty Plays,* p. 69.

[55]*Ibid.,* p. 74.

[56]The authorship of *Sekidera Komachi* and *Kagekiyo* is still a matter of some scholarly dispute, though most authorities attribute both plays to Zeami.

[57]Waley, *The Nō Plays of Japan,* p. 127.

"I stay," he said; and she "I go."
The sound of this word
Was all he kept of her,
Nor passed between them
Remembrance other.[58]

Ono no Komachi, Kagekiyo, and Semimaru all suffer alike in experiencing the opposite extremes of life. Poet, warrior hero, and prince, each must face life as a beggar. But only in *Semimaru* is there an implicit religious significance drawn from the suffering:

The world is so unsure, unknowable;
Who knows—our grief may hold our greatest hopes.

Herein, I believe, lies the lasting appeal of the Nō *Semimaru* as opposed to *Ausaka Madman*. *Ausaka Madman* has long since fallen from the active repertoire; it has probably not been performed for some four hundred years. *Semimaru* itself was not performed for a couple of decades before and during the Second World War, its treatment of the imperial family then being seen as disrespectful. Yet, revived once again in the postwar years, *Semimaru* is now a popular play retaining its timeless power to move the minds of those who experience a performance, and powerful, as well, even through the partial experience of reading alone.

[58]*Ibid.*, p. 133.

FIVE

Tokugawa Period Reinterpretations of the Semimaru Legend

Beginning in the latter decades of the seventeenth century, the Semimaru legend achieved a period of vitality as the inspiration of about a dozen plays directed at urban audiences in Kyoto, Osaka, and Edo. Semimaru plays were presented both by the live actors of the Kabuki stage and the wooden puppets of the *Jōruri* puppet theater. Of all these various new Semimaru plays, by far the greatest success was one entitled simply *Semimaru*, written sometime between 1688 and 1691 by Chikamatsu Monzaemon (1653–1725). Chikamatsu's *Semimaru* is the only one of these plays with sufficient literary value to stand alone as a text for enjoyable reading. It is therefore the last of the Semimaru literature translated in Part II.

For over two hundred years after Zeami's *Semimaru*, the legend of the blind musician was sustained in part by performances of the Nō play. However, though Chikamatsu's play bears numerous clear similarities to Zeami's text, it was not the Nō alone which inspired Chikamatsu to create his own *Semimaru*. Tokugawa urban commercial theater was the scene of a great flourishing of the Semimaru legend, but it was the humble, itinerant, rural sekkyō narrators who played the greatest part in keeping the Semimaru legend alive into the seventeenth century.

Early Tokugawa Sekkyō

Itinerant sekkyōshi, talented narrators who both entertained and inspired their audiences with their tales of human

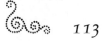

113

tribulations, faith, and their ultimate rewards, had been traveling the Japanese countryside at least since early medieval times. Their veneration of Semimaru of Ausaka as an ancestor deity and Bodhisattva incarnate was also a tradition of long standing. Long before the composition of Nō plays depicting sekkyōshi, such as *Jinen koji* and *Ausaka Madman*, sekkyōshi were active both at Ausaka and throughout extensive areas of the country. Yet the sekkyōshi were but one variety of a large body of virtually nomadic, popular, proselytizing entertainers who were wandering around Japan at this period.

The rootlessness of the sekkyōshi and others like them apparently disturbed the Tokugawa bureaucracy in its desire to establish firm social control over its national population. Though powerless to enforce, all at once, a totally sedentary life on itinerant elements of society, the Tokugawa government established as a means of registration and control a system of identifying and licensing traveling entertainers. The Semimaru shrine at Ausaka became the official authority charged with the responsibility of controlling sekkyōshi. The long-standing connection between sekkyōshi and the shrine at Ausaka became formalized through government sanction.

Though Heian-Kamakura sekkyō preachers had enjoyed some social status and support from major Buddhist temples, the sekkyōshi of late Muromachi to early Tokugawa times were at the very bottom of the social hierarchy. Most of the sekkyōshi who received licenses from the Semimaru shrine were the poorest beggars. They collected what little money they could from the rural peasants who made up the major part of their audiences, and in the worst of times supplemented their income with such lowly and poorly paid activities as selling wicks and flints, and making straw sandals or other simple woven straw products. Some reportedly tried their hands at healing the sick among the poorer strata of society and, perhaps as a result of failure in this endeavor, sekkyōshi are also known to have seen to the disposal of the dead.[1] Though many types of traditional popular entertainers in Tokugawa times became virtual beggars, the sekkyōshi were apparently the lowest of the low and were reduced to the worst paid and most degrading tasks to survive.

Tokugawa sekkyōshi were marginal people in society, the objects of scorn and derision. There is very little known about the nature of their sekkyō performances, which were apparently very simple. The distinguishing characteristic of a sekkyō performance was the use of the sasara, the rudimentary bamboo scraper described in chapter 2. For a time rural sekkyō performers were even called sasara sekkyō.[2] Their performances, needless to say, did not take place in expensive theaters but were presented outdoors at a crossroads or by the gate of a great house or temple where sufficient crowds might be attracted. A sekkyōshi would spread a woven mat, set up a large umbrella, stand before his audience, and narrate his sad sekkyō tale with dramatic punctuation from the rattling sasara. Old drawings of sekkyōshi show tattered-looking fellows, dressed as laymen, with only the front of the head shaven rather than displaying the priestly tonsure of sekkyō preachers of an earlier age. Some sekkyōshi are depicted wearing woven straw hats or carrying a sword, but none has the look of prosperity. Like the scorned beggar sekkyōshi of *Ausaka Madman,* some were doubtless blind.

The geographic range of sekkyōshi licensed by the Semimaru shrine covered a remarkably wide area with Kyoto roughly at its center.[3] Traveling sekkyōshi probably fol-

---

[1] Muroki, *Katarimono,* 240.

[2] *Ibid.* They are so identified in the *Vocabulario da Lingoa de Iapam,* a Japanese-Portuguese dictionary published in 1603.

[3] Shrine records show contributions from chanters performing as far east as Mikawa (modern Aichi prefecture), as far west as Bizen (Okayama), and as far south as Sanuki (Kagawa). Muroki, *Katarimono,* p. 17.

lowed the same routes as the religious pilgrims bound for such major sacred objectives as the great shrines at Ise, Kumano, Mount Kōya, the Shitennōji in Osaka, or Zenkōji in Nagano.[4] Such pilgrims welcomed sekkyō narrations mentioning the deities of the places toward which they were journeying, and in their piety they would modestly reward the sekkyōshi for their performances. It seems unlikely that any single sekkyōshi traveled all over Japan. Rather, the sekkyōshi from a particular area would specialize in tales associated with the deities of their own region. Local dialectisms, from Ise area for instance, are discernible in certain early sekkyō texts.[5] Some sekkyōshi were themselves called "Ise beggars." Recent research is working toward identifying some of the routes regularly traveled by the pre-Tokugawa sekkyōshi.

The question of the religious content of pre-Tokugawa sekkyō is a complicated one. Early in the Tokugawa period some sekkyō performers succeeded in settling in the cities and transforming their art for presentation in urban theaters. With the change to a settled theatrical form, some sekkyō texts were for the first time committed to writing. We have no texts dating from the rural, itinerant phase of sekkyō and can only try to extrapolate backward from the earliest Tokugawa texts. One interesting generalization can be drawn from a comparison of earlier and later Tokugawa texts. The earlier ones tended to have a framework indicating that the story concerned a mortal incarnation of a particular local deity. The sekkyō might never again mention this *honji* (original deity) element, but the framework would serve to localize the sekkyō and make it particularly appealing to an audience gathered at the shrine or embarking on a pilgrimage to the

[4]There are elements of plot indicating a connection with Shitennōji in *Sanshō dayū*, Kōya and Zenkōji in *Karukaya*, and Kumano in *Oguri hangan*.

[5]Araki, "Chūsei makki no bungaku," p. 21.

temple or shrine mentioned in the sekkyō. There are cases where several extant versions of the same sekkyō tale have different introductions associating the story with deities from various places.[6] The honji framework of a sekkyō tale provided the story with a strong sense of place, but the texts themselves did not attempt to encourage any particular system of religious belief. In some cases where the same legend is known both in the form of a Nō play and as sekkyō, the Nō play has the stronger religious tone.[7]

When sekkyō achieved urban theatrical popularity, the honji frameworks were dropped; only the earliest of the texts still retain old-fashioned, stereotyped introductions such as the following, which opens the earliest extant version of the sekkyō *Karukaya:*

> Now, concerning the original deity whose tale I am going to tell, if you ask of the province, he was from the province of Shinano. To the left of the Buddha hall of the Nyorai of Zenkōji, he is the original deity called the Bodhisattva Jizō of parents and children. Now I'll tell you all about him, if you ask me in detail about his history. . . .[8]

Later versions of *Karukaya* begin simply, "At some time in the fairly distant past . . ."[9] When sekkyō were recited in the theaters of Kyoto or Osaka, rather than before the Jizō of Zenkōji or some other pilgrimage location, that honji framework became irrelevant and the sekkyō tale lost some of its original religious significance.

SEKKYŌ TEXTS

The earliest sekkyō text preserved today was printed in 1631. Retaining certain idiosyncratic grammatical features

---

[6]Muroki, "Sekkyō kenkyū no tenbō," p. 42.

[7]*Ibid.* Muroki compares the nō and sekkyō versions of *Karukaya* and the nō *Yoroboshi* with the sekkyō *Shintokumaru.*

[8]Yokoyama Shigeru, *Sekkyō,* II, 3.   [9]*Ibid.,* II, 35.

which distinguish sekkyō from other narrative styles, this text and a handful of others from the 1630s through the 1650s are the best examples for determining the nature of relatively "pure" sekkyō. Sekkyō originally developed independently, but when its performers moved into the cities and strove to attract urban audiences, their style of performance quickly came under heavy influence from Jōruri, a narrative style which ultimately traces its roots back to the influence of Heike biwa musical narration. In the late sixteenth century Jōruri began to be performed with accompaniment on the shamisen, the excitingly shrill three-stringed instrument then recently imported from the Ryukyus. At least as early as the turn of the seventeenth century, Jōruri was performed with puppets as its actors, and it is the Jōruri tradition which was the heart of the highly sophisticated puppet theater which reached its peak of popularity in the late seventeenth and early eighteenth century.

Obviously, the history of Jōruri is a long and complicated one, quite outside the scope of this study.[10] The relevance of Jōruri to sekkyō, however, is enormous. Jōruri and sekkyō theaters in the cities were in direct competition for audiences. The sekkyō chanters felt compelled to emulate the style of their Jōruri counterparts in an attempt to meet this competition, and in a matter of a few decades sekkyō as a distinctive style ceased to exist, having become indistinguishable from Jōruri. Some texts known first in sekkyō style appear later in the manner of Jōruri. Others simply ceased to be performed. Generally speaking, urban audiences preferred the more exciting, lively style of Jōruri to the relatively sad, even morose style of sekkyō. The high point of sekkyō as a narrative art preceded the transplantation of the chanters into the cities and antedated the earliest extant sekkyō texts.[11]

[10] See Dunn, *The Early Japanese Puppet Drama*, and Keene, *Bunraku*.
[11] Muroki, *Katarimono*, p. 251.

In the urban environment, in fixed theaters, however simple, sekkyō chanters copied two major innovative features of Jōruri. Sekkyō narration began to be performed to the accompaniment of the shamisen instead of the sasara, which had always been its hallmark, and the stories were enacted by simple wooden puppets. The first introduction of shamisen and puppets to sekkyō performance was apparently made by the chanter Yōshichirō of Osaka around 1640.[12] Along with the addition of performance innovations from Jōruri there also came rapid changes in the style and content of sekkyō texts.

By 1658, many texts published under the name of sekkyō were virtually identical in style with Jōruri.[13] They had lost the distinctive grammatical elements of sekkyō and were divided into six segments like Jōruri texts. Fight scenes and other typical Jōruri contentual motifs had been added. There is, of course, no precise way of dating the "death" of sekkyō. Whatever may have been happening in the cities, sekkyō survived at least into the nineteenth century as a countryside entertainment for unsophisticated, conservative audiences; and even today some young Japanese report that they were told sekkyō tales as childhood bedtime stories. When writing about the content of sekkyō narrative at its height, however, most critics direct their attention principally to those sekkyō printed in the relatively brief period between 1632 and the mid-1660s.

The phrase "the five sekkyō" has been much used in discussing the most representative texts of sekkyō, though different authors have different lists.[14] Several sekkyō exist in a number of different versions, most of which are dated, making it possible to observe changes brought about by the passage of time. Probably none of the extant sekkyō is an original cre-

[12]Muroki, "Sekkyō kenkyū no tenbō," p. 34.   [13]Ibid., p. 36.
[14]Muroki, Katarimono, p. 255; Araki, "Chūsei makki no bungaku," p. 21.

119

ation invented by the chanter whose name may appear with the printed text. Rather, the plots were traditional, committed to memory, and recreated and elaborated with each new oral performance.

Among the various texts known today, two plots stand out as having been particularly popular. No list of the "five sekkyō" fails to include *Karukaya* and *Sanshō dayū*. They are both the best known and the earliest, the first *Karukaya* text dating from 1631, and the earliest known version of *Sanshō dayū* from 1639. A brief synopsis of these two plots is worthwhile since both are quintessential sekkyō, heartrending and horrifying.

Karukaya concerns a family man who deserts wife and children to become a monk on Mount Kōya. Leaving their sickly daughter behind at home, the man's wife, accompanied by their son, goes in search of her husband. As a woman, she is forbidden to ascend Mount Kōya, and remains at the foot of the mountain as her son goes on to seek his father. The son does find the father, yet the father conceals his identity and the boy never knows his true relationship to this Kōya monk. The wife, meanwhile, unsuccessful in reaching her husband, dies before her son's return. The daughter also dies, overcome by her own arduous journey searching for the rest of her family. In some versions of this plot, father and son together preside over the cremation ceremony of the dead mother without the monk ever revealing that the woman was his own wife.[15]

The plot hardly seems calculated to have encouraged others to embark on the life of a monk. Rather it presents a sadly moving picture of the poverty and hardship facing a broken family. The earliest *Karukaya* text ends with a promising

[15]Muroki, *Katarimono,* pp. 270–71; Iwasaki, "Sekkyō *Karukaya,*" p. 55.

thought: reborn along with his family in the Pure Land, the son will then experience the joy of calling his parents' names. The family, disrupted in this life, will be reunited in the next. It seems cold comfort, yet in such bittersweet touches rested the appeal of sekkyō.

Wives separated from husbands, mothers bereft of their children, long and painful jouneys, illness, suffering, beggary, slavery, torture—these are the dominant motifs of sekkyō. The subjects are gloomy, to say the least, and several critics have suggested that the stories reflect the actual realities of the lives of poor country sekkyō chanters.[16] In some sekkyō the hero or heroine is a special child, granted by the gods after lengthy prayers of the parents. The hero may be reborn as a god or Buddha, but overall the emphasis rests more heavily on the worldly sufferings of this present existence, which are elaborated in far more detail than the ultimate rebirth or redemption.[17]

In the case of Sanshō dayū, despite great suffering, some rewards do in fact come in this lifetime. Starting in a similar vein to Karukaya, the plot begins with a wife who has been separated from her husband and sets out in search of him, though in this case the father has been exiled rather than having entered a monastery. The wife, taking her fourteen-year-old daughter and twelve-year-old son, sets off on her difficult search. En route the mother and children are captured by slave traders and are taken off in opposite directions, the mother in one boat, the children in another. The children are sold to Sanshō dayū, a wicked bailiff or estate manager, and are used as his slaves, the boy as a woodcutter, the girl as a salt maker. The boy eventually escapes his serfdom, finding sanc-

[16]This is discussed generally in Iwasaki, "Sekkyō Karukaya," and in Hayashiya, Kodai kokka no kaitai, pp. 316–33.
[17]Araki, "Chūsei makki no bungaku," pp. 22–25.

tuary in a temple. The sister, however, dies—in some versions through suicide by drowning; in others, tortured to death.

The boy then enjoys a change in fortune. After his escape he makes his way to Kyoto, where he is adopted by an adviser to the emperor. Eventually he becomes the governor of the province in which he had been held as a slave. Naturally, one of his first acts as governor is to forbid slavery. In time he is reunited with his mother, who had gone blind after many long years of starvation and suffering working as a bird chaser in farm fields in Tosa province. The mother's sight, finally, is miraculously restored through faith in the Bodhisattva Jizō.[18]

Sanshō dayū is perhaps the most optimistic of all Tokugawa sekkyō. For the son, at least, there is a certain revenge against his former slave master, and the mother does not end her days in blindness. Yet it is clear even from these two brief plot summaries that Tokugawa sekkyō were hardly likely to move the audience to gales of laughter as has been said of Heian-Kamakura sekkyō.

The history of sekkyō is only very imperfectly known. Particularly because the social class and the level of education of its performers in later eras were so low, until recently little attention has been paid to the subject. In the current state of research it is not yet possible to trace fully the antecedents of Tokugawa sekkyō tales. However, something can be said about the later influence of sekkyō on Jōruri.

While some sekkyō plots—notably *Shintokumaru* and *Aigonowaka*—concern the evils of cruel stepmothers who slander their stepsons and drive them out of their homes,[19] many of the female characters in sekkyō are brave, strong, loving women. They are often the most arresting figures in

[18]Kusabe, "*Sanshō dayū* ni tsuite," pp. 71–74.
[19]Here too is seen the influence of the Kuṇāla legend. Keene, "The Hippolytus Triangle, East and West," pp. 167–69.

sekkyō, and the portrayal of strong female characters in later puppet drama in Japan is thought to owe much to sekkyō influence.[20]

One possible explanation for the strong female characters in sekkyō is that women chanters may themselves have had a hand in the development of the plots. While the term sek-kyōshi was apparently used only of men, blind itinerant women storytellers, generally called *goze,* also chanted the plots known as sekkyō.[21] In fact, even in recent years researchers have been able to find, both in the northeast and in Nagano province, old blind women who still carry in their heads garbled, fragmentary versions of sekkyō plots.[22]

Gradually the dividing line between sekkyō and Jōruri became fuzzy. Sekkyō lost their honji frameworks and their special qualities of language. Jōruri overwhelmed sekkyō, but the legacy of sekkyō, its principal influence on Jōruri, may be seen in a rising Jōruri taste for domestic dramas, dealing with family problems instead of supermen or martial heroes.

Sekkyō Identity Papers and the Semimaru Shrine

The legend of Semimaru itself shows many of the characteristic features of sekkyō. Semimaru is a prince, but, like many another sekkyō character, he is separated from his family, undertakes a difficult, painful journey, lives in poverty, is sought out by a strong, driven woman—in this case his sister—and after death is worshiped, along with his sister, as kami of the Semimaru shrine at Ausaka.

These were the salient features of the life history of Semi-

[20] Araki, "Chūsei makki no bungaku," p. 27; Muroki *Katarimono,* p. 19.
[21] Muroki, *Katarimono,* p. 44.
[22] *Ibid.,* pp. 294–98; Iwasaki "Sekkyō *Karukaya,*" pp. 62–65.

maru as presented, in brief and relatively artless outline, in personal identification scrolls issued to sekkyō entertainers by the Semimaru shrine during the Tokugawa period. The earliest extant scroll of this type dates from 1631, almost exactly simultaneous with the first printed text of the earliest sekkyō, *Karukaya*.[23] Though the identification scroll is hardly comparable to a performance text, it suggests that the tale of Semimaru may well have been chanted in sekkyō style by the performers who bore these license-like identification papers.

One sekkyō text printed in 1661 refers to Semimaru and shows that his legend remained alive in the theaters of Osaka as well as in the countrified setting of the shrine itself. This Osaka sekkyō is *Matsura chōja*.[24] The name of the chanter has not been recorded. The text is largely in traditional sekkyō style, though it is divided into the six sections typical of Jōruri. In the third section appears the journey of a girl who has sold herself into slavery. Passing Ausaka she prays to Semimaru that she may be reunited with her mother.

> Groping along her way she comes to Shinomiya-kawara. The god of this place, where people come and go, hurrying on their way, was in the past a prince of the line of the Engi Emperor. He was known as Prince Semimaru. He was abandoned because both his eyes were bad. He was celebrated as the god of the barrier. Oh, wonderful to think of him.[25]

The full text of the sekkyō scroll of 1631 is included as translation P in Part II. Along with the passage from *Matsura chōja* it shows the essentials of the legend of Semimaru as known in the early seventeenth century. Identification documents of this sort probably existed in considerable numbers,

[23] The text is given in Muroki, *Katarimono*, pp. 214–15.
[24] Printed in Yokoyama Shigeru, *Sekkyō*, I, 163–80.
[25] *Ibid.*, p. 170.

124

and many who carried them were the poorest of beggar entertainers. They might venerate Semimaru as a patron god, one
who had like them been discriminated against as a beggar and
outcast, but whose heart was perfectly pure, inferior to none.

Legal requirements as well as personal piety may have led
sekkyō performers to seek identification papers from the
Semimaru shrine. The informal association between sekkyō
performers and the Semimaru shrine was clearly of great antiquity, and itinerant folk entertainers, both sekkyōshi and
their predecessors, had been active around the Ausaka area
virtually since the beginning of recorded history. However,
the use of the Semimaru shrine as a formal, government-
authorized agency to license and control the activities of sekkyō performers is a Tokugawa phenomenon.[26] The extent of
shrine control over sekkyō performers who had settled in
the cities was evidently fairly limited, but for performers who
wished to be permitted to travel, official authorization via the
Semimaru shrine was legally advisable if not absolutely indis-
pensable.

The introductory heading of identification papers from the
Semimaru shrine read: "This scroll is a record of seals presented to the sekkyō performer by the Chikamatsu branch
temple of Miidera and by the *hyōjika*,[27] and bears the history of the deity of the pure water at the barrier in Otsu in
Omi province." In order to obtain a new seal updating his
papers, the sekkyōshi was obliged to make an annual contribution to the shrine, to help pay for the festival held in the
ninth month. The offering helped to cover the cost of lanterns
for the festival and ensured that the contributor's name would

[26]Muroki has done the most extensive research on the licensing
system. My account is based mainly on his book *Katarimono*, pp.
195–236, and his articles, "Sekkyō to Semimaru" and "Sekkyō
kenkyū no tenbō."
[27]The *hyōjika* are discussed below.

be written on one of the placards carried in procession ahead of the *mikoshi,* the temporary portable shrine of the deity which was transported around the communities in the immediate vicinity of the shrine as part of the annual festival.

The shrine was evidently at the very peak of its prosperity, with the most extensive daily activity and the most splendid autumn festivals in the 1630s and 1640s. Most of the records still preserved by the Semimaru shrine are of a later date, when the shrine was somewhat in decline. For the years 1656–1746, a record book has survived showing a pattern of small annual contributions, in varying amounts, from individuals and from sekkyō communities such as Ise sekkyō, Uji-Yamada, and Terauchi, a sekkyō community near Hidenji, a Kyoto temple in the area of Awataguchi. Though in theory all sekkyō performers were required to contribute and, in effect, reregister annually, the law was probably never as punctiliously observed as the Tokugawa government would have wished.

The shrine fee collectors, the hyōjika mentioned in the identification scroll, may have been a handful of local families who were descendants of the border guards of the original Ausaka Barrier. This was their own claim. In effect they were the "bosses" of the area, who would periodically "strong-arm" the beggar entertainers who wished to perform within their territory into forking over a little contribution. For those who performed in the countryside, regular contributions were rather more necessary than for urban sekkyō stars. The first communities to drop from the record with the passing years were two sekkyō settlements in Kyoto. Others from outlying provinces who traveled into the Ausaka area continued to contribute regularly.

In 1711 the Chikamatsu temple ousted the hyōjika and began collecting the contributions directly at the temple. Some dunning letters have been preserved, letters sent to individual

performers reminding them of their obligatory "offerings."
Yet their lack of compliance makes it appear that the shrine
licenses had become by this time irrelevant for city performers. Still, there are occasional records of very large contributions from some of the most famous urban sekkyō performers. Perhaps nostalgia, more than any real need of
identification papers, sometimes drew one of these men who
had achieved success in the city back to the shrine to offer his
thanks to Semimaru.

The Semimaru shrine was but one of many religious institutions which issued licenses to itinerant performers.[28] Its particular importance lay in its closeness to the capital, as well as
in the fact that performers carrying papers from the shrine
could identify themselves as the "descendants" of a prince,
using this to gain some social status.

In response to the Tokugawa government's desire to identify
and control its entire population, many sekkyō beggar performers found it expedient to give up traveling and to settle in
fixed communities. Such sekkyō districts were the poorest of
the poor, very much at the bottom of society. Suffering extreme exclusionary treatment, sekkyō villagers generally
could marry only within their own community or perhaps into
one or another sekkyō settlement with which their group
maintained social communication.[29]

As time passed the Chikamatsu temple ceased to observe
strict differentiation among the many types of beggar performers. Papers were issued to a wide variety of simple entertainers, such as goze and biwa hōshi, medicine sellers (the
sales pitch being a form of entertainment), performers of
something called "crossroads Nō," and many more.[30] Evi-

[28]Suwa, "Chikamatsu," p. 53, gives some other specific examples.
[29]Muroki, "Sekkyō to Semimaru," p. 158.
[30]Muroki, *Katarimono*, pp. 216–17 includes an old document showing the full range of licenses.

127

dently there was considerable jockeying for status even among beggar communities. Dancers of *kōwakamai* looked down on Nō performers. Nō actors considered themselves quite superior to those who acted in Kabuki. The remnants of the mōsō tradition, while they had themselves venerated Semimaru before sekkyō performers adopted him, in later days sought assiduously to differentiate themselves from sekkyō performers and establish themselves as socially superior.

The fine points of the workings of the shrine-based identification system need not concern us. However, it is obvious that throughout the Tokugawa period the Semimaru legend remained alive and familiar at the Semimaru shrine and that during this period Semimaru came to be considered the patron deity of many different sorts of popular entertainers.

The Semimaru Shrine and Chikamatsu Temple

It is actually something of an oversimplification to speak of the relationship between sekkyō entertainers and "the" Semimaru shrine, for in fact there were two principal Semimaru shrines, plus a third minor offshoot, founded in 1660 after a community dispute about the route of the autumn festival procession. The two principal Semimaru shrines are known as "upper" and "lower," according to their relative positions on the slope of Mount Ausaka. The upper shrine had long been treated as a branch of the lower one, and it was the lower shrine, the shrine by the "pure water," which issued licenses and which is currently the repository of all documents pertaining to the Tokugawa registration system. Appropriately, the vicinity of the lower shrine is known as "Shimizu-chō, Shimizu meaning "pure water."

In earlier centuries there may have been a close connection between the Semimaru shrine and Sekidera (Barrier temple), a temple at Ausaka which had fallen into ruin by Tokugawa times but which had been well-known because of legendary associations with Ono no Komachi. After Sekidera declined, the Chikamatsu temple, a five-minute walk from the lower Semimaru shrine, took over administration of the shrine. The official name of the temple was Kinshōji, but it was popularly known as Takakannon, "High Kannon," because it was located high up the slope, with a good view of Lake Biwa, and there housed an impressive statue of Senju Kannon. Another popular name for the temple, based on alternate readings for the characters which wrote the name Kinshōji, was Chikamatsu-dera, "Chikamatsu temple."[31]

As mentioned at the beginning of this chapter, Chikamatsu Monzaemon, the greatest master among the puppet playwrights of Osaka, in the late seventeenth century wrote his own *Semimaru*, a major Jōruri. We know that the Semimaru legend was familiar in Osaka from sekkyō performances there, and it is quite possible that knowledge of the Nō play *Semimaru*, perhaps combined with inspiration from some earlier playwright's attempt at fashioning a Jōruri version of the Semimaru legend, was the only direct inspiration for Chikamatsu's play.

Still, there is the question of the name. Why did the great Jōruri playwright bear as his self-chosen surname the name of the temple which issued identification documents to sekkyō performers? Perhaps it is sheer coincidence. Various explanations have been presented to justify the playwright's pen name.[32] But several scholars have suggested, rather irresistibly, that there is more than coincidence to be considered here.

The details of Chikamatsu's early life are sketchy indeed. We know that he was originally named Sugimori Nobumori,

---

[31]Suwa, "Chikamatsu," pp. 49–55, describes the shrines and temples and their locations in detail.

[32]*Ibid.*, pp. 45–48, reviews various other theories traditionally offered to explain the name.

that he was born in 1653 in Echizen province into a minor samurai family, served in Kyoto as page to a noble family, then decided, about the age of twenty, to leave this household. Though Chikamatsu was himself born in Echizen, his family was from Omi province, and it seems quite likely that Chikamatsu, on deciding to take up the life of the theater, might have headed for Ausaka and spent some time residing at the Chikamatsu temple.

The Chikamatsu pen name theory has been carried furthest by Suwa Haruo. It is not by any means universally accepted, but several sekkyō specialists have found it convincing. If the theory is correct, Chikamatsu's pen name is a secret self-identification of the playwright with Semimaru himself. The surname Chikamatsu then refers to the Chikamatsu temple, and the given name Monzaemon, the *mon* element of which means "gate," points to the Semimaru shrine which stood directly in front of the original main gate of the Chikamatsu temple. Suwa believes that Chikamatsu chose his theatrical name through reverence to Semimaru. He adduces Chikamatsu's decision to treat the story of Semimaru in one of his earliest plays as evidence of his strong interest in the shrine and its legends. The theory can doubtless never really be proved or disproved.[33] In any case, whether this is a charming fantasy or a clever deciphering of a code created by Chikamatsu, Chikamatsu's interest in the Semimaru legend is indisputable. In his hands the Semimaru legend grew and prospered, and his *Semimaru,* as a great popular success, set off a spate of recreations of the Semimaru legend as plays for Kabuki and Jōruri presentation.

Chikamatsu's Semimaru

The year 1688 is the likeliest date of composition of Chikamatsu's puppet play *Semimaru*. Though the printed text is un-

[33] Muroki rejects this theory, but it is accepted by Kanai.

dated, the style of the woodblocks used for printing is similar to that of the blocks used for other 1688 play books for plays presented at the Takemoto-za in Osaka.[34] A guidebook to the teahouses of Osaka and Kyoto, bearing a preface from the first month of 1692, mentions the popularity of the michiyuki from Chikamatsu's *Semimaru*, thereby placing Chikamatsu's work unquestionably no later than 1691.[35]

Chikamatsu was thirty-five in 1688 and a newly established success in Osaka as house playwright for the Takemoto-za, managed by the chanter Gidayū. In 1684 Gidayū chose Chikamatsu's *Yotsugi Soga* (*The Soga Successors*) as the play with which to open his new theater. With this play Chikamatsu first established himself as an independent playwright, following a period of apprenticeship to the Kyoto playwright and chanter, Uji Kaga no jō, for whom he may have written some ten plays. *Semimaru* was evidently the third notably successful play presented with Chikamatsu's name as playwright. It followed *Yotsugi Soga* and *Shusse Kagekiyo* (*Kagekiyo Victorious*) of 1685 or 1686, as well as several less memorable endeavors by Chikamatsu presented by either Uji Kaga no jō in Kyoto or Gidayū in Osaka.

Semimaru was so successful the first time around that Chikamatsu chose to revive it for a special performance celebrating a very auspicious occasion some years later. On June 12, 1701, a special celebratory performance took place at the Takemoto-za when Gidayū was honored with a new professional name, Chikugo no jō.[36] Since the play dealt with Semimaru, who had by this time become a general god of musicians, its theme was suitably auspicious for celebrating Gidayū's present

[34] Yūda, "Chikamatsu nenpyō," pp. 115, 121.

[35] Yokoyama Tadashi, "Jōruri *Semimaro*, p. 1.

[36] This was long thought to have been the first performance of *Semimaru*, prior to the discovery of materials proving otherwise. Most collected editions of Chikamatsu's plays give 1701 as the date of *Semimaru*.

131

honor and promoting his future success. In fact, the next few years were notably prosperous ones for Gidayū and Chikamatsu's collective efforts.

In his apprenticeship with Kaga no jō, Chikamatsu absorbed several influences which are evident in his handling of the *Semimaru* material.[37] Kaga was an avid Nō enthusiast. His plays are divided into five acts rather than the six which had before his time been typical of Jōruri. Printed texts of Nō plays, which included musical notation, inspired Kaga to begin including musical information in his Jōruri texts. Most important of all, in many of his plays he borrowed extensively from Nō, sometimes embedding virtually whole Nō plays as part of a Jōruri. Chikamatsu himself may have written some of the earlier Nō-derived jōruri attributed to Kaga; but in any case, he adopted Kaga's practice and used Nō reminiscences artfully in his *Semimaru*.

Another important influence on Chikamatsu concerned the subject matter of the plays. Starting in 1677, Kaga began writing plays which dealt with the love affairs of famous historical figures (*sewa jidaimono*), and Chikamatsu's *Semimaru* was precisely such a play. Its revival in 1701 preceded by just two years Chikamatsu's first *sewamono* or "domestic play," a category of works concerning contemporary events in the lives of common people, principally complications ensuing from love affairs.

Chikamatsu's *Semimaru* is set in the reign of Emperor Daigo (r. 897–930), here—as in the Nō—presented as the father of Semimaru. Though technically a history play, it does not describe a single historical event; its concerns are entirely private, involving the complex emotional entanglements of Semimaru and three women who are in love with him. The women

[37] Dunn, *The Early Japanese Puppet Drama*, pp. 100–107, gives a nice account of Kaga no jo's place in the history of Jōruri and of his influence on both Chikamatsu and Gidayū.

involved— a court lady, a court servant, and a commoner—are ostensibly figures from the tenth century, but Chikamatsu portrays them almost identically with the eighteenth-century heroines of his domestic plays. They are interesting because of their emotions, not their alleged historical identities.

ACT ONE

The play opens with a paean of praise for the virtuous, compassionate monarch, Semimaru's father, who remains an awesome, distant figure, significant mainly because of his position. In the introductory section of the first act the emperor is on a tour of inspection of his realm, "imitating the tours of inspection made by the ancient sage kings of China." None of the lines of Act One are taken from the Nō *Semimaru*, but the conception of the emperor as a compassionate "father" to his subjects is mentioned in the Nō. Given the greater length of Jōruri in comparison to Nō, Chikamatsu here has margin to elaborate a theme implicit in the Nō but not so fully developed there.

No sooner has the emperor expressed his joy over the prosperity of his people than he comes upon an abandoned baby crying by the road. Here, in an inversion of the familiar theme of the father abandoning his son Semimaru, the emperor rescues the baby, attributing the infant's unhappy fate to a lack of virtue on his own part.

The image of the emperor as a kindly father to his people is further developed by his reaction when the infant's mother appears soon afterward. The mother—a credit to the emperor's reign!—has been feeding both her child and her aged mother, who is too weak to partake of anything other than breast milk. The infant had been temporarily set aside to give the elderly woman a chance to eat. The young mother describes herself as a widow, and the emperor responds by offering to care for her family, entrusting their welfare to one of his courtiers. It is one

133

of the play's ironies that the baby is—unbeknownst to the emperor, or even to the audience—actually the emperor's own grandson, the child of Semimaru.

After this auspicious introduction, the action of the play shifts to the court itself, and to the first appearance of our ever-changing hero, Semimaru. Though Chikamatsu's text is not annotated to indicate staging, it seems likely that as this scene opened Semimaru was at one side of the stage and his wife at the other, unseen by him. Semimaru is not blind. He is described by the narrator as handsome, deeply loved by his father, and marvelously skilled at playing the biwa. His wife is equally adept at playing the koto. Semimaru himself receives little attention in the first act. The women with whom he is involved are somewhat more fully presented here.

The first of the three women is Semimaru's wife, or *kita no kata*, who is referred to throughout the play by this formal title. We never learn her name. Her first appearance is effectively dramatic. We first hear her voice, singing a song of lamentation to the accompaniment of her koto. Her song is a woman's threnody of grief as she waits for a lover who fails to visit her. Attracted by her song, Semimaru finds her, and she soon makes it abundantly clear that it is of her own situation that she sings. Before Semimaru's eyes she slashes in two the long double headrest which is a part of their conjugal bedding. Symbolically she "punishes" the headrest for Semimaru's failure to have slept with her.

His response is the first of several points in the play where religious motives are used as convenient justifications for a character's behavior. Reassuring his wife that he understands her resentment—they have, after all, been married for two years—he tells her that he had consented to the marriage only out of a sense of duty to his father. He claims that it had been his lifelong intention to become a monk and that he had made a vow to avoid all contact with women.

Typically in Chikamatsu's plays, as well as in the works of other Jōruri writers, surprising revelations often change the apparent motivation of a character's action. As rapidly becomes evident, Semimaru's vow is only a pretext to stave off his wife's unwelcome attentions. Even as a temporary excuse rather than true motivation, however, Semimaru's claim is interesting. Those who were already familiar with the legend of Semimaru knew of him as one who had been forced to give up the life of a prince. Here Chikamatsu has Semimaru considering taking priestly vows on his own initiative.

In this context Chikamatsu effectively portrays the strength of the young woman's passion for Semimaru. She immediately responds that she too will enter Buddhist orders, so that they may be reborn together as man and wife. Yet her true feelings are still clearly this-worldly. "If tonight, for once in our lifetimes, we were to spend the night in love, even Buddha would surely understand" she says as she presses herself upon her unwilling husband. Her vow, like Semimaru's, is purely expedient, aimed at somehow satisfying her own desires. Here, as later in the play, Chikamatsu treats Buddhist values with humor. The contrast to the somber religious tone of Zeami's *Semimaru* is striking.

Chikamatsu's audiences were primarily the merchants and artisans of Kyoto and Osaka. In his depiction of the tenth-century imperial family he focuses on the one aspect of life which would have been common to princes and shopkeepers—love and lust. The most effective scenes in his play are those in which various young women declare their passions, jealousies, and resentments. These powerful female characters are in the tradition of sekkyō, while also owing something to the style of Uji Kaga no jō.

A second scene of passion follows immediately upon the complaints of Semimaru's wife. Semimaru is left alone on stage after rebuffing his wife, and next a palace guard reveals herself to Semimaru as a woman in man's disguise. She is none other than the young mother from the introductory scene, now identified as Naohime, a woman with whom Semimaru had spent "but one brief night a year ago in the village of Kasuga." The "abandoned" infant of the opening scene is Semimaru's baby, conceived on that fateful night. Like Semimaru's wife, Naohime is suffering from jealousy. She has seen Semimaru with his wife and imagines that she has detected signs of his great fondness for the wife. Naohime now is about to burn a written pledge of love from their earlier meeting in the watchfire she tends in her disguise as palace guard. But at the moment Semimaru is protesting his love for Naohime and his indifference toward his wife, the wife's brother appears and penetrates the girl's disguise. Pandemonium breaks loose. Semimaru and Naohime flee in confusion, leaving the wife and her brother together on stage. The wife's anger rises to fury when her brother shows her the written love pledge, accidentally dropped by Semimaru and Naohime in their flight. So great is her rage, her hair stands on end and tears of blood well up in her eyes.

The motif of hair which stands on end is, of course, reminiscent of Sakagami. Chikamatsu's *Semimaru* seems to have been the first Jōruri play to use this device, which can be very effectively executed with a puppet. It reappears in a later Semimaru-related Jōruri and is best known from the Kabuki *Saint Narukami and the God Fudō*, wherein a princess is afflicted with hair which stands on end for a reason which turns out to be most bizarre.[38]

There is a change of scene following the wife's hair-raising exit. The following passage, "The Pilgrimage to Kibune

[38] Lodestones having just been discovered in Japan, the plot has recourse to a giant magnet which pulls up the princess's hairdo full of iron hairpins! See Brandon, *Kabuki*, pp. 124–25.

Shrine," was adapted from an earlier work, called *Aoi no Ue*,[39] written for Uji Kaga no jō.

"The Pilgrimage to Kibune Shrine" is one of the most absorbing scenes in the play. Here a third young woman appears and reveals her love for Semimaru. In the middle of the night, at a shrine by the bridge over the river Uji, a ceremony of black magic is being performed. It is accidentally witnessed by Semimaru's retainer Kiyotsura, who has been searching for Naohime ever since she disappeared from court after her disguise was broken. As Kiyotsura watches, hiding in a tree, a woman approaches the shrine and offers her prayers. Before long a second woman enters in similar attire, and they quickly establish that a common purpose has brought them. By revealing her emotions and praying at the shrine in the dark of night, each hopes to cast a spell upon her rival in love. Surprised at finding another in the same straits, the two women resolve to tell each other their troubles in a "jealousy session."[40]

The first to speak is a court servant, Bashō, who confides that she has been thinking constantly of Semimaru ever since she was "young" (she is now sixteen). She claims that he had promised to fulfill her wishes one night, but failed to keep his word. She imagines that her rival is the prince's wife.

The other woman is Semimaru's wife herself, who declares

[39]The nō *Kanawa* is an earlier source for this tale of a jealous woman who goes by night to the Kibune shrine to case a curse on her rival in love. Sanari, *Yōkyoku taikan* I, 704. Translated by Eileen Kato in Keene, *Twenty Plays of the Nō Theatre*, pp. 194–205.

[40]*Rinki-kō*, a gathering of women expressly for the purpose of airing their resentments against their husbands. The Tokugawa moral code required strict monogamy of women while giving men free reign to visit the licensed quarters. Compare the "jealousy meeting" of a daimyō's wife and her ladies-in-waiting which appears in Saikaku's *Kōshoku ichidai onna*. Ivan Morris, trans., *The Life of an Amorous Woman*, pp. 164–72.

that she too has been cast aside, because of his love for Naohime. Bashō and Semimaru's wife become immediate allies
and set about working a curse on Naohime, venting their jealousy and resentment on Naohime and Semimaru rather than
on each other. Together the two women drive spikes into a
tree at the shrine, with each spike cursing a specific part of
Naohime's body.[41] Blood flows from the tree as the nails bore
in, but the ceremony is without effect because they have been
observed by an outsider: Kiyotsura shows himself and tells his
master's wife her behavior is shameful.

Realizing now that the curses will come to nothing, the jealous wife throws herself into the roiling waters of the river by
the shrine. The act ends dramatically as the wife's corpse,
transformed into a fire-breathing snake, rises from the river,
wraps itself about the *torii* of the shrine, the vows to wreak its
resentment and bitterness for incarnations to come.[42]

Since we have no opportunity to see this play performed,
because it has dropped from the repertory, we can only fall
back on our imaginations to judge its theatrical effectiveness.
It seems clear that this final scene superbly exploits the special
resources of the puppet theater. The appearance of each successive woman has built up the level of outrage and resentment to this climax of jealous wrath. The use of puppets allows
the instantaneous transformation of woman into snake, and
the act ends in a flash of fire and smoke mingling with the
mist over the river Uji.

[41] The pilgrimage, the driving of nails, and the "jealousy session"
are all borrowed from *Aoi no Ue*, *Chikamatsu zenshū*, I, 321–25. The
authorship of *Aoi no Ue* is a matter of controversy, and it has often
been attributed to Chikamatsu.

[42] There is a similar scene in *Tsurezuregusa*, *Chikamatsu zenshū* I,
680–82. This is another unsigned early work often attributed to Chikamatsu; as in the case of *Aoi no Ue*, the attribution is not conclu-
sively proven. The scene also resembles the Nō *Dōjōji*.

ACT TWO

The mood and action of Act Two present a striking contrast to the first act: we are confronted now with scenes of violence, even mayhem. Hayahiro, the brother of Semimaru's wife, roaming around the countryside with an armed band of thirty-odd men, twice attacks a young *rōnin*, or masterless samurai, named Tadamitsu, who has accidentally met Semimaru and Naohime and has undertaken to protect them out of loyalty to the court.[43] Both times Tadamitsu, with superhuman martial skill, singlehandedly holds off Hayahiro and his troops, first with bow and arrow, then with his sword.

The rōnin is a Tokugawa period anachronism in a play set in the reign of the Emperor Daigo. Such swashbuckling, tough-fighting, larger-than-life characters as Tadamitsu were extremely popular in Jōruri, especially in styles which had developed in Edo during the first seventy years of the seventeenth century.

We learn that Tadamitsu is the brother of the court servant Bashō, the third of the women in love with Semimaru. Hayahiro's only wish is to avenge his sister's suicide, but when Tadamitsu soon after is faced with a parallel situation, the death of his sister Bashō, he places greater importance on his loyalty to Semimaru. For Tadamitsu and his parents—who have helped him shelter Semimaru and Naohime—duty and honor override personal, private concerns.

It is Semimaru's retainer Kiyotsura who kills Bashō. Having heard her express her resentment against Semimaru, Kiyotsura fears she will someday cause his master harm. He stabs her in front of the gate of her parental home, when Semi-

[43]This is a glaring inconsistency of plot. Semimaru and Naohime were separated when they fled the court in Act One. Kiyotsura, we know, had been searching for her. Yet in this second act they are together again without explanation.

maru and Naohime have taken refuge from Hayahiro and his armed band. As she dies she laments having wasted her life on a hopeless, impossible love; but freed now of any bitterness toward Semimaru, she asks only that he pray for her and that her relatives continue to protect him.

Obedient to her request, her relatives show no resentment toward Semimaru, or even toward Kiyotsura. Calling Bashō's death a "trifling matter," the family remains resolutely dedicated to Semimaru. In the final fight scene of this act Tadamitsu's father dies at the hands of Hayahiro. The fighting gives Kiyotsura time to escape with Semimaru while Tadamitsu escapes with his aged mother and Naohime.

With its four deaths (besides Bashō and her father, Naohime's mother and infant son are gratuitously cut down by Hayahiro, who has kidnaped them and brought them with him as hostages) and two prodigious displays of martial valor against overpowering odds, the second act was undoubtedly quite exciting in actual performance. Passion dominates the first act, honor and bravery the second. The contrast made between the villainous Hayahiro and the virtuous Tadamitsu is sure evidence that the morality of the play demands that loyalty to the imperial family transcend any personal concerns of the samurai. The first act demonstrated that sexual passion is the hardest of the emotions to control, but at the moment of death Bashō, mastering her feelings for Semimaru, dies a death that brings honor to her samurai family.

ACT THREE

The third act of Chikamatsu's play is modeled directly on Zeami's *Semimaru*, with two basic changes: Semimaru's sudden blindness is attributed to the resentment borne him by the women he has spurned, and the woman with whom he is reunited at Ausaka is not his mad sister but Naohime, the one woman he has really loved.

An unspecified period of time, probably a few months, has

140

passed since the action of the second act. During this interval Semimaru has gone blind. In reporting Semimaru's blindness to the emperor, Kiyotsura blames it on the ill effects of the jealousy felt toward him by the many women who have been dazzled by his extraordinary beauty.

The emperor responds to Kiyotsura's news by ordering that Semimaru be left alone in the mountains at Ausaka. Because of his physical handicap Semimaru is now unfit to remain at court. The emperor here faces exactly the same kind of human dilemma that often confronts the shopkeepers and prostitutes of Chikamatsu's domestic plays—a conflict between personal feelings and a sense of duty. His duty overrides his sympathy for his son. In ordering that the blind Semimaru be abandoned, he makes an example of his own son for all people. The emperor justifies this decision as showing compassion for all his subjects, the virtue for which he was praised at the beginning of Act One.

The michiyuki, the poetic passage describing Semimaru's journey from Kyoto to Ausaka, is longer and more complex than the comparable passage in the Nō. The pathos of Semimaru's blindness and the misery of his fallen state are ideas common to both Zeami's and Chikamatsu's conceptions. The most significant addition in Chikamatsu's michiyuki is the grief expressed over Semimaru's separation from his love. In Chikamatsu's *Semimaru* the prince is pitiful not merely because of his blindness but, even more significantly, because powers beyond his control have separated him from Naohime. Zeami's restrained, disciplined Semimaru tries to accept his fate with quiet dignity, but Chikamatsu's Semimaru is a creature of passion. He says of himself, "My heart, like a wild horse / A thousand times this day goes rushing / Off in thoughts of the one I love." Even some crows which fly by at dusk are said to be longing for their mates. They are called *tsumagoi karasu*, literally "wife-loving crows."

The abandonment scene after Semimaru arrives at Ausaka is

141

most closely borrowed from the Nō. The courtiers Kiyotsura and Mareyo provide him with various items of rustic clothing, each—as in the Nō—accompanied by an appropriate poetic allusion. Lamenting over Semimaru's new-found poverty and isolation, they leave him and return to the capital.

Since sexual passion is the unifying emotion of his play, it is inevitable that Chikamatsu substitutes Naohime for Sakagami in the reunion scene at Ausaka. This is the high point of the play, a scene rife with dramatic tension phrased in powerful poetry. Semimaru's blindness is utilized to full dramatic effect: he cannot see and therefore does not know that Naohime is near him, listening as he plays his lute and sings of his grief. The narrator tells us, "He cannot forget his past—a vanished dream / Even the call of a lovesick deer / Sounds painful to his ears."

Presumably, Semimaru remained on stage after being left by Kiyotsura and Mareyo. Two temple page boys then enter, bringing Naohime with them. Semimaru cannot see, and Naohime cannot speak. The page boys have prevented her throwing herself into a river to end her life. They have learned her identity and brought her to Semimaru, but they caution her against speaking, warning that Semimaru is embarrassed to be seen and will run into hiding if he hears the sound of another human being. Unable to bear listening to Semimaru's protestation of love and longing in silence, Naohime faints.

Here Chikamatsu has again inverted a theme of the earlier Semimaru legend. In earlier versions of the legend Semimaru welcomed an occasional visitor in his loneliness. Here he rejects human company, and not for reasons of religious discipline, but of vanity.

Chikamatsu resolves the act by having Semimaru undergo a sudden change in mood which brings him instant enlightenment. Suddenly he realizes that he must not think of Naohime, but must concentrate only on the impermanence of life.

Chikamatsu here returns his Semimaru to the state of enlightened awareness characteristic of him in the Nō.

In one of the most heightened moments in the play Semimaru "composes" his famous Meeting Barrier poem. "Travelers' journeys / Are only the delusions of dreams," he says. In writing his play Chikamatsu has created a new context for the famous old poem (A) which in Chikamatsu's day was enjoying renewed popularity.

The temple boys disclose that they are manifestations of the spirits of two great poets of antiquity, Hitomaro and Akahito. They attest to Semimaru's enlightenment revealed in the ideas underlying his poem, specifically the principles that meeting is the beginning of parting and that all who are born must die. They assure Semimaru that he will achieve Buddhahood and be reborn into the Tuṣita heaven.

Chikamatsu was writing for an audience which delighted in seeing overt displays of rapidly changing emotion. Semimaru's fate upon his enlightenment is curiously ambivalent, emotionally complex.

Semimaru's enlightenment is depicted as the result of conquering his passions, but ascetic cessation of desire does not fit the structure of Chikamatsu's play. Even in the act of gaining enlightenment, Semimaru is reunited with Naohime. Together they wander off along a mountain path. The act ends with an air of auspicious finality: "The couple are miraculously reunited, and his fame as the poet of Mount Ausaka has remained until this day."

ACT FOUR

Act Four includes a short passage which proves Chikamatsu's familiarity with the *Konjaku* legend as well as with the Nō. In Chikamatsu's play Hakuga no Sammi is described as Semimaru's disciple in playing the lute. This had been his identity in *Konjaku monogatari*, but in the Nō he is merely a local peasant who builds Semimaru's hut at Ausaka. He is never there described as a disciple of the blind man. Chikamatsu borrows the master-disciple relationship as in *Konjaku*, and has Hakuga shelter his teacher Semimaru in his country cottage. Here too Chikamatsu has overturned earlier legend. For in *Konjaku* Hakuga came to Semimaru's hut. Here Hakuga has been living in the countryside and Semimaru has come to him.

In contrast to the highly emotional, poetic third act, Act Four returns to the atmosphere of swaggering bravado that pervaded Act Two. Hayahiro, Kiyotsura, and Tadamitsu each in turn stumble on Hakuga no Sammi's cottage. Twice we see the evil Hayahiro held off by a lone figure faithful to Semimaru.

The charm of the fourth act lies in its humor. Passion, the theme that unified the first three acts, is humorously exploited in Act Four. To this end Chikamatsu uses a standard Jōruri technique, the substitution of one character for another. The result is a parody of the several earlier scenes in which one or another of the women protested her love for Semimaru.

Tadamitsu's aged, white-haired mother is substituted for Naohime. A cupboard under the Buddha shelf in Hakuga no Sammi's cottage affords a hiding place for Naohime while Semimaru and Hakuga no Sammi are temporarily away from the dwelling. But in the course of this act, Naohime leaves her hiding place, and Tadamitsu, coming by chance on the hut, deposits his frail old mother in the same spot. There Semimaru finds her on his return to the cottage. Semimaru must now suffer the humorous confusion of touching his beloved's skin and finding rough bones covered with dry wrinkles. Unable to see her, he hears her description from Hakuga: a white-haired grandmother! Semimaru must listen to the old hag's apparent protestations of love. "Oh, my Prince! My beloved, how I wanted to see you!" exclaims Tadamitsu's mother in feudal devotion.

Chikamatsu uses Semimaru's blindness to full dramatic effect. In the reunion of Semimaru and Naohime in Act Three, Semimaru's blindness had increased the pathos of the scene. Here his blindness increases the humor. One can almost imagine an enthusiast in the audience calling out to reassure Semimaru that the old crone is not really Naohime. The humorous, yet poignant, treatment of Semimaru's blindness is reminiscent of several kyōgen concerning the blind.[44] It is also in the tradition of even earlier tales told by blind biwa hōshi in which, with self-deprecating humor, they used the miscalculations of the blind to amusing effect.

As the fourth act closes, Semimaru, Naohime, and Kiyotsura have all happily reassembled. Tadamitsu leaves his elderly mother in their care and sets off by himself, still seeking to vanquish Hayahiro and avenge his father's death. The others depart for the Kyoto palace of Semimaru's sister Sakagami, here relegated to the most minor of roles.

ACT FIVE

In every Jōruri history play, good ultimately triumphs over evil. Thus it is no surprise that Tadamitsu achieves his goal in the final act, meeting his enemy Hayahiro in battle and slashing off his head. Hayahiro's death resolves the struggle which had run through the preceding acts, but there is one thread of plot as yet left dangling. Three women had fallen in love with Semimaru. Bashō's passionate attachment was resolved and ended at the moment of her death. Naohime's longing has been fulfilled and she remains with her prince. But the most raging passion, the burning jealousy of Semimaru's wife, continues to work its evil curse. Semimaru is still blind.

Sakagami suggests that the spirit of Semimaru's dead wife must be placated in order to cure his blindness and to assure the safe delivery of the baby we now learn Naohime is expect-

[44] See Golay, "Pathos and Farce. Zatō Plays of the Kyōgen Repertoire."

145

ing. A priest is called upon to perform forty-nine days of ceremonies for the repose of her soul.

The play approaches its conclusion with the last day's rites by the bank of the river Uji. The priest performs a ritual in which he describes the ten lunar months of pregnancy. In complex terminology each stage of the development of the fetus is enumerated. For each month there is an appropriate guardian deity. The entire ceremony is almost word by word identical with one which concludes the early unsigned play *Kinoene matsuri,* a work sometimes attributed to Chikamatsu. The complex ritual works to good effect. In a final flash of excitement, the spirit of Semimaru's wife manifests herself, now transformed into the goddess of mercy. Her miraculous glow illuminates Semimaru, and his eyesight is suddenly restored. The last resentment has been resolved. Semimaru and his descendants will prosper eternally.

Chikamatsu's Semimaru as a Whole

The overall structure of Chikamatsu's *Semimaru* is more tightly controlled than that of many of his history plays. The time elapsed is on the order of a single year; all the action develops in and around Kyoto, with variety provided by scenes at court, in the countryside, or in shrine precincts. Thirteen scenes, alternating three-two-three-two-three per act, suffice for the action of the entire play.

In general, with its relatively tight structure, and its focus on private, emotional concerns, Chikamatsu's *Semimaru* bears considerable similarity to his later "domestic" dramas. As I have suggested, passion and jealousy are the principal subjects unifying the play. Of the three women who declare their love for Semimaru, Bashō is the least significant and is done away with in the second act. Semimaru's wife's jealousy is important to the structure of the play, connecting the first and fifth acts and providing the rationale behind the recurrent fighting. But the wife is not a fully developed character.

Naohime, however, lives in the imagination as a believable human being. Chikamatsu portrays her as filial in her concern for her aged mother, enterprising in disguising herself to get into court, and constant in her devotion to Semimaru even after he has lost his sight and suffered abandonment.

Aware that a prince experiences all the emotions of any man, particularly the emotion of love, Chikamatsu still does not portray the prince in the same way as he would a warrior or shopkeeper. It is one of the great strengths of Chikamatsu's work that he effectively captures the character of Semimaru as a prince, a man whose gentle sensibilities contrast with those of the rougher male characters, Hayahiro and Tadamitsu.

Semimaru now has far more individual identity than in the earlier versions of the legend. He is young, gentle, and—compared to the violently passionate women—quite passive. Faced with Hayahiro's enmity, he flees, unlike the others who stand their ground. Chikamatsu's principal device for depicting the gentleness of the prince is especially evident in the third act: in large measure, Semimaru speaks in poetry. This is not merely poetry borrowed from the Nō, though there is some of that. Portions, such as the michiyuki, are original with Chikamatsu. Another dimension is added by classical allusions, ever ready in the mind of a prince. Chikamatsu develops Semimaru's identity as a poet more than as a musician. His poetry demonstrates his enlightenment and is responsible for all the good that befalls him.

In my analysis of the play I have emphasized those elements which contribute to the coherence of the whole as a work of literature to be read. Though printed Jōruri texts were fairly widely read, the interest of the play was naturally enhanced by its stage production. Audience attention did not remain constant throughout a Jōruri performance, and the connection between acts is often quite disjointed. In the case of *Semimaru* the third act was doubtless the high point of the play, whereas the ceremonial felicitous ending of the last act would have been less easily comprehensible and less interesting.

Chikamatsu transformed the legend of Semimaru into a love story, the story of Naohime's undying affection for her prince. Yet at the same time Chikamatsu retained the traditional identity of Semimaru as an enlightened poet whose most famous poem shows the futility of man's emotional attachments to others. There is some logical inconsistency evident in this, but no lack of drama.

In Chikamatsu's play the most basic elements of the Semimaru legend remain intact. A blind musician living at Ausaka Pass sings of the impermanence of life and the inevitability of parting. But, like Zeami before him, Chikamatsu makes many new additions to the basic story. Downgrading while not completely rejecting the Buddhist moral implications evident in the Nō, Chikamatsu's most important additions are the love interest, Naohime, and the threat of the enmity of Semimaru's brother-in-law, Hayahiro. *Semimaru* is recast in Jōruri form as a struggle between the forces of good and evil. Accomplishing this required the creation of new characters and diminished emphasis on some preexisting characters, most notably Sakagami.

In all subsequent Semimaru literature, whether for Jōruri or Kabuki, the good-evil power struggle remains implicit, and Semimaru is always on the side of the good. All later plays show extensive addition of new characters and elaborate departures from the original core meaning of Semimaru's life. The later plays appeared in rapid succession and some of the audience's pleasure derived from its awareness of the variations wrought by each new playwright on the themes created by his predecessors.

Tokugawa Period Reinterpretations

Additional Tokugawa Semimaru Plays

There were at least eight other Semimaru Jōruri or Kabuki produced in the century following Chikamatsu's work, several of them now known by title only. In one case the dating of the play is uncertain, and it may actually be an earlier work than Chikamatsu's. The work in question, a Jōruri entitled *Semimaro*, was written by the Edo playwright Tosa no shōjō. Tosa was active in Edo between 1673 and 1710 and was famous for Jōruri of a rough, vigorous style. The only extant text of Tosa's *Semimaro* dates from 1708, but the date of its first performance is unknown. Both *Semimaro* and *Semimaru* borrowed some lines directly from the Nō, but there are additional similarities between the two plays which are shared inventions not found in Zeami's text. Unquestionably, one of these Jōruri has borrowed from the other, and on the basis of stylistic comparison it is likely that Chikamatsu's play is the later of the two.

In both plays Semimaru makes his vow of chastity, he is visited at Ausaka by his lover rather than his sister, and his blindness is a debility which has begun in mid-life rather than existing from birth. In passages borrowed from the Nō, *Semimaro* generally shows closer similarity to the language of the Nō, while Chikamatsu's work shows greater complexity of plot than does Tosa's. Comparison of the two texts shows greater reliance on divine intervention as a means of advancing the plot of *Semimaro*, whereas the action of *Semimaru* unfolds mainly by the actions of men, not gods. The greater complexity of Chikamatsu's play is the mark both of his superior skill as a writer and of his relatively more modern consciousness concerning causality in human existence.[45]

[45]Yokoyama Tadashi, "Jōruri *Semimaro*," presents a brief yet detailed comparison of these two plays. Much of the interest of this comparison lies in the indication that Edo jōruri influenced early Genroku jōruri in Osaka.

Though Chikamatsu may not have written the first of the Tokugawa *Semimaru* plays, his was certainly the most successful. His success in turn inspired further efforts, the first a Kabuki called *Semimaru nido no shusse* (*Semimaru's Return to Greatness*). This play was staged in 1698 in both Osaka and Kyoto.[46] The titles and lists of dramatis personae suggest that these two productions were identical in every detail.[47] As Kabuki, *Semimaru's Return to Greatness* attracted an audience mainly through the talents and physical appeal of the actors, an aspect which is entirely lost to us. We are left with a text which is hardly more than a simple plot summary. Though we know the names of every actor who took part in the Kyoto and Osaka performances, the identity of the author is a mystery and was presumably a matter of utter indifference to the audience.

Reduced to comparing plot alone, we cannot but conclude that *Semimaru's Return to Greatness* was inferior to Chikamatsu's *Semimaru*. Nearly every scene in the Kabuki is derivative from the Jōruri, but the sequence of scenes is somewhat changed. More important, the characters involved in any particular scene are often shifted from those in the Jōruri. As a result, much of the action in *Semimaru's Return to Greatness* is entirely unmotivated.

Sakagami, who played such a small part in Chikamatsu's play, is assigned a major role in the Kabuki. Here, rather than being Semimaru's elder sister, Sakagami is his elder brother. The basic conflict is a succession struggle between Sakagami

[46] The Osaka version was produced by Iwai Hanshirō I, at his theater, the Iwai-za. In Kyoto the work was performed at the Hoteiya-za, managed by Murayama Heiemon, who was probably responsible for both the Osaka and Kyoto productions. He is known to have spent the year 1697 at the Iwai-za, returning to Kyoto the following year to become head of the Hoteiya-za.

[47] Yūda and Torigoe, *Kamigata kyōgen hon*, pp. 8–11.

and Semimaru. To complicate the situation further, the two brothers are also both in love with Naohime and are struggling for her attentions. As in Chikamatsu's version, Semimaru is gentle and passive; but Sakagami is wildly aggressive and uncontrolled. Sakagami—upturned hair—is here used as a theatrical device to highlight moments of unbridled rage. In one scene Sakagami attempts to carry Naohime off with him. In order to seize her he disguises himself as a woman, a rather unremarkable stratagem unless one remembers Chikamatsu's *Semimaru* and realizes the "allusion" to Sakagami's femininity in the earlier play.

Semimaru, though still gentle and passive, here lacks the dignity with which Chikamatsu treated him. In this version of the Ausaka abandonment scene, Semimaru is left on the mountain while asleep and has no idea what is happening. A few lines of Chikamatsu's michiyuki are borrowed, but they do not suffice to create the mood of pathos present in the Jōruri. There is no talk of karmic causation in connection with Semimaru's affliction. He describes his blindness only as a "punishment" for having led many women astray.

Semimaru's abandonment comes near the conclusion of the play. By this time Naohime has disappeared from the action without the playwright's apparent notice or concern. Rather than Naohime, it is Semimaru's wife who comes to him at Ausaka. She passes Kiyotsura and Mareyo on the road and tells them she has made a vow of silence. Her silence is, of course, modeled on Naohime's silence in Chikamatsu's play, but here it is unmotivated. The "vow" constrains her from speaking when confronted with Semimaru, yet does not prevent her speaking to Kiyotsura and Mareyo.

When Semimaru awakens at Ausaka and realizes that he has been abandoned, he prepares to throw himself into the stream and end his life, exactly as had been Naohime's intention in Chikamatsu's text. This is another instance of the playwright's transferring from one character to another an incident taken from Chikamatsu's play. It is hard to imagine how this play could have made sense to the audience unless it was already familiar with Chikamatsu's version, yet herein lay the secret pleasure of the plot. The audience *was* familiar with the earlier play and appreciated the Kabuki's versatility in twisting and recasting elements of plot, just as some in Chikamatsu's audience may have delighted in the ways he transformed certain Nō motifs in his own *Semimaru*.

A 1721 Kabuki called *Semimaru yōrō no taki* (*Yōrō Waterfalls Semimaru*) is today known only by title, but the next Semimaru play, a 1724 Jōruri called *Onna Semimaru* (*Female Semimaru*), is extant. *Female Semimaru* was the joint creation of Nishizawa Ippū and Tanaka Senryū, a team who wrote a half-dozen collaborative works in Osaka between 1723 and 1726. Nishizawa in addition ran the Osaka bookstore-publishing house which printed the text of his play.

Female Semimaru was first performed on December 2, 1724, when the Toyotake-za had just been rebuilt after the great Osaka fire which leveled it in April of that year. Osaka playgoers held great hopes for *Female Semimaru* and turned out in large numbers for its first performance. Like Chikamatsu's *Semimaru*, *Female Semimaru* was considered a "felicitous" play, appropriate for performance at the reopening of the Toyotake theater and likely to help ensure long prosperity for it.[48] The very large cast of characters reflects the fact that the performance for which the play was written was a *kaomise* "face showing" performance inaugurating the new season in the newly rebuilt theater and designed to show off the talents of the company's entire complement of chanters and puppeteers.

The authors were familiar with both Chikamatsu's *Semimaru* and the Kabuki play *Semimaru's Return to Greatness*. Numerous

[48] Yokoyama Tadashi, "Onna Semimaru," p. 35.

lines from *Semimaru* are reused in *Female Semimaru*, and the central conception of the Kabuki has been borrowed and successfully elaborated upon: in this play also, Sakagami and Semimaru are brothers. The issue of appropriate succession to the throne is crucial. In fact, the most unifying element of plot is a recurrent discussion—running through all five acts—of the nature of kingship and the importance of benevolent government. Throughout, Sakagami's evil violence contrasts with Semimaru's gentle goodness. Good ultimately triumphs over evil, but Sakagami's role as evil incarnate is bigger and far more interesting than Semimaru's.

Semimaru's nature is extremely passive in this play. In no sense can he be said to be struggling with Sakagami for the throne or for the love of Naohime, though both ultimately are his. In the first act, Naohime contrives to speak with Semimaru, with whom she has had previous secret contact. As in Chikamatsu's version, it is Naohime who takes the initiative, not Semimaru. Once Semimaru and Naohime are together, and Sakagami realizes what is happening, he rounds up a gang of toughs in an attempt to seize Naohime by force and to murder Semimaru. The scene epitomizes their diametrically opposed natures. Sakagami is active, evil, and fascinating, but Semimaru is a vapid character who interests the playwrights hardly at all. As one of Sakagami's retainers tells another, "It seems that serving a virtuous master could become rather uninteresting."[49]

Semimaru does not appear at all in the second act, although he is the subject of discussion. Sakagami learns of the emperor's decision: the throne is to pass to Semimaru. Rushing to court in a rage to protest his father's choice, Sakagami is

[49]Quotations from this play are my translations from a woodblock edition in the possession of Kyoto University. The play has never been published in a movable type edition.

153

told by his father, "Did you think I wouldn't hear of your plan to kill Semimaru? Semimaru and you are both of the same flowing royal stream, but one is clear and one is muddied in his heart."

Into this scene enter Semimaru's retainers, Kiyotsura and Mareyo, to report that Semimaru is unable to come to court and unable to accept the throne. He has gone blind. Even the reason for Semimaru's blindness is made trivial in this play. His blindness is not of karmic origin, nor is it caused by the wrathful curse of a jealous woman. He has gone blind from eyestrain:

> From the beginning, ever since he was a little boy, the prince never set aside his poetry and musical instruments. He followed the teachings of white-haired old men, heedless of study's strains on mind and body. From these accumulated stresses there came an eye disease. We searched the great and esoteric laws of every shrine and temple, searched the ten thousand volumes of classical medical treatises. Though we gave him good medicines it was no use. Finally, both his eyes went blind.

Because of his physical imperfection, his courtiers report, Semimaru feels himself unfit to take the throne. The emperor disagrees, believing that the virtue of Semimaru's character outweighs the significance of his blindness. He finds Sakagami unfit to rule, and tells Semimaru's courtiers to return and inform Semimaru that he is to ascend the throne despite his blindness. Again Sakagami takes violent action. He seizes the throne, orders the emperor taken away and killed, and demands that Naohime be sent to him to be his empress.

In fact, the emperor is not killed, but merely taken captive. In the third act, through the actions of Semimaru's allies, the emperor is freed, and we learn that Semimaru's blindness was merely a ruse to avoid conflict with his brother. We next see Semimaru in the fourth act as he and the emperor together are wandering aimlessly about the vicinity of Ausaka. There, in a complete reversal of the roles as depicted by Chikamatsu, Semimaru is reunited with Naohime who had been blinded by her stepmother and abandoned at Ausaka. Their reunion is the occasion for Semimaru's recitation of the by now so very familiar poem, "This, now this . . ."

The final act focuses on Sakagami, who is desperately ill from the effects of a rite of black magic. Without allies, and in this weakened condition, he is forced to hand over the throne to Semimaru. Thanks to an act of sacrifice on the part of a former retainer of Sakagami's, Naohime's sight returns. Her benefactor gouges out his own eyes and holds them up to heaven as an offering, whereupon Naohime is cured. The play closes with the promise of peace and prosperity under the reign of Semimaru.

Female Semimaru includes a few entirely original scenes which must have been of dramatic interest. One shows Semimaru's loyal follower Tadamitsu swimming through rough seas pulling with his teeth the towrope of a small boat in which Semimaru and Naohime had been cast adrift. Another original scene is a horrifying suicide enacted by a follower of Sakagami who had disobeyed him by protecting the emperor. Unable to resolve his conflicting loyalties in any other way, Sakagami's henchman Kunitsura disembowels himself before the eyes of his uncomprehending young children. A retainer decapitates the dead Kunitsura and his children then set off, carrying their father's head, to Sakagami's palace. His little daughter complains to the bundle she carries, "Please say something, Papa. You're so heavy, please walk." Grisly as this scene may be, it shows a greater degree of originality in the composition of *Female Semimaru* than in *Semimaru's Return to Greatness*.

Most interesting in *Female Semimaru* is the obvious, consistent technique used to elaborate the plot, increase the cast, and generate complexities not found in the Chikamatsu version. The technique is one of doubling. For each of several characters borrowed from Chikamatsu there is created here a parallel role of opposite nature or sex. The most openly opposed pair are Semimaru and Sakagami. In addition, Semimaru's loyal retainers Kiyotsura and Mareyo are balanced by Sakagami's men, Kunitsura and Maretsumi, each the brother of his counterpart.

In another sense, Naohime is the double of Semimaru, and Naohime's stepmother is the character balanced against the emperor. After gouging out her daughter's eyes, Naohime's stepmother orders her abandoned at Mount Ausaka. Many details of Semimaru's abandonment in Chikamatsu's play are borrowed and attributed to Naohime, and this accounts for the play's title, *Female Semimaru*. Naohime's robes are changed from those of an elegant court lady to those of a beggar, and like Semimaru she is handed a straw rainhat, raincoat, and blind man's staff. She carries the biwa and plays it in the falling rains at Ausaka; and in the most grotesque variation on Chikamatsu, she refuses to allow those around her to call her stepmother's actions heartless.

Just as the brothers Semimaru and Sakagami are an opposed pair, Naohime is contrasted with her stepsister, called Kashiwadehime. Semimaru and Sakagami are two candidates for the position of emperor, and the mother sees both Naohime and Kashiwadehime as possible empresses. In one scene the emperor discusses the two sons and weighs their moral characters. In a later parallel scene, Naohime's stepmother compares the girls' potential as wives for the new emperor.

The play suffers from the moral absolutism of its roles. Semimaru in particular is too good to be true, and certainly too good to be interesting. The play was written during a period of rapidly advancing complexity in the construction of puppets. No doubt the puppet head used for Sakagami had hair which could indeed stand on end, since at several points in the text it is said to do so. The interest of the play must have centered on the dramatic tricks possible with the Sakagami puppet. Semimaru is important only as a foil for his evil brother.

Female Semimaru was moderately successful at the box office. Though the last two acts were dropped, the first three continued to be performed in the first two months of 1725. A Kabuki called *Semimaru Onna Mōyō* (*Female Pattern Semimaru*) was staged in that same year in Edo. It does not survive, but based on the title alone we can be sure that it shared with *Female Semimaru* the inversion of male and female roles, and it may have been simply a Kabuki staging of Nishizawa and Tanaka's play itself.

Two additional Kabuki were staged later in the eighteenth century, but nothing is now known about their contents or their relationship to the earlier works. Ironically, the very last title listed in a chronological bibliography[50] is identified as a sekkyō. This is a work dating from 1813, entitled *Semimaru miya yurai* (*The History of Prince Semimaru*). Only the vagaries of history can account for our having this record of a very late performance of a Semimaru sekkyō when the many presumed earlier performances all passed by undocumented.

Tokugawa Essayists' Comments on Semimaru

Tokugawa playwrights clearly took a lighthearted approach toward the "facts" of Semimaru's life, amusing themselves and their audiences by inventing one new incident after another in successive waves of allusive variations on earlier plays. In contrast to the playwrights, however, many literary scholars and learned essayists of the day considered it impor-

[50]*Kokushō sōmokuroku*, V, 173–74.

tant to comment on the truth behind the ever-changing Semi-maru legend.

The issues addressed by these essayists were twofold: they questioned the reality of Semimaru's blindness while uni-formly agreeing, on the basis of their scholarly inquiries, that he had never been a prince. As mentioned previously, Semi-maru's poem (A) about the passing travelers at Ausaka en-joyed tremendous popularity during the Tokugawa period be-cause of its inclusion in the card game based on the poetry collection *Hyakunin isshu.* The essayists pondered the question of how Semimaru could have written this poem if he were truly blind and could not see the passers-by. All commentators worried over the headnote to this poem in the *Gosenshū.* Some concluded that Semimaru was not blind, as the headnote read, "On seeing the passers-by . . ." Others took the op-posite view, thought Semimaru was blind, and considered that the word "seeing" in the headnote was not to be taken lit-erally. The details of each commentary need not concern us, but the large number of essays mentioning Semimaru indicate the great vitality of his legend in the Tokugawa period.[51] One writer deserves quoting, however, as his comment might serve as a coda to this whole book. The novelist Takizawa Bakin, writing in 1809, began his discussion with the under-statement, "Many different things have been said about Semi-maru."[52]

The Semimaru Shrine and Legend Today

Today the Semimaru shrine is in disrepair. Though articles written in the 1960s quote documents preserved at the lower

[51] Aside from Bakin, there are comments concerning Semimaru in: Kamo Mabuchi, *Tabi no nagusa;* Amano Nobukage, *Shiojiri;* Ozaki Masayoshi, *Hakunin isshu hitoyogatari;* Najima Masamichi, *Gogo;* and more.

[52] Takizawa Bakin, *Enseki zasshi,* p. 306.

shrine, on a visit there in 1970 I could find no one familiar with the history of the shrine or sure of the whereabouts of its records. The spring of "clear water by the barrier" has long since gone dry, and a recently widened highway out of Kyoto passes right by the foot of the steps leading up to the shrine. Ausaka is still a place where "people come and go," but it is no longer a spot where travelers pause to pray for safe travel or to enjoy entertainments directed in equal parts to the traveler and the gods. A police station stands on the spot of the original Ausaka Barrier, while Semimaru's name now adorns a tunnel which speeds traffic through the pass.

Still, we cannot pronounce the legend dead. Semimaru's claim to royal blood, first invented by biwa hōshi seeking dignity in their profession, has been accepted by the administrative authorities of the imperial family. The Imperial Household Agency maintains a gravestone bearing Semimaru's name at the Jūzenji, a temple at Shinomiya-kawara.[53] The Nō *Semimaru* remains popular, and as recently as 1971 a new dance piece with shamisen accompaniment and a libretto based on the Semimaru legend received its premier performance. "Many different things have been said about Semimaru," and given the longevity of the legend, no one can claim to have spoken the last word.

[53] Hayashiya Tatsusaburō *et al.*, "Semimaru o megutte," p. 28.

Part II

TEXTS

Poems and Prose Selections

A. *Gosenshū*, 951

"On seeing the passersby when living in a hut at Ausaka Barrier."

Kore ya kono	This, now this!
Yuku mo kaeru mo	Where people come and people go
Wakaretsutsu	Exchanging farewells
Shiru mo shiranu mo	For friends and strangers alike
Ausaka no seki [1]	This is Meeting Barrier. [2]

B. *Shinkokinshū*, 1206

Yo no naka wa	Our lives,
Tote mo kakute mo	This way or that,
Onaji koto [3]	Pass just the same.
Miya mo waraya mo	Whether in a palace or a hovel
Hate shi nakereba [4]	We cannot live forever.

C. *Toshiyori zuinō*, 1114 OR 1115, COMMENTING ON POEM B

This is Semimaru's poem. He lived at Ausaka Barrier, sustaining himself by begging from those who passed by. Surely

[1] No. 1090, *Gosenwakashū*, [Kochū] kokka taikei, III, 319.

[2] Keene, *Anthology of Japanese Literature,* p. 92, slightly amended.

[3] The third line here is as it appears in *Shinkokinwakashū* and *Wakan rōeishū*. In *Gōdanshō* and *Konjaku monogatari* it is *sugoshitemu,* and in *Toshiyori zuinō* it is *arinubeshi.*

[4] No. 1851, *Shinkokinwakashū*, NKBT, XXVIII, 374.

he played the koto. I wonder if it was because people felt sorry for him that he was able to survive. When they saw he had built a miserable grass hut and thatched it with straw, they laughed at him exclaiming, "What a dreadful looking house!" or, "He's arranged it nicely even though it's only straw." Because of this he wrote that poem.[5]

D–F. Kokinshū, 905; Hekianshō, 1226

D. *Yo no naka wa* What home can I
   Izure ka sashite Point to as my own
   Waga naran In this uncertain world?
   Yukitomaru o zo Wherever my feet take me,
   Yado to sadamuru I'll call that my place.

E. *Ausaka no* At Ausaka
   Arashi no kaze wa The storm winds
   Samukeredo Blow chill, and yet,
   Yukue shiraneba I sleep here in suffering
   Wabitsutsu zo neru Knowing no future destination.

F. *Kaze no ue ni* A speck of dust
   Arika sadamenu Tossed aimlessly
   Chiri no mi wa On the winds,
   Yukue mo shirazu It seems I've become
   Narinubera nari[6] One with no known future.

---

[5]*Toshiyori zuinō*, Nihon kagaku taikei, I, 136. There is a nearly identical passage in *Kohon setsuwashū*, a collection of tales thought to have been completed about 1130. *Kohon setsuwashū sōsakuin*, pp. 67–68.

[6]*Hekianshō*, in *Gunsho ruijū*, X, 600. In the *Kokinshū*, too, the poems are grouped together and are said to be of unknown authorship and topic. They are nos. 987–89. *Kokinwakashū*, NKBT, VIII, 302.

Poems and Prose Selections

G. *Shinkokinshū*, 1206

Akikaze ni	This world of ours:
Nabiku asaji no	Dewdrops trembling
Suegoto ni	In uncertainty
Oku shiratsuyu no	On every reed-tip
Aware yo no naka [7]	In the autumn wind.

H. *Shokukokinshū*, 1265

Ausaka no	In the violence
Seki no arashi no	Of the storms
Hageshiki ni	At Ausaka Barrier
Shiite zo itaru	I plan, somehow, in blindness
Yo o sugosu tote [8]	To pass my days.

I and J. **Konjaku Monogatari**, APPROXIMATELY 1100

I. The Story of How Lord Minamoto
no Hiromasa Went to the Blind Man's Place
at Ausaka [9]

Once upon a time there was a man called Lord Minamoto
no Hiromasa. He was the son of Prince Katsuakira [10] of the
War Ministry, the son of the Engi emperor.[11] He was an accomplished gentleman, especially skilled in the musical arts.
He played the lute with great delicacy and also played the flute

[7] No. 1850, *Shinkokinwakashū*, NKBT, XXVIII, 374.
[8] No. 1734. *Shokukokinwakashū*, [Kochū] kokka taikei, V, 633.
[9] *Konjaku monogatari*, Book 24, tale 23, NKBT, XXV, 312–14.
[10] Prince Katsuakira (903–26) was the first son of Emperor Daigo.
[11] Here, as in many references, the emperor is identified by the
name of one of his reign eras, Engi. For consistency of identification,
in all future references the name will be translated uniformly as "Emperor Daigo."

165

with indescribable charm. This man was, at the time of Emperor Murakami,[12] a member of the court.

At this time there was a blind man living by the Ausaka Barrier in a hut he had built. His name was Semimaru.[13] He had been a servant of Prince Atsuzane of the Ministry of Ceremonial.[14] This prince, the son of Emperor Uda,[15] was extremely skilled at playing musical instruments. Though he himself had played the lute for many years, whenever he heard Semimaru the prince was astonished by the subtle delicacy of his style.

Now it happened that Hiromasa became passionately interested in playing the lute; when he learned of the great talent of the blind lute player at the Ausaka Barrier, he felt a strong desire to hear him play. Yet, since the blind man's hut was such an unfamiliar place, he did not go there himself, but sent someone else to Semimaru with the message, "What an impossible place to live! Why don't you come live in the capital?"

Semimaru did not respond to this suggestion, but merely said,

Yo no naka wa	Our lives,
Tote mo kakute mo	This way or that
Sugoshitemu	Pass just the same.
Miya mo waraya mo	Whether in a palace or a hovel
Hate shi nakereba	We cannot live forever.

When his messenger returned and reported this answer, Hiromasa was bitterly disappointed and thought to himself, "I care very deeply about this art, and I really want very much to

[12] R. 946–67.

[13] The name is read Semimaro in the NKBT edition of *Konjaku monogatari*. I have changed it to Semimaru for consistency's sake.

[14] Prince Atsuzane (893–967), the eighth son of Emperor Uda. Some scholars read the name as "Atsumi" rather than "Atsuzane."

[15] R. 887–97.

meet this blind man; but it's hard to know how long he will live, nor can I even be sure of my own life span. The lute melodies called 'Ryūsen' and 'Takuboku' should not be lost to the world. Only this blind man knows them."

So thinking, Hiromasa went at night to Ausaka Barrier, but Semimaru did not play those melodies. For three years afterward Hiromasa went every night to the vicinity of the blind man's hut at Ausaka. In secret he stood and listened, always thinking, "Now surely he'll play them!" But Semimaru did not play the melodies. On the final night of the three years—the night of the full moon in the eighth month—when the moon had just risen and breezes were gently blowing, Hiromasa thought, "Oh, it is a delightful night! Surely tonight the blind man of Ausaka will play 'Ryūsen' and 'Takuboku.' "

So he went to Ausaka Barrier and stood listening. The blind man was plucking his lute; it was a very moving sight. As Hiromasa listened, overcome with delight, the blind man, believing himself to be alone, recited:

Ausaka no	In the violence
Seki no arashi no	Of the storms
Hageshiki ni	At Ausaka Barrier
Shiite zo itaru	I plan, somehow, in blindness
Yo o sugosu tote	To pass my days.

Deeply moved, Hiromasa listened to Semimaru's lute and wept.

The blind man spoke to himself, "Ah, what a pleasant night! If only some other connoisseur were with me. If only someone of understanding were to come here tonight—we could talk."

As he spoke, Hiromasa listened, then made a noise.

"Hiromasa from the capital has come," he said.

"Who said that?" the blind man asked, and Hiromasa answered, identifying himself.

167

"Since I love this art very much I have been coming to your hut for three years, and, to my joy, tonight I have met you."

When he heard this the blind man was delighted. Then Hiromasa, also deeply pleased, went inside the hut. They spoke together and told each other stories. When Hiromasa said, "Let me hear you play 'Ryūsen' and 'Takuboku,' " the blind man said, "The late prince played them this way,"[16] and he revealed the traditions of those performances to Hiromasa.

Since Hiromasa did not have a lute with him, he learned the melodies simply by spoken instruction; and rejoicing very greatly, at dawn he returned home.

Reflecting on this, we realize that all the arts should be appreciated in just this way, but such has not been the case lately. Through all ages there are few real masters in any art. Truly this is a sad state of affairs.

Although Semimaru was a lowly person, in years past he heard the prince play the lute and thereby became very skilled at it. Because he became blind he was living at Ausaka. And since his time it has been said that he was the first of the blind lute players.

J. The Tale of How Prince Kuṇāla's Eyes Were Plucked Out and Then Regained through Reliance on the Power of the Law[17]

Long ago in India there was a king called Aśoka. He had one son, the Prince Kuṇāla. The prince's appearance was attractive and his character impeccable. In all things he surpassed other people. Therefore, his father's love for him knew no bounds. This prince was the son of the king's former wife. The present queen was his stepmother. Seeing the prince, the queen began to feel passionately attracted to him. She had no

---

[16]I.e., his master, Prince Atsuzane.
[17]*Konjaku monogatari*, Book 4, tale 4, NKBT, XXII, 273–76.

thoughts but of him. This queen's name was Tisyaraksita.

The queen suffered from her obsession for him, and finally, seizing an opportunity when no others were about, she secretly approached the prince. She grasped hold of the prince and suddenly revealed her feelings toward him. The prince, who did not share her feelings, was alarmed and ran from her.

The queen then became very bitter toward him and found a quiet opportunity to speak to the king. "The prince became infatuated with me. Now that you, oh king, have become aware of this, you should punish the prince."

Hearing this the king thought, "Surely the queen slanders him." Secretly he called the prince to him and said, "If you two are together in the same palace, inevitably evil will come of it. I shall give you a province to rule. You should go live there and follow my orders. If you receive any royal directives supposedly from me, do not follow them unless they bear the imprint of my teeth."

The king sent him off to the distant province of Taxila.

While the prince was living there, his stepmother the queen thought more of what had happened and became extremely uneasy. She contrived a scheme and gave the king a great deal of wine to drink. She got him very drunk, and as he was lying in a stupor, she secretly took an impression of his teeth. Afterward she sent a messenger with a forged royal decree to Taxila where the prince was. It read, "Immediately gouge out the prince's eyes and expel the prince outside the borders of the province."

When the messenger reached the province he delivered the decree. When the prince read the decree he said, "Gouge out my eyes and drive me out." Since the impression of the king's teeth in fact was there, there could be no doubt of the decree's validity. Though deeply depressed and grieving, he said, "I must not disobey my father's command." He immediately summoned an outcast who, weeping, gouged out his eyes. At that time all those about the prince's court were grieving desperately.

After that the prince left the court and wandered about on the roads. Only his wife accompanied him and guided him as they wandered about everywhere. There were no others accompanying them. The king knew nothing at all of this. Thus it happened that the prince chanced to wander near the king's palace. Not knowing where he was, he walked up close to the elephant pen. There people saw him, a blind man, led by a woman. Because he had been wandering about this way his clothing was tattered and his physical appearance greatly worsened, so none of the people of the palace recognized him as the prince, and they had him stay in the elephant pen.

As evening came he played his lute. The king in his high tower faintly heard the sound of the lute and thought it resembled the music of his son, Prince Kuṇāla. He sent a messenger to ask, "Who is playing the lute like that?" When the messenger arrived at the elephant pen he found there was a blind man playing the lute in the company of his wife. He asked, "Who are you?" and the prince replied, "I am Prince Kuṇāla, the child of King Aśoka. While I was in Taxila, according to my father's command, they gouged out my eyes and drove me outside the borders of the country, and so I have been wandering about this way."

Amazed, the messenger hurried back and reported this. The king, hearing this, was shocked and devastated. He summoned the blind man and asked him about this, and the blind man repeated what he had said before. The king realized that this must have been the queen's doing. Immediately he was going to punish the queen, but the prince restrained him and had him withhold the order of punishment.

The king wept and lamented. At a temple by the Bodhi tree there lived a sage. His name was the great sage Ghosha. That sage was versed in the three wisdoms and the six supernatural powers,[18] and in his ability to help others he was like a Buddha. The king summoned this sage and spoke to him, "I beg of you, holy man, through your compassion, restore the eyes of my son, Prince Kuṇāla, to their former state." When he spoke these words, weeping, the sage said, "I shall recite the great teachings. Have everyone in the land come listen to me. Each person should bring a bowl. When the people hear the teachings we will catch in those bowls the noble tears they will shed. If we wash his eyes using those tears, his eyes will become as before." When he said this, the king gave the order and gathered all the people of the land. From near and far they gathered like clouds.

At that time the sage expounded the law of the twelve-linked chain of dependent origination, and the assembled people, hearing the law, all wept. They caught their tears in the bowls and poured them into a golden vessel. And the sage spoke vowing, "All the laws I have expounded are the truths of Buddha. If they are not true, if my teachings are false, this will be ineffective. If they are true, I beg that when I wash this blind man's eyes using the congregation's tears, he will gain sight and will see just as before." After he had said this he washed the prince's eyes using the tears. His eyes reappeared and regained their brightness as before. At that time the king bowed and paid homage to the sage in boundless joy.

Afterward he summoned the ministers and officials. He demoted some. Others he found blameless and pardoned. Some he sent to foreign lands. Some he had executed. The place where the prince's eyes were gouged out was outside Taxila,

[18] The powers of an arhat or Buddha: (1) knowledge of previous existences; (2) universal sight; (3) insight into the end of the cycle of transmigration; (4) absolute freedom, the power to appear at any place; (5) the celestial ear, the ability to hear all; (6) intuitive knowledge of the minds of others. The first three are called the three wisdoms.

on the north of a mountain to the southeast. On that spot he built a stupa over one hundred feet high. Afterward, in that land, when men were blind they would pray at this stupa. And it is said that sight was restored to all of them.

K. *Mumyōshō*, 1211

The tutelary spirit of Ausaka Pass was Semimaru of old. When one passes the spot now, it calls to mind how at the time of Emperor Fukakusa,[19] Yoshimine no Munesada went back and forth to that place to learn to play *wagon*.[20]

L. *Tōkan kikō*, 1242

Long ago Semimaru, a man who had renounced the world, built himself a straw hut near this (Ausaka) pass. He regularly calmed his feelings by playing the biwa and expressed his thoughts by reciting poetry. He lived there suffering from the roughness of the storm winds. It is said that because Semimaru was the fourth son of Emperor Daigo, the area near this barrier is called Shinomiya-kawara.[21]

M. *Heike Monogatari*, 1371 KAKUICHI TEXT

They came to Shinomiya-kawara. This is the place where, long ago, Semimaru, the fourth son of Emperor Daigo, calmed his feelings in the storms at the barrier by playing his lute, and where the man called Hakuga no Sammi came every night for three years. On windy days and windless days, on rainy nights and nights of no rain, he came on foot and stood and

---

[19]R. 833–50.   [20]*Mumyōshō, NKBT, LXV*, 53.
[21]*Tōkan kikō*, Nihon koten zensho, LXIV, 161.

listened. Seeing the floor of that straw hut where the three melodies were passed on, he thought of those bygone times and was deeply moved.[22]

N_1 and N_2. *Gempeiseisuiki,* APPROXIMATELY 1371

N_1 In our country Semimaru of Ausaka—the fourth son of Emperor Daigo—who was very skilled at playing biwa, was taught this melody by a heavenly being. He guarded and preserved it and passed it on to no one; but when Hakuga no Sammi came to his hut at the barrier night after night for three years, he taught it to him. Sammi also guarded it closely and did not lightly pass it on to others.[23]

N_2 When they passed Shinomiya-kawara it made them think of how Prince Semimaru, the fourth son of Emperor Daigo, had played the secret melodies for the lute when he was abandoned in a straw hut, and of how Hakuga no Sammi came every night for three years and the melodies were passed on to him.

Azumaji ya	Oh, the eastern road!
Sode kurabe	Sleeves brushing,
Yuku mo kaeru mo	Those who come and go
Wakarete ya	Are parting
Shiru mo shiranu mo	For friends and strangers,
Ausaka no	Meeting Slope

[22]*Heike monogatari,* NKBT, XXXIII, 258. For a complete translation of *Heike monogatari,* see "Heike monogatari," Arthur L. Sadler, trans., in *Transactions of the Asia Society of Japan,* XLVI, 2 (1918), 1–278; XLIX, 1 (1921), 1–354. The passage cited here is XLIX, 187. The comparable passage of earlier textual varients may be found in *Hiramatsuke kyūzōbon Heike monogatari,* p. 799, and *Yashirobon Heike monogatari,* p. 686.

[23]*Gempei seisuiki,* Kokubon sōsho, VIII, 174.

kyō wa seki o zo	Today we have passed the
torarekeru [24]	barrier.

O. *Tōzai zuihitsu,* APPROXIMATELY MID-FIFTEENTH
CENTURY

Semimaru of Ausaka was a servant of Prince Atsuzane (Shikibukyō). Having gone blind, he played the biwa, and he built himself a hut in which he lived in the area of Ausaka.

Hakuga no Sammi [25] (grandson of Emperor Daigo, son of Prince Katsuakira; Genji clan) was taught the melodies "Ryūsen" and "Takuboku" by him. [26] Prince Atsuzane was a skilled musician. Semimaru took up playing the lute after hearing the prince play. The practice of blind men playing biwa began with him. [27]

P. *Sekkyō* LICENSE DOCUMENT [28]

First, Semimaru was blind in both eyes. Therefore, he was not suitable to be a prince and became an exile. And so he was abandoned at Mount Ausaka. His attendants were in tears, but since it was an imperial order both went home. Thereafter Semimaru's elder sister, feeling deep longing and great sadness, thought she wanted to find where Semimaru was. She

[24]*Ibid.,* p. 444.

[25]Hakuga of the Third Rank, i.e., Minamoto no Hiromasa. The parenthetical information is included in small characters in Kanera's text.

[26]The Yūhōdō text has *kore ni ryūsen takuboku no shirabe o tsutaetari.* This seems to be an error for *kore yori,* as the context makes it clear that the author views Semimaru as the teacher. In citing *Tōzai zuihitsu,* Tashiro quotes the text as *kore yori* without comment.

[27]*Tōzai zuihitsu* in Yūhōdō bunko, Series 2, VII *Ujishui monogatari,* 493–94.

[28]This document appears in Muroki, *Katarimono,* p. 214.

set out for Mount Ausaka and went searching about by night. Thereupon she heard the music of koto and biwa, and thinking that it was no ordinary person, but must be Semimaru, she approached the door of the straw hut. From inside he heard footsteps and opened the door. When the older sister saw Semimaru she took his hands in hers, and together they could only weep.

Seeing his pitiful, weakened body, the elder sister was driven to distraction. When she was in a state of madness her hair stood on end. Therefore she was called Sakagami. The brother and sister together after their deaths were enshrined in the same shrine. The parishioners of those tutelary spirits up until the present day wear their forelocks trained upward— an odd fact.

Ko no Norinaga from Shirakawa finally went up to the capital and from time to time came round to see him. Those who stayed with him were Mototsune, Morosuke, and the beauty from Furuya, and this was in the year Engi 22 (922), the second month.

They say that in that same year he finally got his sight back, but since it was after a period of living in poverty, he was not called back to the capital after that. His pitiable dwelling at Mount Ausaka was a lonely place, like a straw hut or very tiny shack. As time went by, it collapsed to the ground.

The lady from Furuya plaited wild vines and supported Mototsune and Morosuke.[29] There in the mountains with no means of livelihood, they gathered fruit and the roots of grasses and passed their days. In the ninth month of Tengyō 9 (946) Semimaru died. It is said he was thirty-one years old.

Thereafter Mototsune lived in a village in Shiga. The beauty from Furuya became a prostitute, and the sekkyō performers of today are the descendants of Morosuke.

[29] Possibly by weaving baskets; the phrase is obscure.

Sometimes Semimaru has been considered a manifestation of the original Bodhisattva Myōon. The Bodhisattva Myo-on divides himself into thirty-four, and to provide salvation for all mankind shows himself in many varied forms. Therefore at times he shows himself as blind, and coming in close contact with the blind men of this world, he aids them. At times, at the top or the bottom of the slope at Ausaka, he begs from travelers, praying for their benefit. Such is an expedient means taken by a Buddha or a Bodhisattva. Since Semimaru was the Engi prince, though he lived in a hut of straw, his heart was admirable. He always calmed himself with koto or biwa. In his absolute blindness he played various melodies on the instruments, showing the adornment of the celestial music of the Pure Land. Though as expedient means he was temporarily manifest as a beggar, why should his inner soul be thought in any way inferior?

Zeami's *Semimaru*

Cast of Characters

TSURE:	Prince Semimaru
WAKI:	Kiyotsura, an imperial envoy
WAKIZURE:	Two palanquin bearers
KYŌGEN:	Hakuga no Sammi
SHITE:	Princess Sakagami, Semimaru's sister
PLACE:	Mount Ausaka in Omi Province
TIME:	The reign of Emperor Daigo; the eighth month

The stage assistant places a representation of a hut at the waki position. Semimaru enters, wearing the Semimaru mask. He is flanked by two palanquin bearers who hold a canopy over him. Kiyotsura follows them.

	KIYOTSURA	The world is so unsure, unknowable;[1]
	and	The world is so unsure, unknowable,
	ATTENDANTS:	Who knows—our griefs may hold our greatest
shidai		hopes.
	KIYOTSURA:	This nobleman is the Prince Semimaru
sashi		Fourth child of the Emperor Daigo.
	KIYOTSURA	Truly in this uncertain world
	and	All that befalls us comes our way
	ATTENDANTS:	As recompense for what we've done before.
		In his previous existence
		He observed intently the laws of Buddha
		And in this life was born a prince,

[1] The text translated is that included in Sanari, *Yōkyoku taikan*, III, 1671–88.

177

> Yet why was it—ever since he lay,
> An infant wrapped in swaddling clothes
> His eyes have both been blind: For him
> The sun and moon in heaven have no light;
> In the black of night his lamp is dark;
> The rain before the dawn never ends.

KIYOTSURA:
> His nights and days have been spent this way,
> But now what plan has the emperor conceived?

KIYOTSURA
and
ATTENDANTS:
> He ordered us to escort the prince in secret,
> To abandon him on Mount Ausaka
> And to shave his head in priestly tonsure.
> The emperor's words, once spoken
> Are final—what immense pity I feel!
> Yet, such being the command, I am powerless;

KIYOTSURA
and
ATTENDANTS:
> Like lame-wheeled carriages
> We creep forth reluctantly
> On the journey from the capital;

sageuta
> How hard it is to say farewell

ageuta
> As dawn clouds streak the east!
> Today he first departs the capital
> When again to return? His chances are as
>   fragile
> As unraveled threads too thin to intertwine.
> Friendless, his destination is unknown.
> Even without an affliction
> Good fortune is elusive in this world,
> Like the floating log the turtle gropes for
> Once a century: The path is in darkness
> And he, a blind turtle, must follow it.[2]

---

[2] In certain Buddhist texts the rarity of meeting a Buddha is compared to the difficulty of a blind sea turtle's chances of bumping into a log to float on. The turtle emerges to the surface only once a century

Zeami's *Semimaru*

>Now as the clouds of delusion rise
>We have reached Mount Ausaka
>We have reached Mount Ausaka.

(*Semimaru sits on a stool before the chorus. Kiyotsura kneels at the* shite *pillar. The bearers exit through the slit door.*)

mondo SEMIMARU: Kiyotsura!

KIYOTSURA: I am before you.

(*From his kneeling position, he bows deeply.*)

SEMIMARU: Are you to leave me on this mountain?

KIYOTSURA: Yes, your highness. So the emperor has commanded, and I have brought you this far. But I wonder just where I should leave you.

>Since the days of the ancient sage kings
>Our emperors have ruled the country wisely,
>Looking after its people with compassion—
>But what can his majesty have had in mind?
>Nothing could have caught me so unprepared.

SEMIMARU: What a foolish thing to say, Kiyotsura. I was born blind because I was lax in my religious duties in a former life.

>That is why the emperor, my father,
>Ordered you to leave me in the wilderness,
>Heartless this would seem, but it's his plan
>To purge in this world my burden from the
>   past,
>And spare me suffering in the world to come.
>This is a father's true kindness.
>You should not bewail his decree.

KIYOTSURA: >Now I shall shave your head.
>His majesty has so commanded.

SEMIMARU: >What does this act signify?

---

and tries to clutch the log, but it eludes his grasp; this was a metaphor for the difficulty of obtaining good fortune.

KIYOTSURA: It means you have become a priest,
               A most joyous event.

(*Semimaru rises. The stage assistant removes his nobleman's outer robe and places a priest's hat on his head. The section which follows is considered a* monogi—on-stage recostuming.)

SEMIMARU: Surely Seishi's poem described such a scene:
               "I have cut my fragrant scented hair
               My head is pillowed half on sandalwood."[3]

KIYOTSURA: Such splendid clothes will summon thieves, I fear.
               Allow me to take your robe and give you instead
               This cloak of straw they call a *mino*

(*Semimaru mimes receiving the* mino.)

SEMIMARU: Is this the mino mentioned in the lines
               "I went to Tamino Island when it rained"?[4]

KIYOTSURA: And I give you this *kasa* rainhat
               To protect you also from the rain and dew.

(*He takes a* kasa *from the stage assistant and hands it to Semimaru.*)

SEMIMARU: Then this must be the kasa of the poem
               "Samurai—take a kasa for your lord."[5]

(*Semimaru puts down the kasa.*)

KIYOTSURA: And this staff will guide you on your way.
               Please take it in your hands.

(*He takes a staff from the stage assistant and hands it to Semimaru.*)

[3] The poem referred to is by Li Ho and is actually a description of Hsi-shih (Seishi) rather than a poem by her. The meaning of the original verses was that Seishi's fragrant locks rivaled the perfume of cloves or sandalwood; however, the dramatist here misunderstood the Chinese and interpreted it as meaning she had cut her locks and now would have to rest her head on a hard pillow of sandalwood.

[4] From a poem by Ki no Tsurayuki, no. 918 in the *Kokinshū*.

[5] From an anonymous poem, no. 1091 in the *Kokinshū*.

SEMIMARU: Is this the staff about which Henjō wrote:
             "Since my staff was fashioned by the gods
             I can cross the mountain of a thousand
                years"?[6]

(*Kiyotsura kneels at the shite pillar.*)

KIYOTSURA: His staff brought a thousand prosperous
                years.[7]

SEMIMARU: But here the place is Mount Ausaka,

KIYOTSURA: A straw-thatched hut by the barrier.

SEMIMARU: Bamboo pillars and staff, my sole support.

KIYOTSURA: By your father, the emperor,

SEMIMARU: Abandoned.

CHORUS: I met my unsure fate at Mount Ausaka.
             You who know me, you who know me not[8]
             Behold—this is how a prince, Daigo's son,
             Has reached the last extremity of grief.

(*He lowers his head to give a sad expression to his mask.*)

             Travelers and men on horses
             Riding to and from the capital,
             Many people, dressed for their journeys,
             Will drench their sleeves in sudden showers;
             How hard it is to abandon him,
             To leave him all alone;
             How hard it is to abandon him,
             To tear ourselves away.

(*Kiyotsura bows to Semimaru.*)

             But even farewells must have an end;
             By the light of the daybreak moon
             Stifling tears that have no end, they depart.

[6] From a poem by the priest Henjō, no. 348 in the *Kokinshū*.

[7] There is a pivot word embedded here: the *saka* used in meaning *chitose no saka*, the slope of a thousand years; and *saka yuku tsue*, the staff that brings steady prosperity.

[8] An allusion to poem A.

(Weeping, Kiyotsura goes to the bridgeway.)
> Semimaru, the prince, left behind alone,
> Takes in his arms his lute, his one possession,
> Clutches his staff and falls down weeping.

(Semimaru picks up the staff and kasa, comes forward, and turns toward the departing Kiyotsura. Kiyotsura stops at the second pine and looks back at him, then exits. Semimaru retreats, kneels, drops his kasa and staff, and weeps. Hakuga no Sammi enters and stands at the naming place.)

HAKUGA: I am Hakuga no Sammi. I have learned that Prince Semimaru has been abandoned on Mount Ausaka, and it pains me so much to think of him at the mercy of the rain and dew that I have decided to build a straw hut where he may live. *(He opens the door of the hut, then goes to Semimaru at the shite pillar.)* The hut is ready at last, I shall inform him of this. *(He bows to Semimaru.)* Pardon me, sir; Hakuga is before you. If you stay here in this way, you will be soaked by the rain. I have built you a straw hut and I hope you will live in it. Please, come with me. *(He takes Semimaru's hand and leads him inside the hut, then steps back and bows.)* If ever you need anything, you have only to summon me, Hakuga no Sammi. I shall always be ready to serve you. I take my leave of you for now.

(He closes the door of the hut, then exits. Sakagami enters wearing the young woman mask called zō. Her robe is folded back from her right shoulder indicating that she is deranged. She stops at the first pine. The orchestra plays the entrance music, issei.)

SAKAGAMI:
sashi
> I am the third child of the Emperor Daigo,
> The one called Sakagami, Upturned Hair.
> Though born a princess, some deed of evil
> From my unknown past in former lives
> Causes my mind at times to act deranged.
> And in my madness I wander distant ways.

My blueblack hair grows skyward;
Though I stroke it, it will not lie flat.
(*She smooths down her hair.*)
Those children over there—what are they
laughing at?
(*She looks to the right as if watching passers-by.*)
What? You find it funny that my hair stands
on end? Yes,
I suppose hair that grows upside down is
funny.
My hair is disordered, but much less than
you—
Imagine commoners laughing at me!
How extraordinary it is that so much before our eyes is
upside down. Flower seeds buried in the ground rise up to
grace the branches of a thousand trees. The moon hangs
high in the heavens, but its light sinks to the bottom of
countless waters.
(*She looks up and down.*)
I wonder which of all these should be said to go in the
proper direction and which is upside down?
I am a princess, yet I have fallen,
And mingle with the mass of common men;
(*She proceeds to the stage while chanting.*)
My hair, rising upward from my body,
Turns white with the touch of stars and frost:
The natural order or upside down?
How amazing that both should be within me!
(*She enters the stage. The orchestra begins kakeri, music, which
marks a madwoman passage.*)
The wind combs even the willows' hair
But neither can the wind untangle
Nor my hand separate this hair.
(*She takes hold of her hair and looks at it.*)

183

Shall I rip it from my head? Throw it away?
I lift my sleeved hands—what is this?
The hair-tearing dance?[9] How demeaning!
(She begins to dance in a deranged manner.)

CHORUS: After I set forth from the flowery capital, from
ji ageuta   the flowery capital
            Was that the sound of calling birds at Kamo
            River?[10]
            Not knowing where I went, crossing Shira-
            kawa
            I reached Awataguchi, wondering
            "Whom shall I meet now at Matsuzaka?"[11]
            I thought I had yet to pass the barrier
            But soon Mount Otowa fell behind me.
            How sad it was to leave the capital!
            Pine crickets, bell crickets, grasshoppers,
            How they cried in the dusk at Yamashina!
            I begged the villagers, "Don't scold me, too!"
            I may be mad, but you should know
            My heart is a pure rushing stream:
SAKAGAMI: "When in the clear water
ageha   At Ausaka Barrier
            It sees its reflection
CHORUS: The tribute horse from Mochizuki
            Will surely shy away."[12]

[9] The *batō* dance is described in *The Pillow Book of Sei Shōnagon* (trans. by Ivan Morris): "In the Dance of the Pulled Head the dancer's hair is in disorder and he has a fierce look in his eyes; but the music is delightful."

[10] The name of the river, *kamo*, meant a species of duck.

[11] The name Matsuzaka contains the familiar pivot word *matsu*, to wait.

[12] A poem by Ki no Tsurayuki, no. 118 in the *Shūishū*. The horse referred to was presented as tribute to the moon in a special ceremony held at the height of autumn on the night of the full moon.

> Have my wanderings brought me to the same
>   place?
> In the running stream I see my reflection.
> Though my own face, it horrifies me:
> Hair like tangled briers crowns my head
> Eyebrows blackly twist—yes, that is really
> Sakagami's reflection in the water.
> Water they say, is a mirror,
> But twilight ripples distort my face.

(Sakagami sits at the stage assistant's position, indicating she has arrived at Mount Ausaka. Semimaru, inside the hut, opens his fan and holds it in his left hand as if playing his lute.)

SEMIMARU: The first string and the second wildly
ure sashi   sound—[13]
> The autumn wind brushes the pines and falls
> With broken notes; the third string and the
>   fourth—
> The fourth is myself, Semimaru,
> And four are the strings of the lute I play
> As sudden strings of rain drive down on me—
> How dreadful is this night!
> "Our lives,
> This way or that,
> Pass just the same.
> Whether in a palace or a hovel
> We cannot live forever."[14]

(While Semimaru is speaking Sakagami comes before the shite pillar. Semimaru inclines his head toward her as she speaks.)

The headnote in *Shūishū* attributes this practice to the reign of the Emperor Daigo.

[13] An allusion to the poem by Po Chü-i, no. 463 in the *Wakan roeishū*.

[14] Poem B.

185

SAKAGAMI: How strange—I hear music from this straw-thatched hut,
The sounds of a biwa, elegantly plucked—
To think a hovel holds such melodies!
But why should the notes evoke this sharp nostalgia?
With steps silent, as the rain beating on the thatch
I stealthily approach, stop and listen.

(*She silently comes to stage center. Semimaru folds his fan.*)

SEMIMARU: Who is there? Who's making that noise outside my hut?
Hakuga no Sammi, lately you've been coming
From time to time to visit me—is that you?

SAKAGAMI: As I approach and listen carefully—that's the voice of my brother the prince!
It's Sakagami! I'm here!
Semimaru, is that you inside?

SEMIMARU: Can it be my sister, the princess?
Amazed, he opens the door of his hut.

(*Taking his staff he rises and opens the door.*)

SAKAGAMI: Oh—how wretched you look!

(*She comes up to Semimaru as he emerges from the hut.*)

SEMIMARU: They take each other hand in hand.

(*They place their hands on each other's shoulders and kneel.*)

SAKAGAMI: My royal brother, is that indeed you?

SEMIMARU: My royal sister, is that indeed you?

CHORUS: They speak each other's names as in one voice.
Birds are also crying, here at Ausaka,
Barrier of meeting—but no barrier
Holds back the tears that soak each other's sleeves.

(*Both weep. During the following passage Sakagami returns to the middle of the stage and kneels.*)

CHORUS: *kuri*	They say that sandalwood reveals its fragrance From the first two leaves[15]—but how much closer still Are we who sheltered beneath a single tree![16] The wind rising in the orange blossoms[17] Awakens memories we shall preserve We who flowered once on linking branches!
SAKAGAMI: *sashi*	The love between brothers is told abroad: Jōzō and Jōgen, Sōri and Sokuri;[18] And nearer at hand, in Japan The children of Emperor Ōjin,
CHORUS:	The princes Naniwa and Uji,[19] Who yielded the throne, each to the other: All these were brothers and sisters Bound in love, like us, like linking branches.

[15] An expression used proverbially to indicate that genius can be recognized even in early youth. Here used to mean that a noble person reveals his character spontaneously.

[16] Taking shelter beneath the same tree was an illustration of the concept that even causal contact in a previous existence might bring a karmic connection between people in their next incarnation. Because of some connection in a previous life Semimaru and Sakagami were born in this life as brother and sister.

[17] The fragrance of orange (*tachibana*) blossoms, conventionally, summoned up remembrance of people one once knew; here the memories are those shared by brother and sister.

[18] Jōzō and Jōgen were siblings mentioned in the *Lotus Sutra*. Sōri and Sokuri were the son and daughter of a Brahman king of southern India. They were abandoned by their stepmother. After their death, their father found and recognized their skeletons on the island where they had been abandoned. The story is mentioned in the *Taiheiki* and the *Gempei seisuiki*.

[19] Sons of the Emperor Ōjin. The younger, Prince Uji, had been designated by Ōjin as his heir, but declined, saying the office belonged by rights to his elder brother. Prince Uji died first, and the empire went to Prince Naniwa, known posthumously as Emperor Nintoku.

187

SAKAGAMI:	But did I imagine my brother
	Would ever live in such a hovel?
CHORUS:	Had no music come from that straw-thatched hut
	How should I have known! But I was drawn
	By the music of those four strings.
SAKAGAMI:	Drawn like the water offered to the gods
CHORUS:	From deep wells of love and far-reaching ties.
iguse	The world may have reached its final phase [20]
	But the sun and moon have not dropped to the ground.
	But how can it be, then, that you and I
	Should cast away our royalty and live like this,
	Unable even to mingle with common men?
	A madwoman, I have come wandering now
	Far from the capital girdled by clouds,
	To these rustic scenes, a wretched beggar,
	By the roads and forests, my only hope
	The charity of rustics and travelers.
	To think it was only yesterday you lived
	In jeweled pavilions and golden halls;
	You walked on polished floors and wore bright robes.
	In less time than it takes to wave your sleeves,
	Today a hovel is your sleeping place.
	Bamboo posts and bamboo fence, crudely fashioned
	Eaves and door: straw your window, straw the roof,

[20] A familiar concept. Believers in medieval Pure Land Buddhism were convinced that the world had reached the period of the end of the Buddhist law (*mappō*). According to one method of calculation, this period began about A.D. 1000, and was to continue for another thousand years.

	And over your bed, the quilts are mats of straw:
	Pretend they are your silken sheets of old.
ageha SEMIMARU:	My only visitors—how rarely they come—
CHORUS:	Are monkeys on the peak, swinging in the trees;
	Their doleful cries soak my sleeve with tears.
	I tune my lute to the sound of the showers,
	I play for solace, but tears obscure the sounds.
	Even rain on the straw roof makes no noise.
	Through breaks in the eaves moonlight seeps in.
	But in my blindness, the moon and I are strangers.
	In this hut I cannot even hear the rain—
	How painful to contemplate life in this hut!
(*Both weep.*)	
SAKAGAMI:	Now I must go; however long I stayed
rongi	The pain of parting never would diminish.
	Farewell, Semimaru.
(*Both rise.*)	
SEMIMARU:	If sheltering under a single tree
	Were our only tie, parting would still be sad;
	How much sadder to let my sister go!
	Imagine what it means to be alone!
(*Sakagami moves toward the shite pillar.*)	
SAKAGAMI:	Truly I pity you; even the pain
	Of wandering may provide distraction,
	But remaining here—how lonely it will be!
	Even as I speak the evening clouds have risen,
	I rise and hesitate; I stand in tears.
(*She weeps.*)	
SEMIMARU:	The evening crows call on the barrier road,
	Their hearts unsettled

TEXTS

SAKAGAMI: As my raven hair,
              My longing unabated, I must go.
SEMIMARU: Barrier of Meeting, don't let her leave!
SAKAGAMI: As I pass by the grove of cedars . . .
(She goes to the first pine.)
SEMIMARU: Her voice grows distant . . .
SAKAGAMI: By the eaves of the straw hut . . .
SEMIMARU: I stand hesitant.
CHORUS: "Farewell," she calls to him, and he responds,
              "Please visit me as often as you can."
(Sakagami goes to the third pine and turns back to look at Semimaru.)
              Her voice grows faint, but still he listens,
(Sakagami starts to exit. Semimaru takes a few steps forward, stops and listens. His blind eyes gaze in her direction.)
              She turns a final time to look at him.
              Weeping, weeping, they have parted,
              Weeping, weeping, they have parted.
(Sakagami exits, weeping. Semimaru also weeps.)

Zeami's *Ausaka Madman*

Cast of Characters

SHITE:	The blind man of Ausaka
WAKI:	A traveler, returning from the east
KOKATA:	The blind man's child companion
KYŌGEN:	A local innkeeper
PLACE:	Mount Ausaka in Omi Province
TIME:	Unspecified

ki-shidai

TRAVELER: Moon of the Eastern Road brings with it autumn [1]
Moon of the Eastern Road brings with it autumn
To the moonlit capital I shall return.

nanori I am a man from a western province. I had one child, but
he was stolen from me by slave traders and vanished late in
the year. Since I heard that they had gone toward the east, I
followed after them, going here and there, and now in no
time three years have gone by. I think I shall go back up to
the capital.

sashi   If the Aneha pine in Mutsu
Were a person, waiting,
I'd say "Come along
As a souvenir
To the capital." [2]

[1] The text translated is that included in Tanaka, "Osaka monogurui," in *Yōkyoku kyōgen*, pp. 253–58.
[2] This poem is a slight variation on one in section 14 of *Ise Monogatari*, NKBT, IX, 120. *cf. KKS 1090.*

191

Even these words fill me with longing for my child.
How many years have passed pillowed on grass?
I would return for autumn in the capital,
I thought, but traveled long, far off
Toward unknown journey's end,
From Shirakawa, passing the barrier,

sageuta I set off with the mist.
Spring, too, in the capital
Has now come round three years

ageuta Again I cross autumn grasses at Musashino[3]
Again I cross autumn grasses at Musashino
With the moon never ending, lingering at dawn
Enveloped in morning mist
Far distant peak, so called in poetry
Fuji, snow about its base
And in its traces, pines of Miho.
I have passed Kiyomi barrier, passed over Urayama.
Now quickly I have reached the Omi road
Quickly I have reached the Omi road.

tsuki-zerifu In no time I have arrived at Matsumoto in the province of Omi. The day is already drawing to a close, so tonight I will stop here at this inn. And I think tomorrow I will go on up to the capital.
Is anybody here?

mondo INNKEEPER: What do you want?

TRAVELER: I'm a traveler. Please give me a place to stay.

INNKEEPER: I understand. Please come this way. By the way, traveler, I want to tell you something. On the road you'll be

[3] In the preceding lines the traveler was remembering his journey eastward away from the capital. He here begins narrating his return.

taking up to the capital, at Ausaka Barrier, there is a blind man. There's a little boy with him, and they carry a bamboo rattle and a drum. They do all sorts of weird, crazy things. I don't know anything else about him, not even where he's from. You ought to go along with me and get an eyeful of his madness.

TRAVELER: That's fascinating. Let's go together.

issei	**BLIND MAN** **AND CHILD:**	When shall we be reunited in this world At Ausaka of the tangled vines? Unknowing are the hearts of those who pass
	CHILD:	On this side of the barrier
ninoku		The years move on and yet
	BOTH:	They do not stay with us— The months and days.
	BLIND MAN:	To offer a comparison, with all humility,
sashi		In India Prince Kuranu[4]
	BOTH:	And in our court, Semimaru Though both of these were princes The turnings of the wheel of Karma came. The clouds of the blind turtle did not clear. Moonlight on the snow at night, Reflected bright as morning sun, All this unknown, painful their fates The dark road of the heart, how wretched. As mortals like ourselves, ever deluded, They happened to be born in blindness People who knew no shapes or colors Unable even to flee from sadness

[4] This is Prince Kuṇāla, son of King Aśoka. Through metathesis the name here has been corrupted to Kuranu. The most common characters used in Japanese for his name are read Kunara, but Mochizuki's *Bukkyō Daijiten* lists Kuranu, with the characters used here, among the variants.

193

<table>
<tr><td>*sageuta*</td><td>My rain of tears, unending also
Out of darkness
Into a path of darkness
I have entered.
Shine on me from afar
Moon on the mountain ridge.[5]
Where might that moon linger?
Where might that moon linger?</td></tr>
<tr><td>*ageuta*</td><td>The place is the Ausaka Barrier
When in the clear water
At Ausaka Barrier
It sees its reflection
The tribute horse from Mochizuki
Will surely shy away
We've grown accustomed to the sound of horses' hooves
Travelers on foot and those on horseback
Pass by us seeking other places' feelings.
At dusk they draw near, at dawn depart.
Now making his way, someone has arrived
Now making his way, someone has arrived
At our straw hut in mountain shadows.</td></tr>
</table>

mondo TRAVELER: Say there, blind man, how long have you been living here?

BLIND MAN: I have lived here since long ago. This lad is from another province. He was carried off by slave traders but got away and ended up here. And since you're asking about us, let me say that we get by in life by begging together.

TRAVELER: That's odd. Though you say you've lived here since long ago, the people hereabouts say that they've never seen you here before.

BLIND MAN: I hesitate to have to say this, but the people who

[5] This poem is by Izumi Shikibu and appears in the *Shūishū*, no. 1342.

told you that are fools. Even among people who live in other places, there certainly are some who know me. And surely there are some who associate with me yet do not know me.

Here is not so deep in endless mountains that I should be of no account to everyone. It has been written, "To be unknown by men, remain in hiding." Since I appear like your known self, you do not realize I am unknown. For known and unknown this is Meeting Slope Mountain. Here, wandered astray, a hidden spring, how should I, of no account, be known by men?

TRAVELER: A fascinating answer!

> Since you are blind, your sense of poetry
> Can't be expected to show on your face.

Still, since this is the famous place where people come and go, your hearing them must be a blessing for you. From time to time it surely must be so.

BLIND MAN: Just as you've said, this slope of meeting is true to its name. When I hear the storm winds I understand the pathos of flying flowers and falling leaves.

TRAVELER: The flowing spring of running mountain water
              Clears the heart's hearing
BLIND MAN: The sounds of people at the barrier
TRAVELER: Going and returning, cries of birds of parting.[6]
BLIND MAN: Do you hear the birds' calls now?
ageuta   Truly they call their name, Yūtsukedori.[7]
              Although I hear their cries
              Were I a bird, in my blindness

[6] This line incorporates the third line—*yuku mo kaeru mo*—of Semimaru's most famous poem, A.

[7] *Yūtsukedori*, "cotton-attached bird" is another name for the common chicken. The name derives from the fact that chickens were kept at the four border barriers about the capital area and were used in purification ceremonies in which cotton cloths were attached to the birds. Another alternate title for this play is *Ausaka niwatori* "Ausaka chicken."

I would cry out your leaving.[8]
Why can I not see?
Endlessly repeating, envy at the cries of cocks
Truly, eight-voiced birds I've heard they're called
And having heard them, dawn has come.
Now their cries have numbered more than eight.
Are they true cries, or shall I sleep again?[9]
Mad, unreal hearts of birds![10]

INNKEEPER: When travelers are passing by you act mad. Why today are you not madly playing the rattles and the drum? Moreover many travelers are passing by . . .

CHILD: Yes, many travelers are passing by . . .

BLIND MAN: What? Do you say travelers are passing by?

CHILD: Yes, they have come up here to us as travelers toward the capital.

[8] This is an allusion to a poem by Kan'in in the *Kokinshū*, no. 740:

Ausaka no	If only I were
Yūtsukedori	A chicken at Ausaka
Araba koso	Although in tears
Kimi ga yukiki o	I then could see
Naku naku mo mime	You leaving.

[9] This is a reference to a poem by Sei Shōnagon in *Makura no sōshi*. Translation by Ivan Morris, *The Pillow Book of Sei Shōnagon*, p. 140.

Yo o komete	There may be some who are deceived
Tori no sorane wa	By the cock's crow that falsely breaks
Hakaru tomo	The stillness of the night.
Yo ni Ausaka no	But such a fraud will not beguile
Seki wa yurusaji	The Barrier of Osaka
	Where lovers have their trysts.

[10] The lines from "Were I a bird . . ." to this point are included in *Kanginshū* in NKBT, XLIV, 172–73.

BLIND MAN: Travelers have come deliberately to see me
                   Because there is some special bond between us.
CHILD: They stop, yet will they see the slope of meeting?
BLIND MAN: Barrier grove of cryptomeria.
CHILD: Do they now pass by?
BLIND MAN: For a time, so many people

ageuta   Ever growing travelers' numbers
                   Ever growing travelers' numbers.
                   No matter how they hurry
                   This being barrier mountain
                   It's not an easy meeting.
                   Meeting slope mountain wind
                   Rattles the leaves of trees, dancing
                   Drums the waves of Shinomiya-kawara
                   Here—there—blind reeling madness
                   Passionless pity—feel for me!

TRAVELER: Interesting. I had thought him a man without feelings, but just now, how fascinating he is.

BLIND MAN: As usual with men who're blind, my ears are sharp, you know. You just called me a "man without feelings." Don't go on saying things like that! Here at this meeting slope, a blind man builds his hut to live, but for you to say, "Is he one without feelings?"—Now, that is madness!

TRAVELER: Well, well, the blind man says he's built himself a straw hut and is living here at Ausaka; but he says he is a man with feelings.

BLIND MAN: As I mentioned before, Shinomiya-kawara is nearby here. This is its name, river bed of the fourth prince, because here the fourth son of Emperor Daigo, Semimaru, ended his days.

CHILD: And he who was called Semimaru, being blind, lived as a beggar.

BLIND MAN: I hesitate to mention it, and yet, Semimaru was a blind man like myself.

197

CHILD: Separated from his father, he lived as a beggar. In that way, I think, he was like me.

BLIND MAN: That was in the distant past.

CHILD: Now we have come to these final days.

BLIND MAN: Well-born or low-born

CHILD: The levels differ.

BOTH:
All feel the same
The floating world
He sang of in his poetry.

BLIND MAN:
Our lives,
This way or that,
Pass just the same
Our lives,
This way or that,
Pass just the same.
Whether in a palace or a hovel
We cannot live forever.[11]
Of the four strings
The first string and the second wildly sound[12]
The third and fourth sound clear.
Autumn wind gives voice to the season's rains.
What's sounding now—the drum?
Which is it? Either one
Makes music for my dance.
Perfected Bodhisattvas also dance.
Is that "without feelings"?
Ah, traveler, traveler, you're a fool
Praise the three treasures!

INNKEEPER:
Now sing and dance that famous *kusemai*,
"Descending the Eastern Sea Road."

[11]This is poem B, attributed to Semimaru, which also appears in the Nō *Semimaru*.

[12]An allusion to a poem by Po Chü-i. Lines shared with the Nō *Semimaru*.

CHILD: I have heard my father, too, went off along that eastern sea route. Hearing this, in longing for my father, I sing along. And having sung so often, the words flow from my lips.

BLIND MAN: Because he has expressly requested it, now let us sing—together.

CHORUS:	Even on a withered branch in snow[13]
shidai	Even on a withered branch in snow
	Flowers may bloom once again.[14]
kuri	Now the man known as Morihisa[15]
	Was a warrior of the Heike clan,
	A brilliant man of arms,
	Well-known even to the Lord in Kamakura[16]
sashi	So, thinking him a problem,
	They send him off to the East.[17]
	After he sets forth from the flowery capital
	Is that the sound of calling birds at Kamo river?
	Not knowing where he goes, crossing Shirakawa,
	He reaches Awataguchi, wondering,
	"Whom shall I meet now at Matsuzaka?"[18]
	Shinomiya-Kawara, then the four crossroads,

[13] In the printed text of *Ausaka Madman* included in Tanaka, "Osaka monogurui," the *kusemai* is not given. I have supplied it from the version included in *Rankyoku kusemai yōshū* in Nihon kayō shūsei, V, 272–73.

[14] These lines form the closing shidai of *Azuma kudari*.

[15] Taira Morihisa, a Heike warrior captured by Minamoto troops. He is the subject of the Nō *Morihisa*.

[16] Minamoto Yoritomo (1148–99), founder of the Kamakura Bakufu.

[17] Morihisa was sent as a live captive to Yoritomo. *Azuma kudari*, the *kusemai* here incorporated in the Nō, presents Morihisa's journey to the east.

[18] The preceding five lines, in very slightly different form, are also quoted in Zeami's *Semimaru*.

kuse   Heavy autumn rains on the barrier mountain road
Will wet his sleeves yet more.
For known and unknown alike
Meeting Barrier[19] and the sounds
Of heavy, stormy winds blow cold.
A stop at Matsumoto on Uchide beach
The reflection of the moon
Seen mirrored in the waters of the lake
Strikes the waves to rippled ice.
We think "That's how it must have been
When in a little boat propelled by oars
Fan Li rowed off from Yüeh
On the smoky waves of the five lakes."
From long ago in Nagara mountain village
The name of the old capital also lingers.
When offering prayers at Ishiyamadera
He remembers with trust Kannon's deep vow,
Salvation for all beings of this world.
Seeing the reflection of the long bridge at Seta
The long rainbow linked to it in the water,
He grieves for this transient world.
Through Noji's autumn grasses
And morning dew on bamboo grass at Shino-
wara
He parts and passes on the way of travel
How many, now how many nights?

ageha   The rains and dew together seep through at Moriyama
Even to the lower leaves of colored maples.
And in the evening light, the color's stronger
Kagamiyama reflects the past and present.
Who can forget its form?
Ah, though it has no feelings,

[19] The last two lines of poem A are incorporated here.

In name alone, brave, Musa no Yado
Still passing on the way at Asagaya
Little fields of shallow reeds,
He looks onward from a stop at Ono
And there is Suribari Pass
Where once they polished ax blades.
At famous Bamba the sounds of horses are in
    fact
Storm winds of evening in the mountain
    pines.
Awakening from a traveler's dream
By the waters of Samegai
Pillowed on grasses which he bound together
At Kashiwara who will lend him lodgings
Where even the moonlight is rare?
Deep within the mountains, indestructible,
Fuha no Seki, eaves at barrier inns.
Even on short journeys one longs for the
    capital
When he passes the inn at Tarui
The plains of Aono, green only in their name
For all is evening frost's mysterious white
Dripped on withered leaves, no living grasses.
Such is the floating world he finds at Aohaka
He cannot free himself of feelings
At Kuisegawa, crossing Sunomata, Ashika
And on beyond Oritsu and Kaya shoals.
When he comes to Atsuta no Miya

ageha   The Hōrai shrine is there in name alone.
For one near punishment by death
There is no elixir of immortality.[20]

[20]The "one near punishment by death" is Morihisa. Hōrai was a mythological island of immortals in the Eastern Sea. Borrowed from Chinese mythology, it struck the Japanese imagination and is mentioned in many Japanese literary works.

The winds through reeds cry out at Narumi
lagoon
A little boat has been abandoned on the shore
Sure to drift off on the tide
Waves fill up the dry salt beds at Shiomisaka
The cliffs join with the sky
The boat in the offing rows into the clouds
Wu and Ch'u are separated to the east and
south [21]
Day and night, heaven and earth are floating.
He does not know if he will return at Shira-
suga
And dismounting for a while he listens
To waterbirds with hearts uneasy in their
depths. [22]

BLIND MAN: At meeting slope

chū no mai [23]   Ausaka Barrier, gate of stone
Tread on it, it makes a sound.
The horse of Kiribara
The horse of Kiribara
Sets forth from the mountains
The heart of a god
A wild horse drawn by men and ridden on-
ward.
Do you not know I am a god?
Fools!

TRAVELER: That's odd. The appearance of the blind man has
changed. He asks, "Do you not know I am a god?" Perhaps
these are the words of a god.

---

[21] From Tu Fu's poem, "Climbing Gakuyō Tower."

[22] Even all this is only about half of the complete *kusemai, Azuma kudari*. A complete translation is given by P. G. O'Neill in Appendix I of his *Early Nō Drama*, pp. 153–60.

[23] The editor of the text, Tanaka Makoto, indicates some doubt as to whether the dance *chū no mai* was performed at this point.

BLIND MAN: True, so it is, the barrier god, manifest for your sake

TRAVELER: "Yes," he says, "for your sake"; what is he saying?
What is that he carries? Folded cotton offerings

BLIND MAN: Remembrances of the gods of long ago in their straw huts
And this child too was taken from his father.

TRAVELER: I realize this world's . . .

BLIND MAN: Pathos.
Thinking to guard the path of father and child[24]
When I bring forth this child and show him to you
Without a doubt father and son
Drawn together by the god.
Meeting slope, its name is true, a gratifying promise
Saying, "I have stayed this long."
The blind one, unlike men, immortal
Draws back the brocade of the barrier shrine
It seems he may have entered
In confusing glow of moonlight
He vanishes—miraculous
He vanishes—miraculous.

[24] Though unmarked with a specific structural pattern label in the text, this closing passage is highly poetic.

Chikamatsu's *Semimaru*

In performance all lines of a puppet play were delivered by the chanter or chanters, and for this reason most printed editions of Chikamatsu's works publish the texts of the plays as a single continuous narrative with no indications as to the speaker of any given line. Obviously, in order to facilitate the reading of the translation, it is necessary to attribute the lines either to individual characters or to the chanter as narrator. In so doing I have followed the *Chikamatsu Monzaemon shū* (Shinshaku) Nihon bungaku sōsho series, which indicates by means of brackets those lines attributable to a specific character rather than to the narrator. References to this edition in the footnotes to the translation are marked by the abbreviation CMS. *Kessaku* abbreviates *Chikamatsu kessaku zenshū*, and *Zenshū* is used to abbreviate *Chikamatsu zenshū*.

Where the format of the translation makes their inclusion unnecessary, I have deleted very short lines of the narrator's which would amount to nothing more than "He said," following the speech of another character.

I have added scene headings in each act, marking the obvious changes in location which are evident from the play's content. For the most part I have simply given a brief identification of locale such as "At the Court," or "At Ausaka." The longer scene titles for Act I, scene 3 and Act III, scene 3 are exactly as they appear in the original text. In the original, Act III, scene 2 is called *Semimaru michiyuki*, which I have made more explicit as "Semimaru's journey to Ausaka." Other than the division into five acts, these three scene headings are the only breaks indicated in the original text.

Chikamatsu's *Semimaru*

Cast of Characters

Emperor Daigo
Naohime, mistress of Semimaru
Prince Semimaru
Semimaru's wife
Hayahiro, elder brother of Semimaru's wife
Kiyotsura and Mareyo, Semimaru's attendants
Bashō, a low-ranking court servant in love with Semimaru
Tadamitsu, Bashō's brother, loyal to Semimaru's cause
Tadamitsu's father and mother
Temple boys
Kitōda, woodcutter employed by Hakuga no Sammi
Hakuga no Sammi, Semimaru's disciple in lute playing
Sakagami, Semimaru's elder sister
The Priest of the Agui, exorcist

ACT ONE

SCENE 1: The Emperor's Tour of Inspection

NARRATOR: The moss lies deep on the drum of remon-
              strance
              The birds are not frightened by its sound
              The cattails have rotted in the punishment
              whip
              The fireflies fly off idly[1]

[1] The "drum of remonstrance" refers to a drum kept by the legendary ancient Chinese ruler Yao. A petitioner seeking to have the ruler resolve a legal dispute would strike the drum. The poem presents images of a reign of perfect peace in which there is no discord and the drum need not be struck.
   The punishment whip is a similar image and refers to a whip, described in an episode of the *History of the Later Han Dynasty*, as employed by the ruler Liu Kuan to punish erring subordinates. Chi-

Now in times of just such peace our ruler is the Emperor
Daigo. Even to speak of his illustrious virtues is deeply gratifying. He stated his wish to observe directly the lands and
peoples under his rule, to see how well they prosper. So
imitating the tours of inspection made by the ancient sage
kings of China, now he has come out to the imperial hunting ground of Katano,[2] famous for its cherry blossoms.
Today he lingers over the sight of autumn maple leaves. As
moon and clouds attend the sun, his courtiers preceding
him have called out ahead to clear his path. Five are the
cords on his royal carriage, five like the constant virtues.[3]
The roadside grasses reverberate, heavy with the dew of his
blessings, as his carriage passes by. How magnificent is this
royal procession!

He passes out of the forbidden fields and comes to Nagisa
no In.[4] In his subjects' fields, outside their gates, smoke
from cooking fires rises faintly visible among the tall,
flourishing rice plants. The peasants living in this happy
reign have no need to lock their doors. They rejoice with all
their hearts over the music of his procession's flutes and the

kamatsu has here inverted the lines of the poem by Ōe no Otondo
which appears in the *Wakan roeishū*, NKBT, LXXIII, 220.
 [2] A plain by the bank of the Yodo River in the area of present-day
Ōsaka. During the Heian period it was reserved as a royal hunting
ground. Katano is used as a poetic image because of the fame of its
flowering cherry trees.
[3] The five cords binding the blinds on the front of the emperor's
carriage mark it as the vehicle of a person of high rank. *Tsune no michi*
"the constant paths" refers to the five basic Confucian virtues—
benevolence, righteousness, propriety, wisdom, and fidelity—and is
a pivot word with *michi shiba* "roadside grasses."
[4] A detached palace used by the emperor on his hunting excursions
to Katano. In *Ise Monogatari* this is the site where Ariwara no Nari-
hira composes one of his most famous poems celebrating the beauty
of the cherries. NKBT, IX, 158–59.

beauty of his banners.⁵ Even the birds in the skies await the royal procession with an air of expectation and flock about his cart chirping their affection for him. Truly this shows that the love of a wise ruler extends even to the birds and beasts. It is a sign that the people are safe and happy.

Now beneath a pine ahead of them they hear the sound of a baby crying. When the emperor sends his archives keeper to investigate, it turns out to be an abandoned baby, still too young to have been weaned. The emperor is moved to tears.

EMPEROR: Although I care for the people of my land with compassion, there is within my country someone so cruel as to abandon a baby. This indicates a lack of virtue on my part.

NARRATOR: His eyes fill with tears.⁶ At this point a young woman of eighteen or nineteen comes rushing in, all flustered.

NAOHIME: Oh! Please give back that baby! Return my child, please!

NARRATOR: She sobs, choked with tears.

NAOHIME: He's not an abandoned child at all! I have a toothless, aged mother, like an old tree from which the leaves now fall, and there is no way for me to feed her. I am keeping her alive by letting her drink my own milk. Because the baby was crying and fighting to get to the breast, I left him out here for a little while to calm him. I certainly wasn't abandoning him! Please, give him back!

NARRATOR: She weeps. Suddenly the emperor claps his hands together.

⁵"The music of flutes" and "the beauty of banners" are phrases from Mencius, Book One ("King Hui of Liang"), Part II. Their import, there as here, is that the people will rejoice in the king's pleasures if, by his benevolent government, he has also brought them pleasure. See Legge, *The Works of Mencius*, pp. 152–53.

⁶*Zenshū* and *Kessaku* both have the compound *ryūgan*, lit. "dragon face," meaning the emperor's face. CMS has *ryōgan* "both eyes." I follow the latter interpretation.

EMPEROR: Well! So he's not an abandoned baby! You act as a filial child toward your mother by treating her lovingly. You should be considered a wise woman. But don't you have a husband?

NAOHIME: No. My husband vanished from this life with the autumn haze last year. This child is the lingering shadow which I have as a keepsake in remembrance of him.

NARRATOR: She can speak no more, choked in tears which fall for good reason. She has dark eyes and the manner of a well-bred woman. The emperor is moved by her and summons the Middle Counselor Mareyo.

EMPEROR: To care for unfortunates was the way of the past.[7] I entrust her, together with her aged mother, to your care. You should invite them into the court and care for them well. In fact, it will be a sign to bespeak to heaven our happiness over this prosperous year. We should hold the Banquet of the First Chrysanthemums,[8] perform music in the inner imperial hall,[9] and pray for the fertility of the five grains.

NARRATOR: This is an excellent imperial decree to be followed by the people.

SCENE 2: At the Court of Emperor Daigo

NARRATOR: The first frosts
            In the first frosts

---

[7] This is probably also a reference to *Mencius,* Book One ("King Hui of Liang"), Part II, in which Mencius advises his king that the virtuous King Wen of Chou made the care of widows and widowers, elderly childless people, and orphans his first order of concern. See Legge, *The Works of Mencius,* p. 162.

[8] This may refer to the last of the five festivals (*go sekku*) held annually, the *Kiku no sekku* "Chrysanthemum Festival" held on the ninth day of the ninth month.

[9] The *shishinden,* the central ceremonial hall of the imperial palace.

If you want to pick the flowers
Pick them, at the flower banquet.[10]

At the royal chrysanthemum viewing among the many assembled musicians is the fourth child of the present emperor, the prince called Semimaru. He has natural good looks and is deeply loved by his father the emperor. He is marvelously skilled at playing the lute, and his wife is very talented at playing the koto. Well, now, his wife is the younger sister of Hayahiro, the major controller of the right.[11] She is a girl just past the age of eighteen, who dresses in robes with free-hanging sleeves. They are a couple only two years different in age, well-matched in marriage and in the instruments they play.

The emperor has ordered that the music be begun when the moon rises, so the imperial guards, with heads inclined, are waiting for the advent of the moon. Even the beacon fires they have lit while waiting give an elegantly pleasing appearance.

Semimaru is all alone, looking out from the railing of a corridor in the interior of the court and wondering if the moon has risen yet. He hears the sleepy voice of a woman who has pillowed herself on her koto and is singing this song:

[10]These lines are based on a poem by Ōshikōchi Mitsune in the *Kokinshū*, no. 277, as follows:

Kokoroate ni	If we pick them
Orabaya oran	We'll pick by guessing:
Hatsushimo no	Blossoms of white chrysanthemum
Okimadowaseru	Where first frost has settled
Shiragiku no hana	And deceives the eye.

[11]*Udaiben.* I have adopted the practice of using a character's full name and title only on his first appearance, thereafter using a consistent short form for the name.

209

SEMIMARU'S WIFE:
> Evening—at evening, the river of my tears
> Can I not even be with him, pillowed on the
> waves
> At the shoals of meeting?
> Wishing for that chance, I have laid myself
> down
> For all these months and years.

NARRATOR: Startled, the prince goes to look and discovers his wife. He draws close to her and speaks.

SEMIMARU: Say, say, the music tonight is cheerful. Be careful, if you nap on your koto you'll ruin its tuning. Who's around? Hey! Hey!

NARRATOR: When he calls out her ladies-in-waiting answer, "Yes!" and bring out her pillow.[12]

His wife quickly moves up close to him. Suddenly she draws out the prince's long sword. Pulling over the long double pillow, she cuts it right in two. The prince is shocked and seizes her.

SEMIMARU: What's this? Are you mad?

NARRATOR: He is absolutely dumbfounded. His wife listens to him and answers.

SEMIMARU'S WIFE: It is not in the least insane! Since you and I became husband and wife, two years—how many nights— have passed, yet will we never be together? Don't I please you? We have not spent even one night together, our bodies touching, sharing one pillow. Even the Buddha Shakyamuni didn't behave that way.[13] Was it in name alone that I was wed? It's of no use, this long double pillow. Although it is not at fault, I have punished it!

---

[12] A hard wooden headrest used as a pillow.

[13] The Buddha Shakyamuni had married and fathered a child before renouncing his life as a prince. The wife's words anticipate Semimaru's "vow," soon to be revealed.

Chikamatsu's *Semimaru*

NARRATOR: She weeps in sorrow and resentment. The prince nods.

SEMIMARU: Ah, it seems you feel resentful. I have had no opportunity to talk to you about this, and the time has just slipped away without my telling you about it. I did not go against my parents' wishes and so we became husband and wife, and yet, ever since I was a young boy I have wanted to become a monk and have made a lifelong vow of celibacy. Since this is my sacred vow to Buddha, please resign yourself to the situation.

NARRATOR: He speaks, weeping along with her. His wife stifles her tears.

SEMIMARU'S WIFE: Oh, well then—is that the way things are? In that case I too will enter a Buddhist order. This life lasts hardly any time. We will truly be husband and wife in our hearts for all eternity. Now I shall make a written vow to Buddha and we will both bear the shame of our hearts' earthly passions. We will not defile our bodies so that we may both joyously achieve a state of purity. But—for the sake of this vow, if tonight for once in our lifetimes we were to spend the night in love, even Buddha would surely understand.

NARRATOR: She says this leaning against Semimaru's knees. Her words are wildly disordered like wind-tossed plume-grass, and with them falls a dew of tears. She enters deep inside the blinds of her room.

NARRATOR: Is it not the moon which touches all with a red glow? An imperial guard, while kindling a beacon fire, is weeping bitterly. Semimaru looks at him.

SEMIMARU: It is the occasion of a happy festival, yet strangely enough your tears are falling. This is hard to understand.

NARRATOR: When Semimaru speaks the guard flings aside his ceremonial headgear and answers.

GUARD (NAOHIME): Look at me! Have you forgotten me? I am the girl with whom you spent but one brief night a year ago in the village of Kasuga. I am Naohime! The waters of our river of meeting settled, the months passed by, and then I gave birth to your child. It's odd, but my old mother and I have been taken under the care of your father the emperor. Fearing a scandal about you, I lied and said that my husband had died. We are being cared for by Lord Mareyo. By any means possible I wanted to see you, so I disguised myself as a palace guard. Since I am a very lowly person it is not appropriate for us to be together as lovers. The vow we pledged to each other, sealed in blood, is meaningless now. I shall burn it up, seeing how beautifully you get along with your wife. The relationship is lovely as the first cherry blossoms at Yoshino.[14]

NARRATOR: She is about to commit the paper to the sparkling scented flames when Semimaru stops her and pulls it back.

SEMIMARU: Day and night I have never forgotten you for even an instant. I sent out my childhood retainer Kiyotsura to search for you; and I lied when I said I wanted to become a monk. I have not slept a single night by my wife's side. You shouldn't treat me so cruelly. Isn't it wrong for you to say, "Let's burn the vow"?

NARRATOR: When he complains this way Naohime embraces him and their feelings of love well deeply like Tsukuba River.[15] At the moment of meeting their hearts are numbed and their breasts aflutter to the point of trembling.

[14] The phrase is *onaka yoshino no hatsuzakura* and fuses *onaka yoshi* "good relations" with *yoshino no hatsuzakura* "the first cherries at Yoshino."

[15] This is an allusion to a poem by the Emperor Yōzei in the *Gosenshū*, no. 777.

Tsukubane no	From Tsukuba peak
Mine yori otsuru	The Mina river
Mina no kawa	Flowing downward,
Koi zo tsumorite	As a river of love,
Fushi to narinuru	Wells deeply into pools.

At this point Semimaru's wife's elder brother, Hayahiro, sees just what is going on.

HAYAHIRO: The court guard tonight is Semimaru's secret mistress. We must question her!

NARRATOR: The court officials and their attendants come rushing out calling "What's up? We're coming!" Frightened by the sound of their voices, everyone runs off into the shadows of the palace's earthen walls. Hayahiro picks up the slip of paper on which the vow was written.

HAYAHIRO: Aha! I've got evidence! I'll report this to the emperor.

NARRATOR: When he raises such a clamor, Semimaru's wife speaks, unembarrassed by the eyes of others gazing at her.

SEMIMARU'S WIFE: Don't be vulgar. This matter concerns the reputation of a prince. Please handle it discreetly, brother.

NARRATOR: She speaks in tears. Hayahiro, squinting at her, answers.

HAYAHIRO: There's no point talking about it. What's right depends upon the circumstances. When the prince became your husband, it brought glory to our whole family. Do you want to destroy your brother? Don't you resent having your husband stolen right out of your bed? Look at this evidence!

NARRATOR: When he thrusts forward the paper Semimaru's wife looks at it. It is the prince's handwriting without a doubt. On her furiously angry face the veins form a bright red net. Her hair stands on end. Her body shakes with rage and her teeth chatter.

SEMIMARU'S WIFE: He deceived me! I'm furious! Jealous! Can't you sense my resentment? I'll show you! See!

NARRATOR: She glares at heaven and earth and tears of blood form drop by drop in both her eyes. As her anger rises she chews up and spits out the paper with their pledge of love. The watchfire is burning brightly, but even fiercer is the fire

213

in her heart. Fuming and crazed she leaves shaking—a frightening and pitiable sight![16]

SCENE 3: The Pilgrimage to Hashihime Shrine[17]

NARRATOR: Well, now, at this time Semimaru's childhood retainer Kiyotsura, the chief of the outer palace guard, has been searching around the southern capital[18] looking for Naohime. Just now he is on his way back up to the capital for a while. The sun is setting behind the long pond at Nagaike as he arrives at the very lonely shrine at Uji bridge.[19] He thinks that he will spend the night here, and taking off his straw hat he looks out across the shrine

[16]The passage describing Semimaru's wife's rage is replete with strings of repeated syllables such as *hara-hara-hara* and *kuru-kuru-kuru*, allowing the virtuoso chanter to work up to an intense pitch.

[17]The section of the play beginning with the line "Though you can tie a wild horse" is headed *Hashihime mōde* in some versions of the original text and *Kibune mōde* in others. I have moved the heading up in the translation to the point where the scene, as described by the narrator, changes.

[18]Nara, while "the capital" is Kyoto.

[19]The bridge crosses the Uji River in the town of Uji, and just to the south of the bridge was the Hashihime shrine. According to a legend associated with the shrine, long ago a jealous woman who resented her husband's relations with other women came every night and immersed herself in the Uji River. In accordance with her prayers she was transformed into a demon with the power to torment those whose behavior causes others jealousy. She became enshrined as the deity of this shrine. This section is called *Kibune mōde* "the pilgrimage to Kibune shrine" in some original editions of the play. The confusion arises because the legendary woman had been instructed by the deity of the Kibune shrine, located in Otagi district, Kyoto, to immerse herself in the Uji River in order to achieve her goal. The Kibune shrine and Hashihime shrine both became the objective of pilgrimages by resentful women. The Nō play *Kanawa* takes this legend as its subject. See Keene, *Twenty Plays*, pp. 194–95.

grounds. What a ghastly sight! Good Lord![20] This is the
shrine of the protector of the jealous, Hashihime. These are
the people who come on secret pilgrimage at the hour of the
ox.[21] Thinking to watch in secret, Kiyotsura climbs up an
old pine tree before the shrine and makes himself as small as
possible, just like a spider on a branch.

> With the web-ropes of a spider
> A wild horse may be tied, and yet
> It is painful to love a man
> Who treads two paths in love,[22]
> Yet not to love him, too, is dreadful.
> The awful hour of the ox,[23]
> The time of the pilgrimage has come
> To the iron crown's three fires,[24]

[20]*Namu sambō* "Praise the three treasures" (the Buddha, the
teachings, and the congregation).

[21]Two to four A.M.

[22]The first four lines are a variant on an old song of unknown origin which runs:

Kumo no i ni	With the web ropes of a spider
Aretaru koma wa	A wild horse
Tsunagu to mo	May be tied, and yet
Futamichi kakuru	Never can you trust a man
Hito wa tanomaji	Who treads two paths in love

It also appears in the nō *Kanawa* and is alluded to in Kenkō's
Tsurezuregusa.

[23]The pivot word here is *monoushi* "horrible" which links with *ushi
no tokimairi* "pilgrimage at the hour of the ox."

[24]The woman entering the shrine courtyard wears an inverted tripod on her head with a flaming firebrand attached to each leg of the
tripod. For an illustration of the prop used to portray this in the Nō
Kanawa, see Keene, *Twenty Plays*, p. 193. *Kanawa* is the source of inspiration for this scene of Chikamatsu's which was first used in the
puppet play *Aoi no ue*, possibly also by Chikamatsu. *Zenshū*, I,
321–25.

Fed by enmity, passion, and hatred,
Add the kindling of wrath
And the blaze will not die down.
In the smokelike evening sky
Float the pillars of the shrine!
An awesome, numbing sight
Oh—do not speak of it!
A woman's boxwood comb,[25]
Bunches of disarranged hair,
Seven—eight—at midnight
The sound of the bell is eerie.
If you clap your hands
And cast a spell[26]
Following your heartfelt wishes,
It is sure to have effect.
Horrifying, horrible
The jealousy within her heart
Here from the high tree branches
The grove glows dark and murky
Do not dawn faintly,
Oh morning sun at Mount Asahi![27]
He sees shadows reflected
In the Yamabuki shoals
Lightning from the peak flashes.
Is it the light of stars?
The glitter of fireflies?
The light of her yearning soul departing?
Truly "outwardly she seems a Bodhisattva,

[25] The pivot word is *natsuge* "do not speak," linking with *tsuge no tsumagushi* "a woman's boxwood comb."

[26] *Ama no sakate o utte ukeeba* "If you pray while clapping [in the rhythm called] *ama no saka.*"

[27] These lines are a good example of the kind of alliteration Chikamatsu often favors: *asaku na ake zo asahiyama.*

Within, her soul is like an evil demon"[28]
Though her appearance may be white
It should be blackened by
The endless raging flames of Hell.
She is in tears, crazed by her love,
The woman's heart is darker than the darkness
At Kurahashi mountain,[29]
Her jealousy boils up,
A river where jewels of bubbling steam
Well up and fall again.
The sound of the waves at the river shoals
Echoes through the branches with the
    midnight winds
Like the storm, her footfalls rumble.[30]
She claps her hands and prays
At the shrine of Hashihime, on Uji bridge.
In this depressing world it is enough
To make the hair upon the body stand on end.

NARRATOR: Kiyotsura now begins to look. He feels uneasy as he holds tightly to a branch and gazes out. At the other side he sees the figure of another similar woman.

KIYOTSURA: Ah, for her too, it is the midnight pilgrimage. How many of them there are! Is this the work of demons? Surely the foxes have bewitched me?

NARRATOR: He dampens his eyelashes with spit.[31] The two women exchange glances and both shiver. The one who had come first speaks in a soft voice.

[28] As a woman, her appearance is gentle, but her heart is raging.
[29] Kurahashi mountain is introduced here because *kura* means "dark."
[30] This passage, beginning "Kurahashi mountain," is replete with repeated nonsense syllables allowing the chanter to establish an eerie mood.
[31] There is a folk belief that this practice can dispel enchantment.

FIRST WOMAN: Who are you?

SECOND WOMAN: And who are you?

FIRST WOMAN: I am the same as you.[32] My prayers must be the same as yours—prayers of jealousy.

SECOND WOMAN: I too am jealous. There are no good men in this world. Well, we have met each other, and things are just the same for both of us. While we are standing here let's speak of our jealousy, and in the telling of it let's dispel our gloom.

NARRATOR: As she speaks, she draws up close to the other woman. Kiyotsura forgets his fears. Suddenly, confessions of jealousy, and in such a strange place! It is so funny it's more than he can stand. He practically bursts out laughing.

SECOND WOMAN: I am a servant girl of the empress. I am called Bashō. Although it is a hopeless love, ever since I was young I have thought constantly of Semimaru. I told him about this and he made me a firm promise that one night my wishes would be fulfilled, but he is tightly tied to his wife and his promise is now nothing but a dream. Rather than pine to death alone, I am praying this way.

NARRATOR: The first woman interrupts her.

FIRST WOMAN: I am the prince's wife! It is wrong for you to resent me! Because of a lustful woman named Naohime I have been cast aside too. The one to hate is Naohime!

NARRATOR: She speaks gnashing her teeth. Kiyotsura hears what she says and sees that it really is the prince's wife. He is thunderstruck. Bashō claps her hands to cast a curse.

BASHŌ: So you are his wife! Not knowing that, I've been speaking my resentment, but our enemy in love is Naohime alone. Well, let's kill her! Together let's satisfy our deep desires!

SEMIMARU'S WIFE: Yes!

[32] Both wear flaming iron crowns.

NARRATOR: They stand side by side under the sacred tree at the shrine.

BASHŌ: Turn me into a demon or a snake!

NARRATOR: As they reveal their innermost feelings, they take out some nails.

SEMIMARU'S WIFE: These are nails to drive into Naohime's eyes. May her eyes be ruined quickly![33]

NARRATOR: She speaks and drives the nails right into the tree trunk.

BASHŌ: Here—her head, her breast—may her whole body rot!

NARRATOR: Forty-four spikes the two together strike. Sinews, bones, and joints. Driving the nails they hope to relieve their feelings. They dance and fly about wildly, and as they strike blood flows from the nail holes.

Because the big tree shakes as it is struck, Kiyotsura bobs about like a floating boat. He has been shaken too much, and everything goes dark before his eyes; he loses his footing on the branch and comes crashing down. Both women are terrified and try to flee rapidly, but Kiyotsura gets hold of Semimaru's wife's arms and pulls her back again while Bashō runs off and disappears. Now Kiyotsura can control himself no longer.

KIYOTSURA: Listen, my lady, think of who you are. You have been behaving shamefully. Get back to the court before dawn comes!

NARRATOR: Though he says this, she does not listen.

SEMIMARU'S WIFE: Since I have been recognized my prayers will come to nothing. My one thought is to die and get my revenge.

---

[33] Though Chikamatsu never elaborates on this point, it seems it is this action which has the effect of blinding Semimaru instead of Naohime.

NARRATOR: She creates a scandal because of her love. At Ko-
jima point at Tachibana,[34] a great red lotus,[35] she throws
herself into the roiling waters and disappears pitifully in
death. Kiyotsura cries out, alarmed.

KIYOTSURA: Torches! Torches!

NARRATOR: When they hear him the villagers bring torches
and lanterns enough to rival the stars. There is a great com-
motion everywhere. Now small waves beat against the
bank. Oh! How awful! The corpse of Semimaru's wife suddenly rises up. She has grown horns and through her jealousy has been transformed into a snake. She shakes her
scales, scatters flames about, and kicking the waves she coils
upward. She wraps herself about the crossbeam of the
shrine arch gate, and as she faces upward to the sky, her
breath is like a rain of fire. The people are terrified by this,
and crying out in alarm they scatter and flee. Then the great
snake plunges back down into the rapids.

SNAKE-WIFE: I changed my life to death and death to life again.
Through world upon world and incarnation after incarnation, I shall tell of my grievances—the resentment! the bitterness!

NARRATOR: Only her voice lingers on as she sinks to her grave
at the bottom of the water. And the water, ever changing,
flows by. In the mist over the river Uji she disappears
faintly with the dawning sky. The eerie scene is terrifying
and her death sadly moving. How painful the way of love
can be!

[34]The place name Tachibana, which cannot be definitely located in
this vincinity, is introduced because of the pun on *ukina o tateru* "to
create a scandal."

[35]Presumably this means the waters are darkened red because of
the flames about her head.

ACT TWO

SCENE 1: At the Village of Kohata

NARRATOR: This place too is called by the name "Road of Love." In the country village of Kohata, near Nasake Pass, there lives a man called Senju Tarō Tadamitsu. He is by nature an unusually good archer, and now, although he serves no master, he is living comfortably in a thatch hut, neither starving nor freezing, but taking pleasure in hunting day and night. Today again he has gone out hunting carrying his bow and plume-grass quiver. When, near Mount Fukakusa,[36] he drives a rabbit out of a cattail field, he puts an arrow to his bow. The arrow released by his bow hand flies straight but misses its mark and comes to a sudden stop after driving up to the feathers into a clump of rice stalks someone had cut and left gathered together. The rabbit runs off and disappears.

TADAMITSU: Holy Hachiman![37] I missed! I'll go get the arrow.

NARRATOR: When he pulls away the rice stalks—what's this! A noble boy of only about twenty and a court lady of some sixteen years are there, weeping, the arrow in her left sleeve. Tadamitsu is quite startled.

TADAMITSU: I had no idea there was anyone here! Now that I see you I find you don't look like commoners. This is strange, tell me about it.

SEMIMARU: I am the fourth son of the emperor. My name is Semimaru. This woman is called Naohime. "In the young

---

[36] Mount Fukakusa is not in this area, though a village called Fukakusa is. Chikamatsu presumably meant some other mountain in the area of the village.

[37] Tadamitsu's expletive is *yumiya Hachiman*, lit. "bow and arrow Hachiman." Hachiman Bōsatsu is the patron of warriors, hunters, and so forth.

221

grasses, never trod upon, my wife too is hidden."[38] The people who are chasing us will surely come soon. I beg you, help me.

NARRATOR: He says this and again begins to weep.

TADAMITSU: Well—so you are Prince Semimaru! I am called Senju Tarō Tadamitsu. In the past I used to ride in court horse races. And what's more, my younger sister is now serving in the lowest ranks of the court ladies, so I have a certain connection with the court. Nobody that I am, I would not hesitate to give even my own life in answer to a plea for help from such an exalted person as yourself. My father is the monk Senju, and though he is old, he has a good reputation. Please come along to our house and you can tell us at your ease all about what's happening. Let's go.

NARRATOR: Just as he says this Hayahiro comes searching about this way and that, accompanied by twenty or thirty armed men.

HAYAHIRO: There they are—Semimaru and Naohime! Capture them!

NARRATOR: He shouts. Tadamitsu stands in front of him and blocks the soldiers' way.

TADAMITSU: Hey! So you're the ones who're chasing after them? I don't know what wrong the prince has done, but I am Tadamitsu, and since I have been asked to help him, you'd better go back at once!

NARRATOR: He shouts these words, and Hayahiro becomes very angry.

---

[38] This is an allusion to a poem in *Ise Monogatari*, NKBT, IX, 119.

Musashino wa	Today do not burn
Kyō wa na yaki zo	The plains of Musashi
Wakakusa no	For in these fields,
Tsuma mo komoreri	Like ears of grasses,
Ware mo komoreri	My wife and I are hidden.

HAYAHIRO: Because of the prince's error, a lack of virtue, there is an imperial order to arrest him. You go against the emperor's orders? Well, are you [39] an enemy of the court?

TADAMITSU: Call me an enemy of the court! Call me a fool! A samurai's word is more binding than an imperial order. Since he asked my help, I give my life to the prince. If you come near me I'll kick you to death.

NARRATOR: Hayahiro answers angrily.

HAYAHIRO: What a young upstart! [40] Take him!

NARRATOR: The group of warriors retreats. Loosening the quiver band which holds his arrows, Tadamitsu shoots rapidly, taking out his arrows and nocking them on his bow. None of his arrows are shot in vain. Since arrows are falling upon them like rain, even Hayahiro cannot withstand them, and everyone scatters out of sight in all directions.

TADAMITSU: Well, time to go.

NARRATOR: He takes Naohime over his shoulder. Leading the prince by the hand he returns to his family home.

SCENE 2: At Tadamitsu's Family Home

NARRATOR: The day has already grown dark. Kiyotsura, having heard that Semimaru has disappeared, is searching in the vicinity of the capital. When he arrives at the village of Kohata it happens by chance that his sandal breaks and it becomes difficult for him to go further on this night of winter showers. However, he does not know that the prince is here on such a night. He stands warding off the rain in the dry space under the thatched roof of the monk Senju's outer gate. As the midnight bell sounds, enveloped by the rain, he peers through a break in the mist and sees a young girl,

[39] Hayahiro insultingly addresses Tadamitsu as *uneme,* a term normally used to address a woman.

[40] *Nisaime* "two-year-old," used as a term of abuse in addressing a young person.

223

dressed in a gown with long hanging sleeves, who appears to be hiding. As he draws back under the trees and watches, the girl strikes roughly on the door of the gate, calling out "Hello!"

TADAMITSU and FATHER: Oh! It's the ones who're after him.

NARRATOR: They cry out and rush to the door.

TADAMITSU: Who is asking admittance in the middle of the night?

BASHŌ: Is that my brother and father? It is Bashō no Mae. I was slandered by my friends and so I left the court secretly. Please open the door.

NARRATOR: Her mother is startled by the sound of her voice.

MOTHER: Is it my daughter? Oh how I want to see her!

NARRATOR: Just as she is about to open the door, Bashō's father, the monk, speaks.

MONK SENJU: Wait! Danger comes from carelessness. Since we are hiding the prince here, it's not wise to open the door in the middle of the night.

Now, Bashō, there are reasons why we cannot open the gate at night. Stay there through the night. When dawn comes we'll let you in.

BASHŌ: I don't understand what you are saying! What sort of hatred do you bear for me? Please, you must open the door. Open up!

NARRATOR: She complains and laments.

MONK SENJU: No, no, though we bear no grudge against you, it would not be right for us to open the door tonight. We'll explain the reasons tomorrow morning. It really won't be long until dawn. Here, spread this out to sleep on for the night.

NARRATOR: They toss a short-sleeved robe from inside the house, and Bashō weakly takes it, wraps it about herself, and lies down.

When Kiyotsura hears that it is Bashō, he thinks to himself, "That girl is the one who made the shrine pilgrimage at the hour of the ox. I shall ask her what is happening at court." He quietly draws up close to her and speaks in a disguised voice.

KIYOTSURA: Say. . .

BASHŌ: Ai! I'm frightened!

NARRATOR: She starts to run away.

KIYOTSURA: Now, now, don't be worried. I'm just a country traveler and I've come to get out of the rain. From what I've heard you say, you seem to be a person from the court. I'm just a humble fellow, a simple country peasant, and folks like me have never seen the goings-on of court ladies even in our dreams. As a gift for me to take back home, tell me a little about life at court.

NARRATOR: His words make Bashō laugh.

BASHŌ: All you peasants talk this way, but it's not especially different at court. Music, poetry, literature—but above all, *love* is fashionable at court.

NARRATOR: Smiling, she speaks kindly to him. With an expression of feigned ignorance Kiyotsura responds.

KIYOTSURA: Even in the countryside and in the mountains the way of love does not go out of style. Surely you must also have the same passions. Well, now, I would like to hear about it.

NARRATOR: When he says this, she thinks, "Even for us to have stopped under the same tree shows that we have some connection to each other from a previous existence." [41] Concealing nothing she tells of her love.

BASHŌ: I am embarrassed to say so, but I fell in love with Semimaru, the most handsome man at court, and I have

[41] Lodging under the same tree and scooping water from the same stream are frequently cited as indications of a connection between two individuals stemming from some occurrence in a previous existence.

loved him with all my heart, drawn to him like a boat pulled through the water. He is a man who has had affairs with many women. Although he promised me that we would spend one night of love together, rolling in each others' arms in the jeweled hail of love, his promise was not fulfilled. Our love has been disrupted by a worthless woman and there has been no end to my longing. My body has decayed in a rain of tears. If the old saying, "The power of thought can penetrate rock,"[42] is no lie, I shall get my revenge whether I live or die. Oh, but I'm embarrassed. Don't spread my indiscreet confessions to anybody.

NARRATOR: Again she breaks down in tears, her sleeves wet enough to rival a rainstorm. As soon as he hears this Kiyotsura thinks, "What an appalling idea; she'll inevitably end up becoming the enemy of Semimaru and Naohime. What will she do? If she harms him, afterward will be too late to feel sorry about it." Finding what has just happened endlessly unpleasant, he unsheathes his long sword and conceals it. Taking hold of her, he draws close and stabs her through the heart.

BASHŌ: Help! Murder!

NARRATOR: At the sound of her voice, her father and brother open the gate and come rushing out. Thinking, "This is bad," Kiyotsura runs into the thicket of small bamboo and hides for a while. Her mother takes the girl in her arms and grieves. The monk and his son both think her murder must be the work of some thief. They rush out to charge after him, but when they think of the prince they can neither go nor stay. Semimaru and Naohime are both flustered and

---

[42]This refers to an episode in the Biography of General Li Kuang in *Shih Chi* (109). Li Kuang shot an arrow at a rock which he thought to be a tiger, and the arrow penetrated the rock. See Watson, *Records of the Grand Historian of China*, II, 146.

bewildered. Bashō, who is breathing her last, looks intently at the prince and speaks while gasping for breath.

BASHŌ: Oh, is that Prince Semimaru and the lady Naohime? I feel resentful and embarrassed, all at once! Thinking that your lying words were true, I was consumed with passion. I tormented my heart with love for you and went mad thinking hopeless thoughts because I was so singlemindedly in love with you. If I was an obstacle to your love affairs, why didn't you tell me, "Resign yourself, give up?" Was it your plan to deceive me and kill me? Your heart is too cruel. Have you no pity? If you hate someone you cannot be in love with him. I regret that I have ruined my reputation because of a hopeless love.[43] But, since you have taken lodging here in my house, it shows a bond between us from another existence. For your sake, from my grave beneath the grasses I will not pray evil upon you. Thinking of the bond between us, I would rather have one prayer offering from you than a hundred or a thousand from other people. I do not lament the passing of my life, as brief as the dew on the offering flowers. Oh father, brother, I only ask that you care for the prince. Oh, mother, how I hate to leave you. Praise Buddha!

NARRATOR: She speaks in a voice as weak as in sleep. Among the flowers on an evening in autumn, after the span of seventeen years, her life fades to nothingness. Parents and son, unable to decide whether it is a dream or reality, take her in their arms and weep. Then Semimaru and Naohime raise their voices in lamentation.

[43] An allusion to a poem by Lady Sagami in the *Goshūishū*, no. 815.

Uramiwabi	So deep in grief
Hosanu sode da ni	My sleeves are never dry
Arumono o	And yet, I think
Koi ni kuchinamu	How dreadful to be called
Na koso oshikere	The one who rotted in tears.

SEMIMARU and NAOHIME: We didn't know things were this way! Please vent your resentment, please forgive us! We feel terrible!

NARRATOR: They take hold of her and fall down weeping. Though they gasp and sob it is to no avail. A pitiful death. Kiyotsura changes his plans. Unable to bear it any longer he gives way and reveals his presence. "Here's what happened," he explains.

SEMIMARU: Is that Kiyotsura I hear? Come right over here!

NARRATOR: Kiyotsura, having been invited in, confronts the others. He greets them with careful polite formalities.

KIYOTSURA: I am very grateful to you for concealing them so well here. Now first of all, I am sorry to see your daughter's untimely death. I shall tell you who your enemy is and let you achieve your heartfelt desire for revenge.

NARRATOR: When he says this Tadamitsu seems delighted.

TADAMITSU: Who was it—from where?

KIYOTSURA: I, Kiyotsura, am that enemy!

NARRATOR: The father and son are both utterly dumbfounded.

TADAMITSU: I don't understand at all. There must be some explanation. Please tell us!

NARRATOR: They speak, knitting their brows. Kiyotsura, shedding heavy tears, tells every detail precisely.

KIYOTSURA: Having no idea that the prince was here, I thought her an enemy for his future, and unpleasant though it was, I stabbed her. But my devotion was, rather, a lack of devotion. Her enmity turned to sympathy. I was hot-tempered and careless. I am mortally ashamed. Take out your resentment against me.

NARRATOR: As he speaks he suddenly draws his great sword, point toward him, ready to commit suicide. The father and son take him by both arms and restrain him.

TADAMITSU and FATHER: Now, Lord Kiyotsura, we too are samurai. Since our whole house have dedicated their lives to the prince, how could we feel any resentment against you? You have great responsibilities. For you to die over such a trifling matter—are you mad, have you gone insane? Well, if you really want to die, try dying!

NARRATOR: Since they soothe and dissuade him this way, even Kiyotsura, who had been quite resolved to die, is swayed by their logic and does not die. Yet he cannot really live, nor can they kill him. The three of them look at each other and, of course, all weep together.

NARRATOR: Just at the first dawn light Hayahiro arrives with some young men he had armed. They have kidnaped Naohime's mother and baby and brought them out as captives at the head of their ranks. They surround Senju's house and call out.

HAYAHIRO: You are sheltering Semimaru who has been disowned. The emperor is exceedingly angry. Anyone who stirs up trouble in the realm of the great ruler of peace is a fool. Now, hand over Semimaru and Naohime. If you object, then I'll just kill these two.

NARRATOR: As he speaks he presses his blade against their chests.

HAYAHIRO: Well, what is your answer?

NARRATOR: They cry out, shouting fiercely. Tadamitsu and his father are troubled because of the hostages. They can not, in any case, go charging out. "What shall we do?" they ask each other. After a little time has gone by Hayahiro speaks.

HAYAHIRO: You've waited too long. Let's make them offering grasses for the gods of war. Let's kill these and go get the others!

NARRATOR: How dreadful! The old grandmother and the baby prince are cut down together by the same sword—a sight too horrible to watch.

TADAMITSU: You animals who know nothing of human ways, not one of you will get away!

NARRATOR: He takes up a long-bladed sword and fights against more than forty men, taking on some with his left hand and holding off the others with his right. Tadamitsu by his own hand kills sixteen men, and his father the monk dispatches eight to their deaths with his long sword. The remaining men sustain severe wounds. Suddenly they withdraw, and then they charge again. Two or three, then four or five times they jostle together. The father and son call out.

TADAMITSU and FATHER: Kiyotsura! Are you here? Take the prince away with you! Don't worry about us here—don't worry!

NARRATOR: Kiyotsura answers, "Right!" and carrying the prince on his back he flees to his own house. During this time Hayahiro breaks down the rear wall of the house and drags out Naohime. He stamps her on the ground and lifts her up on his arms.[44] Crying out, "Praise the Three Treasures!" the monk strikes from the side and, with sparks flying, they cross swords. Tadamitsu, thinking, "Don't kill my father!" joins in the fray, but the monk holds him back.

TADMITSU'S FATHER: Don't protect me! If you let the princess[45] be killed, I will disinherit you until the seventh reincarnation.

NARRATOR: His voice is weak. Carrying Naohime and his mother, one under each arm, Tadamitsu flees to the mountain top. Without looking back, the monk holds off the enemy who chase after them. Hayahiro, in a rage, strikes him on the left shoulder with a blow from his great sword. Like a fragile dream, on a night in the spring of his seventy-first year, the monk's life dissolves into nothingness. Tadamitsu comes back wanting to find out how his father is faring.

[44] He raises her up as if making an offering. The verb *ogamu* "to worship" is used.
[45] He is referring to Naohime.

TADAMITSU: Oh, how awful, he's been killed! You are the enemies of my father!

NARRATOR: He takes on the retreating army. He moves this way and that, back and forth, holding them off in all directions like the threads of a spider web. They maneuver for about an hour. He does not know where Hayahiro has gone.

TADAMITSU: Oh, this is horrible! Get out of here, or I'll kill you and offer you up to the memory of my father!

NARRATOR: He calls out and the few remaining men scatter like windblown waves of leaves, roughly shaken by storm winds. The faint smoke of his father's remains floats into the mist in the valley. If the father is a father, the child is a child.[46] He was truly trustworthy and brave. Such a bold warrior had never been heard of before, and so his fame has remained for us in writing.[47]

ACT THREE

SCENE 1: At the Court of Emperor Daigo

NARRATOR: The prince has barely escaped with his life from the danger caused by Hayahiro's treachery, and now he is at the residence of Mareyo, thanks to Kiyotsura's arrangements. At some point Kiyotsura and Mareyo make a trip to the court.

KIYOTSURA and MAREYO: Since the fifth month, Prince Semimaru has been suffering from an eye disease of an unprecedented nature. We have used both Chinese and Japanese

[46] An allusion to the *Analects* of Confucius, Book XII, chap. 11, in which Confucius advises that good government is dependent on the correct fulfillment of one's personal roles as prince, minister, father, or son. See Legge, *The Works of Mencius*, I, 256.

[47] Though most of the narration of the play is in the present tense, it here slips into the past. The same time shift is evident at the end of Act Three as well.

medicines and have exhausted every means of treating him. Still, by nature the prince is an extraordinarily handsome man. Therefore many women have felt envious of his attention to others, and their resentment concentrated upon him and brought things to the point where medicine cannot help him. Finally he went blind in both eyes. For him,
>The sun and moon in heaven have no light
>In black of night his lamp is dark.[48]

In his blindness he is beyond our powers.

NARRATOR: Speaking together the two of them report to the emperor. Suddenly the emperor's appearance changes. Shedding tears, he speaks.

EMPEROR: Truly, since he was born a prince, my fourth son, he is one who ought to know the state of the ten virtues.[49] And yet, when someone who could see at birth goes blind, the reason for it is his very profound evil in a previous life. It is difficult for anyone with a deformed body to become a Buddha. What is more, even in this life the future is dark and painful for someone who wanders about in the darkness of the blind.

NARRATOR: He breaks down in tears.

EMPEROR: In this life he should confess his shame to everyone. As a way to put an end to this obstacle[50] and to help him in

---

[48] These two lines of poetry are quoted from the Nō *Semimaru*.

[49] The state of the ten virtues refers to the merit to be attained by avoiding committing the ten evils: killing, stealing, adultery, lying, double tongue, coarse language, filthy language, covetousness, anger, and perverted views. (Soothill and Hodous, *Dictionary of Chinese Buddhist Terms*, p. 50.) Avoiding the evils was believed to bring good karma and might allow a man to be born a prince in his next incarnation.

[50] Confession is seen as a means of exonerating him from his evil in a previous incarnation, thus allowing a move upward in the next cycle of rebirth. Elsewhere in the play Semimaru's blindness is attributed to his wife's jealousy rather than to past evils.

his next incarnation, we must abandon him on Mount Ausaka.

NARRATOR: The emperor's words are very moving. The two
courtiers speak as one.

KIYOTSURA and MAREYO: This is the emperor's command. Still,
even a lowly woodsman feels sympathy for a crippled child.
So, compared to such a person, if you abandon a prince of
the realm in the mountain fields, it appears somehow as if
you are lacking in humane feelings.

NARRATOR: They speak in fear and trembling.

EMPEROR: No, no. There is no living creature that does not love
his child. And what is more, as his father I feel that I would
like to take his place. Still, because of his evil deeds in his
previous life, he must leave the ranks of the court. I shall
make this an example for all of my subjects and lead the
many people of my realm into the Way of Buddha. Isn't this
great compassion on my part? My sympathy for my child is
inexhaustible, but since I am the one who must nurture the
people of this country, it is difficult for me to make my son
more important than all my people. Certainly, for you two to
take the least pity on him would, on the contrary, do him
harm. You should abandon him in the mountains quickly.
What an unpredictable world! What a miserable life!

NARRATOR: He bows his head and breaks down in tears, and
all the people at the court must wring their sleeves. The
courtiers Kiyotsura and Mareyo withdraw helplessly. In life
we never know what will come next.

SCENE 2: Semimaru's Journey to Ausaka

NARRATOR: The gods who bind together lovers,[51]
             The creators, do even they deceive us?

[51]*Musubu no kami*, originally considered creator spirits, the *musubi*
or *musubu no kami* came to have a secondary, more specialized meaning as spirits who are responsible for the attraction between lovers.

233

One day a bond between them was begun[52]
Yet now it disappears—a dream
At midnight in sleep's first moments.
Even the ties between them were fragile,
Thin as his own robes of silk.
How pitiful he is—Prince Semimaru
Who brought him the reward of darkness,
Darkness in the world and in his love?[53]
Out of the dark they lead an ox[54]
Which once had drawn the royal cart
And now the wheel has turned.
Today the oxcart is disguised
In rough ropes, for a common pasture beast
As company he has a lute, called *Genjo*.[55]
With Kiyotsura and Mareyo
He sets forth dispiritedly
His appearance so pathetic!

KIYOTSURA: As we lament, our tears obscure the moon.
Although we pass Higashiyama
In his blindness he sees no glimmer.
We cross the waves at the shore of the Kamo
River of the waterfowl[56]
And at Matsuzaka he thinks

[52] A reference to Semimaru's love for Naohime, this sets the stage
for their reunion at Ausaka.

[53] Though it does not ascribe a specific source, *Kessaku* notes this
line as coming from a popular song of Chikamatsu's day.

[54] This line is based on a proverb. *Kuragari kara ushi o hikidasu* "to
lead an ox out of darkness" used to indicate a situation of utter confusion. The image is one of a black ox. The pattern of his hide cannot
be seen any better in bright light than in darkness.

[55] A famous lute, traditionally associated with Hakuga no Sammi,
who later appears as Semimaru's musical disciple.

[56] *Mizudori* "waterfowl" is a pivot word continuing from *hikari no
mizu* "sees no glimmer."

"If my ties to her are ended
I wish that I could die now
Here at Awataguchi."[57]

NARRATOR: On the mountains, where autumn is still
    young,
The first red maple leaves are stealing in.
They are weaving a brocade robe
But whom would they have wear it?
At times the flowers and birds, the wind and
    moon
Are his diversions, yet at other times
The scene brings him a sense of sadness:
A mountain where, like him, the flowers have
    fallen,
The faint and distant sound of a bell striking.
Hurrying toward their evening resting place,
And longing for their mates—two or three
    crows,
Now become four, now five,

KIYOTSURA Five of them, like a verse of characters
and And here on Poem Mountain[58] is the Seiganji
MAREYO: The hedge around the shrine is ancient
And there—behind the mountain to our left—
The mausoleum of the emperor.[59]

NARRATOR: They take his hand and point out the direction to
him, but the prince says nothing.

SEMIMARU: I am descended from the emperor's line

[57] That is, disappear like foam, the *awa* of Awataguchi. There was a
crematorium at Awataguchi.

[58] The Seiganji is in the southeast sector of Kyoto. *Uta no naka
yama*—which I have translated as "Poem Mountain"—is behind the
Seiganji and is introduced here merely because it links with the preceding line—"a verse of characters [in a poem]."

[59] Emperor Tenchi, r. 668–71.

And I have scooped the flowing dew
Of the poetry with which he blessed his
   people,
Yet see how miserably my life is ending!

NARRATOR: As he holds back his tears, Kiyotsura and Mareyo
are disheartened. Even the unfeeling ox droops his tail and
lowers his horns, seeming to shed tears. The plants, too,
show signs of sad sympathy.

SEMIMARU:[60] In autumn fields the wind blows through
            Huts[61] among the harvested grain
            Disturbing the peasants sleeping
            Pillowed on their arms.
            They dry their hair and dry their clothes,
            Harvesting the rice, they dry it too
            But my sleeves have no time to dry.
            Do not cry, you frogs by the marsh edge,[62]
            You cannot know such thoughts as mine.

KIYOTSURA   Under a thicket of mingled bamboos
and   Are young grasses of the spring,
MAREYO: Different bamboo grasses.[63]
            On your sleeves as you pass through
            Wear a straw raincoat, also a straw rainhat.

SEMIMARU: My falling tears are heavier than rain.

[60] I am following my own intuition in ascribing the sections of the
remaining part of the michiyuki to the various speakers. It seems
most effective this way, though it may be, as marked in the CMS edition, that all lines from here to the end of the michiyuki should be
ascribed to the narrator.

[61] Here I follow *Kessaku* and *Zenshu,* both of which interpret the text
as *waraya* "straw hut." CMS has *hara ya* "fields [exclamatory]."

[62] *Naiso-naiso.* This rather odd negative, which means "do not cry"
and links with the preceding line *kawaku ma mo nai* "have no time to
dry," may have been part of a popular song of Chikamatsu's day.

[63] The path of discretion apparently lies in not translating the
names of the grasses, since they include such impossible English poetic images as "giant knotweed" (*saitazuma*).

Are we not in a rainstorm?
The leaves upon these many trees
Are fragile, brittle, crackling in the wind.[64]
At Moroha shrine[65] I pray
Today will be my last visit.

NARRATOR: Travelers move to and from the capital
Even tonight each one is thinking
"With whom shall I pass the night tonight?"
When they see Mount Fushimi,[66] there in the
darkness
It calls to mind again whisperings of love.

SEMIMARU: No matter how I hurry it
My lazy-going ox will pull
The jewel-decked royal carriage slowly[67]
But my heart, like a wild horse,
A thousand times this day goes rushing
Off in thoughts of the one I love
Rushing like the waters at Hashiri-i.[68]
The teeth of my water-dipped comb are fine.[69]
When will I, as I wish, bind smooth
The tangled creepers of my black hair?[70]
Now here we have arrived at Mount Ausaka.

[64]This represents a line of onomatopoetic syllables in the Japanese.

[65]At Shinomiya-kawara. They have very nearly reached Ausaka. *Moroha* means "fragile leaves."

[66]The place name Fushimi is a pivot word linking with *tare to fushi* "lying down with whom."

[67]In fact, of course, Semimaru is now in a rough oxcart. Tamaboko is a pillow word for "road"; usually written with characters meaning "precious spear," it is then a poetic image for a straight journey.

[68]*Hashiri-i* means "running well."

[69]This line appears because of the word play on *mizugushi* "water comb," which links with the "waters" of Hashiri-i in the preceding line, and with the image of binding hair which follows.

[70]*Sanekazura* (or *sanakazura*) "tangled creepers" is a *utamakura* for "meet" (*au*) and is here linked to the place name Ausaka.

SCENE 3: At Ausaka

NARRATOR: The two courtiers, Kiyotsura and Mareyo, set the prince down underneath a tree.

KIYOTSURA and MAREYO: We cannot disobey an imperial order. We have attended you this far, but I wonder where we should leave you? Our rulers have been wise kings, ever since the days of Yao and Shun,[71] so how can it be that the emperor now gives an order to abandon his own child?

NARRATOR: They speak in tears. Semimaru listens to them and answers.

SEMIMARU: How foolish you are! In a previous life I failed in following the teachings, and that is the reason I have gone blind. It appears to you that my father the emperor lacks compassion, but he has a plan to aid me in my next existence, to help me escape my bad karma in this life. This is real parental love. Leave me and go back!

NARRATOR: When he says this the two weep ever harder.

KIYOTSURA and MAREYO:
Such splendid clothes will summon thieves, I fear[72]
Allow me to take your robe and give you instead
This cloak of straw they call a *mino*.

SEMIMARU: Is this the *mino* mentioned in the lines
"I went to Tamino island when it rained?"

KIYOTSURA: Yes, and I will give you this *kasa* rainhat which will also protect you from the rain and dew.

SEMIMARU: Then this must be the *kasa* of the poem
"Samurai—take a *kasa* for your lord."

KIYOTSURA: And this staff will guide you on your way.

SEMIMARU: Is this the staff about which Henjō wrote
"Since my staff was fashioned by the gods

[71] Legendary prehistoric sage kings of China.
[72] The poetry describing the raincoat, rainhat, and staff is quoted from the Nō *Semimaru*.

238

I can cross the mountain of a thousand years"?[73]

KIYOTSURA: That was the staff of a thousand years' prosperity
But here you are at Mount Ausaka
In a hut of straw with bamboo pillars
You meet your uncertain fate.
Oh you who know him,
And you who know him not,
Behold! The life of the prince
Daigo's son, has come to this.

What can all this indicate?

NARRATOR: Raising their voices, they both weep. Since it is the emperor's command, the others, in tears, force themselves to leave him and return to the capital. The prince remains behind all alone; holding his lute and leaning on his bamboo staff, he breaks down, collapses. "Good-by," "Good-by," he can only hear their voices. He takes the sounds of the tree and mountain echoes[74] to be the others' voices calling out in parting, and parting the grasses he enters into a mountain path.

It is the night when the moon tree bears its fruit,[75] the night of the famous full moon of the eighth month, at Ausaka, at the spot known as Pure Water by the barrier, one of the most famous streams in Omi province. Just now some

[73] The original sources of these poems are cited in the notes to the translation of the Nō *Semimaru*.

[74] The terms here translated as "tree and mountain echoes" are *kodama* "tree spirit" and *yamabiko* "mountain lad." Though their contemporary meaning is "echo" and they likely were understood as such by Chikamatsu's time, their etymological, literal meanings were presumably not far from conscious awareness.

[75] A Chinese folk belief, adopted in Japan, holds that a *katsura* (*Cercidiphyllum japonicum*) tree grows on the moon and that the brightness of the full moon comes from the tree's bearing fruit.

239

temple boys from the barrier temple have come out to the source waters of the stream, clear in the autumn moonlight.

TEMPLE BOYS: Here's the bucket for water offerings to Buddha. There's a cord of dew jewels on the ladle, let's scoop up the moon!

NARRATOR: Now a young woman comes running out from the shadows of the willow trees. She gathers up stones and tucks them in her hem, and calling out "Praise the Name of Buddha," she is just about to throw herself into the water. The temple boys restrain her.

TEMPLE BOYS: It's unthinkable to throw away your life here in the most sacred waters of a holy place.[76]

WOMAN (NAOHIME): No—No, I can live no longer! Have mercy, please, ignore me and let me die!

NARRATOR: She tears free from their grasp.

TEMPLE BOYS: There must be reasons for you to be so depressed. Whatever the reasons, in any case, calm down and then tell us about it. Calm yourself, be calm.

NARRATOR: When they say this the woman's face blushes deeply.

NAOHIME: I am embarrassed to tell you, but I am the mistress of Prince Semimaru who has been abandoned on this mountain. My name is Naohime. I longed to know where he had gone and wandered out this far, but I am not sure where he is. When I asked people about him they said that he is ashamed of his deformity and has gone deep into the mountains, absolutely refusing to show his face to others. They don't even know now whether he is alive or dead. When I

---

[76]CMS has *hōjō* "sacred place" or site of a monastery. All other printed editions have *hōshō*, the action of releasing living animals to freedom as a means of attaining merit. This often involves the freeing of small caged birds, or, as might be expected here, releasing small fish into a stream. Since *hōjō* fits the context better I have chosen to follow this interpretation.

heard that, I gave up all hope in this unpredictable life. I want to make of this river the river of death. I will hurry to meet him in the afterlife. Quickly, let me die!

NARRATOR: Again she breaks down and weeps. After hearing her story the temple boys answer.

TEMPLE BOYS: What a sad tale! We are only boys from the temple at the barrier, but from our wanderings in meditation in the mountains we happen to know where he is. Let us show you from a distance. But, if he hears the sounds of people, he will run and hide himself. You absolutely must not speak! If you want just to see him, let's go. We'll show you!

NARRATOR: They wear their rainhats in the evening rains. There on the mountain path their tears, and the rain as well, are falling intermingled.

SEMIMARU: The first string and the second wildly sound [77]
The autumn wind brushes the pines and falls
With broken notes; the third string and the fourth
The fourth is myself, Semimaru
And four are the strings of the lute I play
As sudden strings of rain drive down upon me.

NARRATOR: He cannot see before his eyes
The foam of the rushing river
Nor understand the logic of this life,
So like that water foam.
Unable to judge if yet the moon has set
He has no means to tell the night from day.
He hears the owls and cuckoos in the valley,
The flying squirrels that flit from branch to branch

[77]The lines attributed to Semimaru here are from the Nō *Semimaru*.

241

For what are they grieving—those crying mon-
keys?
On his robe of fallen leaves [78] the dew lies
heavy
His shoulders are too thin and weak
To carry even the light of the moon.
Sad, these changes brought him by time's
passing.
The sun as it sets off to the west
Now seems an old friend from the capital.
Like hands that beckon to him,
The storms from that direction make him
homesick.
As he plays his lute in the bone-chilling wind
He cannot forget his past—a vanished dream
Even the call of a lovesick deer
Sounds painful to his ears.
Vines coil about the spindle trees. [79]
He does not realize that anyone has come,
But pushes aside the mountain pines and oaks
And using his staff to guide him
He shambles along unsteadily
Following the path on the mountainside.

NARRATOR: The minute she sees him, Naohime speaks.

NAOHIME: Is this the man I love? How miserable he looks!

NARRATOR: She is just about to throw her arms around him
when the temple boys push her back.

TEMPLE BOYS: Oh—you're making loud noises. He'll hide himself if he hears the sound of people, so you must not say
anything. As we told you before, don't make any noise.

---

[78] This can refer either to a pattern dyed on a robe or to a pattern
of shifting light shining on the robe through tree branches.

[79] This line is introduced because of the pivot word *kuru* "to coil"
which links with *kuru hito* "people who come."

Chikamatsu's *Semimaru*

NARRATOR: When they say this Naohime's eyes cloud over with tears of frustration.

NAOHIME: Is my love a reflection in a mirror?
We meet and yet we cannot speak.
Can he not sense my love, unspoken,
The scent and color of gardenias, [80]
Does he not know me? Oh, my misery!

NARRATOR: Without raising her voice she whispers these words and is choked with tears.

NARRATOR: Not even aware that she is there, the prince takes up his white-stringed [81] lute and changes its tuning.

SEMIMARU:

Wait, oh wait,
Wild geese of heaven
Bring me word
How is the autumn
In my home town? [82]
Deep in the mountains
I live in loneliness
I have no friends
Beside my lute.

[80]*Kuchinashi no iroka. Kuchinashi* means either "gardenia" or "no mouth," which I take to mean "unspoken." The line then means both "the scent and color of gardenias" and "unspoken love" because *iro* can mean either "color" or "love."

[81]*Shiraito* "white-stringed" pivots from *shira* [*naide*] "not knowing."

[82]This poem is similar to one attributed to Mikuni no Machi in the *Kokinshū*, no. 152.

Yayo ya mate	Wait, oh wait
Yama hototogisu	Mountain cuckoo,
Kotozuten	Carry the message:
Waga yo no naka ni	I have grown weary
Sumiwabinu to yo	Of living in this world.

243

NARRATOR: When he takes up the plectrum, the autumn rain suddenly begins to fall. This is the wind-borne rain called "late red maple leaves." Semimaru is concerned lest his lute get wet, and he recites a few lines.

SEMIMARU: Beneath this tree
                    Or in the shadow of that one
                    Though I get wet,
                    I shall sleep here.[83]

NARRATOR: That is a poem about enjoying oneself among the flowers.

SEMIMARU: I, too, am a humble man, a lowly man. I wear rough straw sleeves as protection from the rain. In these sudden showers of early autumn the leaves of the trees are tossed about.

NARRATOR: He runs about this way and that, his robes soaked by the rain.[84] Because he is not underneath the trees, the rain is unbearable. Watching him even hurts the others' eyes. From behind a low rock hill one of the temple boys thrusts out his rain hat to protect the prince. The prince strains his ears.

SEMIMARU: It's odd. Although the rain is falling, it is not wetting me. I must be underneath a tree. How painful this is! In days gone by wherever I stayed, for even a single night, my bed was laid with brocade quilts and mats. The walls were hung with rose of Sharon, and on the doors were strings of

---

[83] Semimaru's poem alludes to an anonymous poem in the *Shūi-shū*, no. 50, as follows:

Sakuragari	When cherry-viewing
Ame wa furi kinu	What difference if it rains.
Onajiku wa	Even if I want to sleep
Neru to mo hana no	I'll hide myself under the flowers.
Kage ni kakuremu	

[84] Here again there is a string of onomatopoetic syllables.

crystal quartz. Then I was bothered even by the wind which seeped into my magnificent robes inside my royal palanquin.[85] And yet my world has changed so much that now my bed is this lowly moss-covered ground, a quilt that I cannot really spread. If I could only spread my robes in sleep with the woman I love, even my imposing palace would seem of no importance. But Naohime does not know this: how sad her life must be! Oh the love we knew in the past! My beloved Naohime!

NARRATOR: In his pathetic blindness he does not know that she is beside him. Believing himself all alone, he laments loudly.

Now Naohime is unable to bear all she has seen and loses her resolve. She is about to say, "Naohime is here!" when the temple boys stop her saying, "Wait!" She loses her senses, collapses, and faints in anguish. It is an impossible situation for an ordinary mortal.

After a little while Semimaru roughly casts aside his lute and plectrum.

SEMIMARU: Good heavens![86] I have let myself think about unsuitable things! Meeting is the beginning of parting. There is no way for me alone to stay. Colors and scents last only briefly. Ah, I must not think of her. I must not grieve for her.

NARRATOR: In a single poem he captures all these thoughts.

SEMIMARU: This, now this,
            Where people come and people go
            Exchanging farewells
            For friends and strangers alike
            This is Meeting Barrier.

---

[85] The passage beginning "In days gone by . . ." is based on the nō *Sekidera Komachi*. See translation by Karen Brazell in Keene, *Twenty Plays*, p. 79, n. 20, for a discussion of the Nō play's source.

[86] Literally "Praise the Three Treasures."

> They part in the morning
> And meet in the evening
> At Mount Ausaka the travelers' journeys
> Are only the delusions of dreams
> If the rain will fall—let it fall!
> If the wind will blow—let it blow![87]

Deep in the mountains is a fine place to live. Yes, now I am coming to understand the impermanence of life.

NARRATOR: He is about to run off, whereupon the others come rushing out from the mountainside and take hold of him, crying out, "Here is Naohime!" The prince says only, "What!" They hold each other's hands and sleeves and speak together of their love and longings. Their tears are endless. When they understand the lovers' feelings, the temple boys speak as one.

TEMPLE BOYS: Well, Semimaru, you were guided by passion and fettered by your thoughts of love you sank into self-pity. You led a great many woman astray, and the haze of karma clouded your eyes until you became blind, and yet, that poem of enlightenment you composed just now is wonderful. In thirty-one syllables you showed, on the surface, the appearance of travelers, and beneath the surface you showed the principle that all who meet must part, as well as the distress of parting from those we love. You demonstrated how meeting is the beginning of parting. In one poem you revealed the three lives.[88] The gods have softened in their feelings toward you, and you have realized the teachings of Buddha.

The sound of the bells from the temple at the Ausaka Barrier awakens you from your dream of worldly passions. The

---

[87] Several commentators cite a poem by the Zen priest Ikkyū as the source of these lines, but none gives the location of Ikkyū's poem.

[88] Past, present, and future.

246

voice of the Law sounds quietly.[89] When they strike the bell of the evening watch, it echoes the message of the impermanence of all things in this world. When they strike the midnight bell, it echoes the truth that all who are born will die. The echo of the bell of early morning is, "All living things are utterly extinguished." And the bell of evening echoes that Nirvana brings happiness.

The Way to Buddhahood is not dark. The midnight of enlightenment leads to bright dawn. Though both your eyes are dark, the moon of your heart is bright. (*First boy*) I am Hitomaro. (*Second boy*) And I, Akahito. To teach the essence of poetry, our two spirits have manifested themselves. With us you will achieve deliverance to Buddhahood and will be reborn in joy in the Tuṣita heaven.[90]

NARRATOR: Only voices—when he hears them speak, the sound mingles with the noise of the storm in the cedars on Mount Ausaka and disappears. Semimaru sighs.

SEMIMARU: This land of the rising sun is the country of the gods. Through poetry we know the way of the gods. The spirits of the sages of poetry revealed themselves and exchanged words with me. This favor shows that divine providence has not yet abandoned me.

NARRATOR: He speaks as tears of gratitude soak his sleeves.

SEMIMARU: And my meeting with Naohime was also a fate dictated by the gods.

NARRATOR: Each of them gropes along the way wondering if it

---

[89] The passage from "The voice of the Law" through "The Way to Buddhahood" is taken from the Nō play *Miidera*. The four phrases of the bells are found in the Nirvana Sutra. They are the four bells of the Jetvana garden, best known in Japan from the opening lines of *Heike monogatari*.

[90] Tuṣita is the heaven where all Bodhisattvas are reborn pending their final reincarnation as Buddhas. It is the abode of the Buddha of the Future, Maitreya.

is all a dream. A profound example of the way of devotion through poetry, they return together into the mountain path. The couple are miraculously reunited, and his fame as the poet of Mount Ausaka has remained until this day.

ACT FOUR

SCENE 1: At Mount Ausaka

NARRATOR: It has become difficult for Hayahiro to live in the capital because he killed the monk Senju, so he has been wandering about in the far provinces.

HAYAHIRO: In any case my enemy is Semimaru. I shall certainly get my revenge.

NARRATOR: He has taken on a pair of low class fellows as his followers, and they are searching very hard through the peaks and valleys around Mount Ausaka, parting the grasses. But they can't find where the prince has gone. Behind them are Oseki and Fujino-o. You can grow accustomed to the life of even such mountain villages. Here some countryfolk are calling out to each other.

RUSTIC: Say, I've picked up an odd thing to find at Mount Ausaka. Well, what can it be? Come, take a guess!

NARRATOR: He holds up a lute plectrum. The countryfolk gather around.

FIRST RUSTIC: It's shaped like the leaf of a gingko tree. I don't understand it. Is it a monkey's fan?

SECOND RUSTIC: No, no, it must be a demon's hairpin.[91]

NARRATOR: Each of them takes a look and laughs. Just at this point a young woodcutter, over by a small hill, sees them.

WOODCUTTER: Say there, you, that is the lute plectrum of Semimaru who was abandoned here on this mountain. Don't

---

[91] "Monkey's fan" and "demon's hairpin" are each the name of a variety of fungus.

handle it carelessly like something unimportant! Give it to me!

RUSTICS: And then what will you do with it? It all depends.

NARRATOR: The woodcutter interrupts them.

WOODCUTTER: I am a woodcutter, a servant called Kitōda, and I work for Hakuga no Sammi who is living a life of retirement from society in the village of Shiga. My master is Semimaru's disciple at playing the lute, and because of this relationship, lately Semimaru and his wife have been staying at my master's house. Please give it to me; I want to give it to him.

RUSTICS: Is that so? Well, for us to keep it would be useless and irreverent.

NARRATOR: They give it to Kitōda and they all leave. Hayahiro listens carefully and winks at his cronies. They surround Kitōda on all four sides and take him prisoner.

HAYAHIRO: So Semimaru is at the house of your master Sammi, eh? Well, lead the way and take us there! If you refuse we'll stamp you to death.

NARRATOR: Hayahiro speaks threateningly. Kitōda is taken by surprise but nods.

KITŌDA: Yes, I understand. Your blackguards are robbers. Would I lead robbers to my master's house just because they made frightening faces at me? Don't insult me with such a low opinion. I'm not a man who'll do just anything. Get out of here before you get hurt!

NARRATOR: He speaks angrily. Hayahiro too becomes angry.

HAYAHIRO: Pull him up and make him lead the way!

NARRATOR: "Yes, sir!" say his followers, but when they fly upon Kitōda, he throws them off. When they take hold of him Kitōda kicks them down. He picks up his pole and beats them. Hayahiro draws his sword and strikes two or three times, but the country youth is accustomed to mountain paths. Cliff or valley, it makes no difference to him. He runs about, even more light-footed than a monkey, and Hayahiro himself can't do a thing about it. Tumbling and falling he flees. Thinking, "Well, that's that," Kitōda goes back to where he had been before.

KITŌDA: I had to work up a sweat over those worthless fellows!

NARRATOR: He sticks his pole into his brushwood pile and carries it on his shoulders. Humming a little tune to himself, he returns to the village of Shiga.

SCENE 2: At Hakuga's Cottage

NARRATOR: Although he had been following an imperial order, Kiyotsura, who had served the prince ever since his infancy, has come to feel miserable about living on in the world after abandoning the prince in the wilderness. Disguising himself in the black robes of a priest, he travels from province to province performing Buddhist exercises and prayers. But his native place is hard for him to forget. "How is the prince faring, oh you waves which ebb in at the capital?"[92] he wonders, and arrives at the beach at Shiga.

In the past this place had been the capital, and in a village full of falling flowers there is a hut which has an air of significance about it. It is surrounded by hedges and a cypress lattice fence. He goes inside and looks around, but finds the owner isn't there. The incense and flower offerings are scant; the sacred sutras are aged and in bad repair, and the Buddha statue looks old-fashioned. What kind of hermit's

[92]This is an allusion to the following anonymous poem from the *Senzaishū*, no. 66.

Sazanami yo	Waves lap ashore
Shiga no miyako no	At the ruined capital of Shiga
Are ni shi o	Only the mountain cherries
Mukashi nagara no	Are yet as in the past.
Yamazakura kana	

house can this be? Anyone unable to bear the everyday world would surely like to live this way.

While waiting for the priest's return, Kiyotsura thinks, "I'd like to go on after staying and talking for one night." And he settles down on the veranda and waits. Now, from below the Buddha shrine he hears a woman's voice say, "Hello." Very startled he goes to look and stealthily opens the door of the shrine. A snow-white hand reaches out. The woman speaks.

WOMAN (NAOHIME): Please give me some water.

NARRATOR: Kiyotsura, who is a devout follower of Buddha, thinks, "This must be a changeling!"[93] and his knees are shaking hard. "How terrible," he thinks, "it must be a spirit which has been wandering through the hell of hunger." Considering it the duty of a priest, he puts some water into a bowl and hands it in to her.

KIYOTSURA: May your sufferings on the three paths[94] be ended. Praise Amida Buddha!"

NARRATOR: He pulls his hand back again very quickly, but then he gingerly approaches again and peers at her—Holy Hachiman! She is an attractive woman!

KIYOTSURA: Well—so you are the priest's wife! Dear Lord, what shrewd goings-on there are in this world. I don't know who he is, but some pleasure-loving monk lives in this hut and, of all places, has affairs with a woman under the Buddha shrine!

NARRATOR: Thinking this over he finds it funny and laughs to himself. Then she speaks again.

[93]*Keshō*, the term used here, can mean either one born metamorphically, such as a god or Bodhisattva, or secondarily, a ghost or frighteningly supernatural being.

[94]"Three paths" refer to the three possible types of torment facing the dead.

WOMAN (NAOHIME): How good it is, please give me some more.

NARRATOR: She puts her hand out again. Now Kiyotsura feels more lighthearted.

KIYOTSURA: A real priest's wife! Let me have a look at you!

NARRATOR: He takes hold of her hand and pulls her out. When he looks carefully he finds that it is Naohime.

NAOHIME: What! Are you Kiyotsura?

KIYOTSURA: My Lady? Naohime?

NARRATOR: Both clap their hands in amazement, but some doubt still lingers in Kiyotsura's mind.

KIYOTSURA: What are you doing here?

NARRATOR: When he asks Naohime answers.

NAOHIME: Well—this place is Hakuga no Sammi's. Since he is the prince's disciple in lute playing, we have been hiding out here together.

NARRATOR: At this explanation Kiyotsura is delighted.

KIYOTSURA: Where is the prince? I want so much to see him!

NAOHIME: In accordance with his vow to enter the priesthood the prince makes daily pilgrimages to the Sannō shrine at Sakamoto.[95] Today Hakuga went with him to visit the shrine. They will be back soon.

NARRATOR: As she is saying this Kitōda returns. He looks intently at Kiyotsura.

KITŌDA: Is he one of those thieves too? Watch out!

NARRATOR: He changes his grip on his sickle, but Naohime, seeing this cries out.

NAOHIME: Kitōda! He is the prince's childhood retainer, Kiyotsura. Have you lost your senses?

KITŌDA: Oh, is that so? I beg your pardon, beg pardon. You see, it's because I just ran into some robbers on the mountain, that's why I did this.

---

[95] A Shinto shrine, now called Hiyoshi jinja, at the Eastern base of Mount Hiei.

NARRATOR: He explains the details of what has happened. Kiyotsura listens carefully to everything he says.

KIYOTSURA: No, those weren't robbers! I'm sure it's Hayahiro. Surely he's coming to attack here with his mob of men. We will be sorry if trouble comes and we have a weak-footed, long-sleeved woman with us here in this house with its one flimsy fence. You should go and take the lady with you. You should go to Sannō, meet the prince along the way, and take him up to the capital. Go, Kitōda, and take her hand. Quickly! Before it gets dark, go!

NARRATOR: So he says, and they hurry all the way to Sakamoto following along the beach of Lake Nio[96] where the evening waves lap.

Now, since his father the monk was killed by Hayahiro, Tadamitsu also has but one thought constantly on his mind. With his aged mother slung over his shoulder, day and night he prowls through the mountain forests following after Hayahiro. His one ambition is to cut down his father's murderer Hayahiro with a slash of his great sword. His goal is understandable.

Just at this time he spies out Hayahiro at the village of Shiga.

TADAMITSU: Now the time has come to test my fate. A gift from heaven! How fine!

NARRATOR: He speaks impetuously, but then he sees that his enemy is coming surrounded by a great crowd of men.

TADAMITSU: Where shall I leave my old mother? Ah, here's a hermit's cottage. This will do. Excuse me!

NARRATOR: He calls out a quick greeting and goes right inside. He pushes open the door on the lower pedestal of the Buddha shrine and hides his mother inside.

TADAMITSU: Now I needn't worry about her. Now I can fight with all my strength and with all the might of my sword!

[96]This is another name for Lake Biwa.

253

NARRATOR: As he is putting on his armor, Hayahiro arrives with six men.

HAYAHIRO: This must be the hut of Hakuga no Sammi. Let's smash it in and capture them!

NARRATOR: Such are the words he speaks. Crying out, "Me first," the men rush in in confusion. Tadamitsu stands and blocks the doorway.

TADAMITSU: Have you forgotten what Tadamitsu looks like? For you to come to me this way is like a gift from the gods. I'm glad you've come. You're my father's murderer, remember?

NARRATOR: He strikes with singleminded fury, and the first man struck falls. In terror they draw back and when they pause he strikes against them. The enemy returns again, and again he cuts them down. He attacks over and over until he is out of breath. He runs after the fleeing enemy and chases them all the way to Awazu-ga-hara.

Not knowing about this, Hakuga no Sammi, with Semimaru, comes back from the pilgrimage along a road through the rice fields at the foot of the mountain. They had failed to cross paths with Kiyotsura and now return to Hakuga's cottage.

SEMIMARU: Your loyalty to me because of our bond as teacher and pupil has been very deep.

NARRATOR: When Semimaru says this, Hakuga answers.

HAKUGA NO SAMMI: To go on this kind of pilgrimage has been my lifelong wish. Well, Naohime surely must be quite depressed in her loneliness.

NARRATOR: As he speaks he opens the door of the shrine and pulls her out by the hand.

HAKUGA: What's this!

NARRATOR: An old woman of more than seventy years, her snow-white hair done up in a triple bun,[97] emerges, weak

[97] The hair style in question, called *mitsuwa mage,* was typical of mature or elderly women in the Edo period. It involved dividing the

with age. Hakuga jumps back in amazement and the prince too is frightened.

SEMIMARU: What has happened? I am worried!

HAKUGA: Oh! The Lady Naohime has suddenly turned into a white-haired grandmother. To grow old in such a short time—I just don't understand it! Look!

NARRATOR: He takes hold of Semimaru's hand; when Semimaru rubs her hand, the bones are rough, the skin wrinkled with the waves of old age. She is thin and old and her skin has no color or luster. The prince is dumbfounded, and Hakuga is all the more perplexed.

HAKUGA: This morning when we left the cottage, I'm sure it was the Lady Naohime whom I put in here—I think. But was I mistaken? I just don't know!

NARRATOR: As he speaks he wrinkles his eyebrows in a worried expression. How terrible it is! Semimaru is shedding a stream of tears.

SEMIMARU: Even though I became blind, I was happy because of this woman. But now my feelings of tenderness and love have disappeared. Is this the work of the devil?[98] Is it a divine punishment?

NARRATOR: His grief is surely understandable. When the old woman remembers his voice and recognizes his face she speaks.

TADAMITSU'S MOTHER: Oh, my prince? My beloved, how I wanted to see you!

NARRATOR: She takes hold of him.

SEMIMARU: Stop it! Let me go! Let me go!

hair into three rolled portions, one rolled behind each ear, the third at the back of the crown of the head. Here the *mitsu* of *mitsuwa* is a pivot word with *yuki no mitsu* "looked like snow."

[98]Temma, from Sanskrit *Deva Māra*, also called Ma-ō, the lord of the highest heaven in the world of desires, obstructs the devout in their adherence to Buddhist principles. Also called Pāpīyan, "the evil one," he is close to the Christian concept of the Devil.

NARRATOR: He flees to the opposite side, returns and hides himself. One less than one hundred,[99] the white hairs of an aged hag. It is more than he can bear!

TADAMITSU'S MOTHER: Oh, true, true. I didn't say my name and you have probably forgotten me. I am the widow of the monk Senju who was killed by Hayahiro for your sake. I am Tadamitsu's mother.

NARRATOR: She explains what happened previously.

SEMIMARU: Yes, yes, it is she. How amazing! Well, well.

NARRATOR: He claps his hands. All his suspicions are cleared away in a snap, but he still doesn't know where Naohime is.

SEMIMARU: Did our enemies carry her off during that disturbance earlier?

NARRATOR: While he is still feeling so unbearably anxious, Kiyotsura and Kitōda come, bringing Naohime along.

KIYOTSURA: Since we didn't meet the prince, we must have taken the wrong road.

NARRATOR: As he says this, they come back into the hut.

SEMIMARU: Kiyotsura?

KIYOTSURA: My prince?

BOTH: Yes! Yes!

NARRATOR: They all gather together, both laughing and crying. They speak excitedly and loudly about everything to each other. Tadamitsu comes running onto the scene. He has been slightly wounded and is worked up into a sweat. As soon as he sees the others he is startled and delighted and speaks of what has happened.

[99] This is a pun on the shape of the characters for "white" and "100." "White" is written with one stroke less than "100." The woman is very old and her hair is white. The phrase *tsukumogami* also means "pasqueflower," a marine plant which the short, sparse hair of an elderly woman is thought to resemble.

A poem in *Ise Monogatari* is the *locus classicus* of the lines *momotose no / hitotose taranu / tsukumogami* "one less than one hundred, the white hairs." NKBT, IX, 146.

UNISON: Senju! Tadamitsu! We heard the whole story from your mother! But did you kill the enemy?

TADAMITSU: Well, the enemy were many and I had exhausted my strength chasing after them for a long distance, but I fought wholeheartedly. I was worried about my mother, and though I fought, unfortunately, I let them slip away. So then I came back here. How fortunate this is. This way I can entrust my mother to your care and I can go back to hunt the enemy with an unburdened mind. Then I'll be back. Well now, I beg to take my leave.

NARRATOR: Kiyotsura interrupts him.

KIYOTSURA: How fine and heroic! We shall take care of your aged mother. At the palace in Ichijō in the capital is Semimaru's elder sister, the princess Sakagami. We shall take your mother and go there secretly with the prince.

Here, these are the priest's robes I was using. Since I have chanced to run across you, it seems they are robes of good fortune.[100] I will give them to you. Disguise yourself as a monk, draw close to your target, achieve your objective, and return happily to the capital!

NARRATOR: They each offer prayers of departure for him.

TADAMITSU: Oh, I am grateful, thank you. I will take these robes and disguise my body in black, but my heart alone will remain undyed. I shall carry the sharp sword of Amida Buddha.[101] Even supposing the enemy should sprout wings, should flit across the branches and pass through the waves, fly off to Silla, Paekche, Koguryo,[102] China, or even India—

[100]There is a pun here in the line *medetaki mie nari* which means both "they seem auspicious" and "it is an auspicious *mie* [three-layered] priest's garment."

[101]Though here Tadamitsu speaks of using a real sword, *Amida no riken* generally refers to the saving power of the name of Amida. Invocation of Amida's name has the power of a sharp sword.

[102]That is, modern Korea, which was comprised of these three ancient kingdoms.

257

even if they should leave heaven and earth, still I would per-
severe for five years, or even ten. Even after my own death,
my single-minded spirit would remain and achieve my great
desire. Happily I shall return to see the smiling face of my
mother.

TADAMITSU'S MOTHER: I too want to see your smiling face
again.

TADAMITSU: Farewell, my lord. Good-by, mother. I ask all of
you to take good care of my aged mother.

NARRATOR: "Good-by!" "Good-by!" they all call out as he
leaves.

Like the finest flowers, the cherries at Yoshino, he is the
finest sort of man, a warrior.[103] His praises rise like perfume
to the clouds.

ACT FIVE

SCENE 1: At the Shirakawa River Crossing

TADAMITSU: In any case, this world is only a temporary dwelling.[104] Even if I lie beneath a single umbrella, it is enough
hut to hide my body. Wearing black sleeves and a black-
dyed hood, I carry in my bag a number of sutras and commentaries as I go searching after my father's murderer.
Though I may be led astray by my wrath, I lead the people
on the six paths.[105] My cross-roads sermons are praiseworthy.[106]

Truly it is dreadful, it is sad. Throughout their lives the

[103] This is a popular proverb meaning the *best* of anything.

[104] The opening lines of the act are an allusion to the poem found in
Konjaku Monogatari and the Nō *Semimaru*.

[105] The six states of sentient existence through which the souls of
living beings transmigrate: hell, the realm of hungry spirits, animals,
asuras, men, and heavenly beings.

[106] *Tsujidangi* "cross-roads sermon" links with *rikudō no tsuji*
"crossings of the six paths." The lines that follow, down to "There
can be no doubt about this," are the content of Tadamitsu's sermon.

people of today become ever more evil. They wander astray in the filth of passions. In the morning they are angry and in the evening, happy. Misled by the emotions of desire, anger, stupidity, and laziness, they do not know, even for a moment, the teachings of the Buddha. How foolish they are.

It is said: wife, children, and treasures, even kingly rank, none of these can be taken along at the hour of death. In this life people build up a mountain of treasure. Waited upon by their children, grandchildren, and servants, they sing poems among the flowers and declaim them loudly in the moonlight. They carry unsurpassed glory to the extreme, yet, in the storm that cuts off the breath at the moment of death, the fire chariot[107] of greed and selfishness thunders in the clouds born of their worldly evils. When it comes to call for them, their accustomed lackeys do not follow them; they are not clad in their robes of gold and silver; and their headlong plunge into unending hell is faster than the flight of a three-feathered arrow.

Wealth has been likened to a gift to hell, and fame has been compared to kindling for a hell of fire. You may say that each of us will attain enlightenment, no matter what we do, yet in the precious words of the Lotus Sutra: The Buddha Daitsūchishō[108] sat for ten kalpas on the platform of enlightenment,[109] but the Buddha teachings were not yet manifest to him, he did not yet attain enlightenment.

[107]The fire chariot is a chariot of flames in which the tormenting devils carry off those whose evil causes them, at death, to be taken to hell, the lowest of the six states of sentient beings. In other words, Kiyotsura is admonishing his listeners to mend their ways in this lifetime in order to avoid reincarnation in hell.

[108]Mahābhijña jñānābhibhu, a Buddha described in Chapter 7 of the *Lotus Sutra* as having lived at a time countless eons in the past. His sixteen sons each were reincarnated as later Buddhas, the sixteenth being Shakyamuni.

[109]*Dōjō* or *Bodhimanda,* circle of enlightenment. The place where a Buddha attains enlightenment, the plot under the Bodhi tree of enlightenment.

The sense of this text is that there is no law outside the
heart itself. Outside your own heart you cannot achieve Nirvana. The foolish, ignorant common man searches for Buddha outside his own heart, he searches for the Pure Land
outside this mundane world, but rather, this becomes the
source of his delusions. Putting this more understandably, a
poem by Dengyō Daishi[110] says:

> Enlightenment
> To seek it outside
> Your own heart
> Becomes the beginning
> Of delusion.

Also, in the Tendai commentaries it says: Hokke and
Amida are but different names for the same thing. To say
"Shakyamuni" or "Amida" is the same as saying "eye" or
"eyeball." One Buddha with different names, but the Way
is all the same. Outside the heart no Buddha descends to
earth to receive the believer.

As we sit here, this too can be our place of meditation.
Sleeping or waking, meditate on Buddha. Standing or sitting, meditate on Buddha. In every state—walking, standing, sitting, or lying down—if you recite the Nembutsu
with a settled heart, your self becomes Amida and your
mind the Pure Land. If outside your heart there are no dis-
tinctions, then you attain enlightenment within this very
body. Without even changing your position, you will emit a
nimbus of bright shining light in all ten directions.[111] You
will be seated upon a golden lotus pedestal. In an instant,
suddenly you will be in the Land of Tranquil Nourish-

[110]Saichō (767–822) who introduced the Tendai sect into Japan in
806 and founded the Enryakuji on Mount Hiei.
[111]The eight principal compass directions, plus zenith and na-
dir.

e of this text is that there is no law outside the
Outside your own heart you cannot achieve Nir-
foolish, ignorant common man searches for Bud-
e his own heart, he searches for the Pure Land
s mundane world, but rather, this becomes the
is delusions. Putting this more understandably, a
Dengyō Daishi[110] says:

Enlightenment
To seek it outside
Your own heart
Becomes the beginning
Of delusion.

the Tendai commentaries it says: Hokke and
but different names for the same thing. To say
uni" or "Amida" is the same as saying "eye" or
One Buddha with different names, but the Way
same. Outside the heart no Buddha descends to
ceive the believer.

sit here, this too can be our place of meditation.
or waking, meditate on Buddha. Standing or sit-
itate on Buddha. In every state—walking, stand-
ng, or lying down—if you recite the Nembutsu
ttled heart, your self becomes Amida and your
Pure Land. If outside your heart there are no dis-
then you attain enlightenment within this very
thout even changing your position, you will emit a
f bright shining light in all ten directions.[111] You
eated upon a golden lotus pedestal. In an instant,
you will be in the Land of Tranquil Nourish-

ō (767–822) who introduced the Tendai sect into Japan in
unded the Enryakuji on Mount Hiei.
eight principal compass directions, plus zenith and na-

260

UNISON: Senju! Tadamitsu! We heard the whole story from your mother! But did you kill the enemy?

TADAMITSU: Well, the enemy were many and I had exhausted my strength chasing after them for a long distance, but I fought wholeheartedly. I was worried about my mother, and though I fought, unfortunately, I let them slip away. So then I came back here. How fortunate this is. This way I can entrust my mother to your care and I can go back to hunt the enemy with an unburdened mind. Then I'll be back. Well now, I beg to take my leave.

NARRATOR: Kiyotsura interrupts him.

KIYOTSURA: How fine and heroic! We shall take care of your aged mother. At the palace in Ichijō in the capital is Semimaru's elder sister, the princess Sakagami. We shall take your mother and go there secretly with the prince.

Here, these are the priest's robes I was using. Since I have chanced to run across you, it seems they are robes of good fortune.[100] I will give them to you. Disguise yourself as a monk, draw close to your target, achieve your objective, and return happily to the capital!

NARRATOR: They each offer prayers of departure for him.

TADAMITSU: Oh, I am grateful, thank you. I will take these robes and disguise my body in black, but my heart alone will remain undyed. I shall carry the sharp sword of Amida Buddha.[101] Even supposing the enemy should sprout wings, should flit across the branches and pass through the waves, fly off to Silla, Paekche, Koguryo,[102] China, or even India—

[100]There is a pun here in the line *medetaki mie nari* which means both "they seem auspicious" and "it is an auspicious *mie* [three-layered] priest's garment."

[101]Though here Tadamitsu speaks of using a real sword, *Amida no riken* generally refers to the saving power of the name of Amida. Invocation of Amida's name has the power of a sharp sword.

[102]That is, modern Korea, which was comprised of these three ancient kingdoms.

257

even if they should leave heaven and earth, still I would per-
severe for five years, or even ten. Even after my own death,
my single-minded spirit would remain and achieve my great
desire. Happily I shall return to see the smiling face of my
mother.

TADAMITSU'S MOTHER: I too want to see your smiling face
again.

TADAMITSU: Farewell, my lord. Good-by, mother. I ask all of
you to take good care of my aged mother.

NARRATOR: "Good-by!" "Good-by!" they all call out as he
leaves.

Like the finest flowers, the cherries at Yoshino, he is the
finest sort of man, a warrior.[103] His praises rise like perfume
to the clouds.

ACT FIVE

SCENE 1: At the Shirakawa River Crossing

TADAMITSU: In any case, this world is only a temporary dwelling.[104] Even if I lie beneath a single umbrella, it is enough
hut to hide my body. Wearing black sleeves and a black-
dyed hood, I carry in my bag a number of sutras and commentaries as I go searching after my father's murderer.
Though I may be led astray by my wrath, I lead the people
on the six paths.[105] My cross-roads sermons are praiseworthy.[106]

Truly it is dreadful, it is sad. Throughout their lives the

[103]This is a popular proverb meaning the *best* of anything.

[104]The opening lines of the act are an allusion to the poem found in
Konjaku Monogatari and the Nō *Semimaru*.

[105]The six states of sentient existence through which the souls of
living beings transmigrate: hell, the realm of hungry spirits, animals,
asuras, men, and heavenly beings.

[106]*Tsujidangi* "cross-roads sermon" links with *rikudō no tsuji*
"crossings of the six paths." The lines that follow, down to "There
can be no doubt about this," are the content of Tadamitsu's sermon.

people of today become ev
in the filth of passions. In t
the evening, happy. Mis
anger, stupidity, and lazin
moment, the teachings of tl

It is said: wife, children,
none of these can be taken
life people build up a mour
their children, grandchildre
among the flowers and de
light. They carry unsurpass
the storm that cuts off the
the fire chariot[107] of greed
clouds born of their worldly
them, their accustomed lack
not clad in their robes of gol
plunge into unending hell is
feathered arrow.

Wealth has been likened
been compared to kindling
that each of us will attain enl
do, yet in the precious word
dha Daitsūchishō[108] sat for
enlightenment,[109] but the Bu
manifest to him, he did not y

[107]The fire chariot is a chariot o
devils carry off those whose evil cau
hell, the lowest of the six states of
Kiyotsura is admonishing his liste
lifetime in order to avoid reincarnat

[108]Mahābhijñā jñānābhibhu, a
7 of the *Lotus Sutra* as having lived
past. His sixteen sons each were re
sixteenth being Shakyamuni.

[109]*Dōjō* or *Bodhimanda*, circle
where a Buddha attains enlightenme
of enlightenment.

The sens
heart itself.
vana. The
dha outsid
outside th
source of h
poem by D

Also, ir
Amida ar
"Shakyam
"eyeball."
is all the
earth to re

As we
Sleeping
ting, med
ing, sittir
with a s
mind the
tinctions,
body. Wi
nimbus
will be s
suddenly

[110]Saich
806 and fo
[111]The
dir.

ment,[112] the Realm of No Defilements.[113] You will reach the joyful capital of the realm of constant progress toward Nirvana.[114] There need be no doubt about this.

NARRATOR: Since he preaches with the fluency of a Bodhisattva, the travelers all bow to him as they go by.

How Hayahiro comes to the Shirakawa crossing on his way down to Tamba. He is wearing a wattle hat and riding a post horse. Perhaps frightened by the priest's umbrella, the horse on which Hayahiro is riding suddenly stumbles in alarm. It rears up and throws Hayahiro off the saddle and crashing to the ground. He is furious.

HAYAHIRO: You foolish priest! Even though I was on horseback you waved your umbrella around without hesitation, and you made me fall from my horse. Idiot!

NARRATOR: He grabs hold of the umbrella. Tadamitsu looks at him intently.

TADAMITSU: So, my father's murderer Hayahiro! You must recognize Tadamitsu!

NARRATOR: He pulls the pole out of the umbrella and sticks a spear blade into the long handle. He charges, yelling, "You won't get away!"

HAYAHIRO: Lord help me![115]

---

[112]The Pure Land, Amida's Western Paradise.

[113]Vimala, the realm of absolute purity. This is the world into which the eight-year-old daughter of the naga king is instantly transported upon attaining enlightenment. The story of her miraculous enlightenment is told in Chapter 11 of the *Lotus Sutra*. It is the extreme example that any living being, even the young and female, can attain enlightenment.

[114]*Futai* "constant progress" or "no backsliding" is an epithet of all Buddhas. The Pure Land sect refers to the Western Paradise as the Realm of Constant Progress, the land from which none fall away, and teaches that faith in the vows of Amida Buddha assures the believer of such constant progress.

[115]Literally "praise the three treasures."

NARRATOR: Hayahiro pulls up his horse, leaps on, and rides, whipping the animal.

TADAMITSU: Spineless coward! Come back! Come back here!

NARRATOR: Tadamitsu runs after him shouting until he is out of breath. He looks just like the Guardian God Idaten.[116] He chases after Hayahiro about half way, but Hayahiro is riding on a fleet-footed horse[117] and Tadamitsu pauses about fourteen or fifteen chō[118] behind him, under the Sagari pine tree.[119] He intends to start after him again, and yet—what's this?—his feet will not take him. Tadamitsu has been sleeping in the fields and has not eaten for two or three days. His throat is parched and he is staggering, barely able to drag one foot along.

TADAMITSU: My divine protection has run out! Oh, how horrible!

NARRATOR: He stands gnashing his teeth. Then—is it truly a gift from heaven? Here beneath the tree he finds, cast aside, some food which had been put out as an offering cake for the dead.[120]

TADAMITSU: Thank Heavens! How fortunate!

NARRATOR: He eats it in one bite. He gives his body a shake

---

[116]Sanscrit; Skanda, one of eight generals protecting the southern quarter of the world. A statue of this ferocious, heavily armored guardian is sometimes kept facing the main hall of a temple as protection.

[117]Ashinami hayahiro, a pun on Hayahiro's name, haya-"fast," provides the meaning "fleet-footed."

[118]As a measure of distance, one chō equals about 119 yards.

[119]The Sagari pine was a famous old pine tree at Ichijōji in northern Kyoto. The name is introduced here to link with jūyongo chō sagari "[to stop] 14 or 15 chō behind."

[120]Chikamatsu used this same idea, nourishment from an offering for the dead, in the early play Ota-in Kaichō, and it was subsequently borrowed in Semimaru nido no shusse.

and pounds his powerful feet on the ground. He appears as strong as the Kongo Guardian God.[121]

TADAMITSU: Well, a thousand, ten thousand *li* in one bound!

NARRATOR: Saying this he rushes off again. In no time at all he is up to the flowing waters of the Kamiya River[122] and he shouts out. He seizes hold of the rear trappings of Hayahiro's horse and stabs it. The horse collapses, suffering. Hayahiro dismounts.

HAYAHIRO: All right!

NARRATOR: They match swords and Hayahiro wards off Tadamitsu's blows; but a spear thrust with single-minded power, enough strength to penetrate rock, pierces Hayahiro's left ribs. Since he falls backward, the spear suddenly drives in deeply. Tadamitsu pulls it out, lays Hayahiro down and sits astride him like a horse.

TADAMITSU: My father's murderer is the enemy of many people. Know the resentment I have felt all these years!

NARRATOR: He strikes two or three times with his sword.

TADAMITSU: How happy I am! How fine I feel!

NARRATOR: He is weeping tears of joy.

TADAMITSU: Now first I'll go delight my mother by telling her about this.

NARRATOR: So saying he cuts off the head, sticks it on his spear, and hoists the spear on his shoulder. As if flying he hurries off to the mansion of Sakagami at Ichijō Ōmiya where Semimaru is. He feels great happiness.

SCENE 2: At Sakagami's Mansion

NARRATOR: Without even being announced he calls out in a loud voice.

[121] One of two ferocious guardian kings whose statues guard the gate of Buddhist temples. Such statues hold the *kongo vajra* "diamond scepter."

[122] A tributary of the Katsura River, it flows past the west side of the Kitano shrine in Kyoto.

TADAMITSU: Senju Tarō Tadamitsu has come after taking the head of the enemy Hayahiro!

NARRATOR: Mareyo, Kiyotsura, and the prince and Naohime come rushing out calling, "Wonderful, wonderful!"

MAREYO, ETC.: What a praiseworthy deed!

NARRATOR: They rejoice heartily. He tells them in detail of his recent hardships and of how he warded off starvation with a dead man's offering cake when he was starving under the Sagari pine.

TADAMITSU: I want to tell my mother and delight her. Quickly, take me to her.

NARRATOR: When he says this everyone starts weeping, but they don't explain anything.

TADAMITSU: I don't understand. What is it? Tell me!

NARRATOR: Mareyo holds back his tears and answers.

MAREYO: Even now it pains me to have to speak of this, but, about your aged mother, she caught cold about twenty days ago. Though we tried every means of treating her it was to no avail. The evening before last she died. From what you have just told us, the offering cake that you ate must have been an offering for your late mother.

NARRATOR: Before he has finished speaking, Tadamitsu collapses with a gasp and cries without restraint. His heart is pitiful as he weeps more and more.

TADAMITSU: Well, did I sustain my life when I was starving and did I then achieve my goal through a death offering for my mother? My mother thought of her child straight through to her grave. How grateful I am for that warm relationship between us. I had no idea that it would be this way. I came hurrying back here proudly to see her face, but that was useless. What an unpredictable world this is!

NARRATOR: Unmindful of the eyes of the others, he raises his voice, lamenting and weeping.

KIYOTSURA, ETC.: Yes, that is true; you are right.

NARRATOR: Each of the others must wring out his sleeves. After a little while Tadamitsu speaks again.

TADAMITSU: Oh, I ought not grieve. Even though my parents and my sister lost their lives, it was to help your position in the world. Since I have killed the enemy, I want to argue at the court on your behalf and fulfill my filial duty to my parents.

NARRATOR: He stops himself from weeping as he speaks. Kiyotsura interrupts him.

KIYOTSURA: We feel that way too, and yet, since the month before last Naohime has shown signs of being pregnant, and so we have been perplexed and have been delaying. Now let's quickly go report to the emperor.

NARRATOR: As they are consulting about various things the prince's elder sister, the princess, enters in a stately manner.

SAKAGAMI: So you are Tadamitsu. I appreciate your loyalty. I am called Sakagami and I am the older sister of Semimaru. As a deformity caused by karma my hair grows upward, and so my father the emperor hates me and I must live in this lonely place. But this is my fate from past existences and so prayers won't help me. And Semimaru's blindness is only a punishment in this lifetime, wrought by the single-minded will of his wife who died of jealousy. Also there is Naohime's pregnancy. A baby born under such resentment will surely be deformed. Originally Semimaru's wife bore no hostility and was blameless. Let us invite the priest of the Agui[123] to perform ceremonies for her soul for forty-nine days at Uji River. If we can soothe her dead soul, Semimaru's eyes will be opened again, Naohime will deliver safely and it will be a good-tempered, handsome boy baby. Hurry! Hurry!

[123] The Agui school of shōdō popular preachers had its head-quarters in northwestern Kyoto. As discussed in Chapter 2, these preachers had a place in the history of sekkyō.

265

NARRATOR: When she says this everyone agrees that it is reasonable. A messenger is sent to the holy man. Their thoughts turn to Uji, to the southeast of the capital, and now, on a propitious day they begin the ceremonies.

SCENE 3: The History of the
Ten Months of Pregnancy

NARRATOR: The days have accumulated like the fish trapped in woven weirs in Uji River,[124] and today is the day for the ceremony of the fulfilled vow.[125] The prince and Naohime, as the petitioners, are seated to the right and left of the altar. This is a royal temple visit and everyone has heard of it, both in the capital and in the nearby provinces. Devout pilgrims—old and young, men and women, the mighty and the humble, city people and countryfolk—are crowded together sleeve to sleeve in a lively throng. The priest of the Agui, a follower of En no Gyoja,[126] wears a *suzukake* robe[127] in which he had passed through Mount Omine[128] and scat-

[124]The opening line of this section contains a complicated set of puns. *Uji no ajirogi* are weirs woven of bamboo stakes set into the river bed to trap fish. *Hi o kasaneru* means both "the days pile up" and "the *hio* [whitebait] accumulate [against the weir]."

[125]Today is the forty-ninth and last day culminating seven weeks' rites.

[126]The description of the priest is identical to one in the Nō play *Aoi no ue*. En no Gyoja (634–701) was the founder of the Shūgendō (Yamabushi), a sect of Buddhist ascetics who practice mountain-climbing austerities. He founded a monastery on Mount Omine in Yamato province, and this mountain complex is held sacred by the sect.

[127]An over-robe of hemp worn by mountain ascetics on ascents.

[128]Omine is here called the Peak of Both Parts—Womb and Diamond—a reference to two mandalas, the *Kongokai* and *Taizōkai* "world of the diamond" and "world of the womb" respectively. In esoteric Buddhism, Shingon, and the mountain ascetic sects these are used to represent the dual aspect of the cosmos.

tered the sacred dew of the seven jewels.[129] And he wears a robe of forbearance to protect him from impurity. His disciples, also excellent in their knowledge of the rites, attend him on both sides as he approaches the altar. First he recites healing incantations.

PRIEST: I praise Buddha. I bow repeatedly. I speak reverently. Her spirit is calmed. It attains the realm of passionless Nirvana.[130] Now there is no thought of "self" or "other." At the time of enlightenment the entire world is a vacuum. We think of the three worlds only because of delusions.[131] Anger and happiness arise in confusion; because of this both grief and pleasure never cease. They seem to be flowers! It seems to be snow! The brocade of maples at Tatsuta River. The clouds at Yoshino. Since it is not reality, the dream does not end. If there is insufficient water, the moon cannot dwell reflected in it. To these paper offerings which I now flutter I invite the wind of Inherent Existence.[132] May the darkness of illusion be dispelled!

Well, now, as for the ceremonies of the practitioners:

For the first seven days they use mandalas.

For the second seven days they release living animals.

For the third seven days they make water-pouring offer-

[129] A part of the Pure Land paradise is said to be a grove of dew-laden trees of jewels. The seven jewels are variously described in different sutras. One list includes gold, silver, lapis lazuli, crystal, agate, ruby, and carnelian.

[130] *Muro mujō no hōkai* "the dharma realm without illusion and without constancy."

[131] The three worlds are an illusion of the unenlightened. They are the world of desire, the world of form, and the formless spirit world. This sentence of the text and the one preceding it are quoted from the Nirvana sutra.

[132] *Aji-hompushō* "the letter *a* is originally uncreated." A tenet of esoteric Buddhism illustrating the truth that all elements exist inherently and nothing is newly created.

267

ings for the hungry spirits, offerings like that by which the dragon-maiden became a Buddha.

For the fourth seven days they recite the mantra of light.[133]

For the fifth seven days, how exquisite! they chant the Lotus Sutra.

For the sixth seven days they chant the *Rishu-kyō*.[134]

This month, this day, is the forty-ninth, called the great expiration of the vow. It is the ceremony to help a pregnant woman give birth safely. By our ceremonies now may she[135] forget her enmity. May her eyes look protectively upon us.

NARRATOR: He says this and then recites the aspects of the ten months of pregnancy, a laudable recitation.

PRIEST: In the first month a spirit takes form within the body. Its shape is just like a hen's egg. Originally this was one drop of seed. As regards its shape, the chaos has not yet been divided. As far as its name is concerned, it is called the Great Origin and the Great Beginning. In Shinto it is called *Kunitokotachi no mikoto*.[136] The Confucian scholars call it Heaven's Giving Its Essence to the People. In Buddhism it is called the Original Vairocana; this is the original essence of the void. It is the responsibility of Fudō Myō-ō.[137]

In the second month the Yin and Yang spirits harmonize

[133]*Kōmyō shingon* "the mantra of light," a mantra also recited while sprinkling sand over the body of a dead person to insure rebirth in the Pure Land. The mantra destroys evil karma through the power of the light of the Buddha.

[134]The *prajñāpāramitā-naya-sūtra*, also called in Japanese the *Hanya-rishu-kyō*.

[135]Semimaru's dead wife.

[136]According to the *Kojiki*, the first god created in the Age of the Gods.

[137]In each of the ten lunar months of pregnancy the fetus is here said to be guarded or protected by a different Buddha or Bodhisattva. Here, the Buddha Fudō myō-o, Sanscrit, Acala.

and become one spirit. The form is revealed as the shape of a single *vajra*. [138] This is called the Great Beginning. It is the beginning of the form and the continuation of the spirit. It is the responsibility of Yakushi Nyorai. [139]

When we reach the third month, the human consciousness is not individuated. It shows feeling for the first time. In India Shakyamuni called this Buddha consciousness. In China the sages gave it the name Illustrious Virtue, [140] and in our country it is respected as the divine consciousness. Although the names given differ from each other, the three teachings agree. Yes, yes. Now this takes the form of the three-pronged *vajra* and is the responsibility of the Bodhisattva Monju. [141]

Already in the fourth month the five elements [142]—earth, water, fire, wind—are linked together. The shape is that of the five-pronged *vajra* of the five cardinal virtues. It is guarded by the Bodhisattva Fugen. [143]

Then when we reach the fifth month, the six sense

---

[138] The *vajra* "diamond" was originally an ancient Indian weapon. In esoteric Buddhism it is used as a symbol of the diamantine penetrating brilliance of the Buddha mind. The single vajra (*dokkō*) here referred to is the simplest of several shapes for this symbol.

[139] Bhaiṣajya-guru, the Buddha of Healing.

[140] *Meitoku*, the virtue derived by man from heaven. It is discussed as one of the principal subjects in the Confucian classic *The Great Learning*. See Legge, *The Chinese Classics*, I, 355–81.

[141] Mañjuśri, the Bodhisattva of Supreme Wisdom. The left-hand attendant of Shakyamuni.

[142] Chikamatsu actually lists only the first four of the five elements, omitting space. The five elements are also used to name the five parts of the body—arms, knees, and head—and it here may be taken to mean that the fetus has attained recognizably human form.

[143] Samantabhadra-bodhisattva, the right-hand attendant of Shakyamuni; he typified the teaching, meditation, and practice of the Buddha.

TEXTS

organs[144] and the hands and feet are formed. All parts of the body are now completed. From this time on a principal guardian Buddha is decided upon to protect the body. The mother's attendants wrap the stomach obi, and this period is the responsibility of the Bodhisattva Jizō.[145]

When it gets to the sixth month, likes and desires arise spontaneously. It takes hold of the mother's nipples with its mouth and drinks her milk by the gallon.[146] The Kannon of Great Compassion[147] guards this period.

When it reaches the seventh month, graciously the Buddha considers the life in the three worlds bound by karma. He places on the baby's head a round jewel on which is carved the cycle of cause and effect, the wheel of the baby's predestined fate. Now it is the responsibility of the Bodhisattva Miroku.[148]

In the eighth month it is guarded by the Bodhisattva Ashuku.[149] As the round jewel turns it forms the placenta.

In the ninth month it is fully grown; because it has consciousness, the evil demons and evil spirits in the universe blow and blow their malicious vapors, and if the baby is born into this world they watch intently for an opportunity to lead it into their own paths of evil.[150] The baby is influenced by what its mother and father do and by what they think. If they do good, it will be a good person. If they do

[144]Eye, ear, nose, tongue, sense of touch, and faculty of intellect.
[145]Kṣitigarbha-bodhisattva, represented as a monk with shaved head; in Japan he is considered a special protector of children.
[146]No commentator has offered any explanation for this remarkable prenatal feat. The quantity of milk described in Japanese is *san koku roku to*, about 165 gallons!
[147]Avalokiteśvara.
[148]Maitreya-bodhisattva. The Future Buddha.
[149]Akṣobhya-buddha.
[150]This is apparently a folk understanding of the dangers of premature birth.

evil it will become an evil person. This is called the boundary between paradise and hell. The gods of birth are decided on and it is guarded by the Bodhisattva Seishi.[151]

In the tenth month it is the responsibility of Aizen Myō-ō.[152] Among the six types of life and the four types of birth,[153] among the twenty-five abodes,[154] there is none more honored than man since each man has the Buddha nature. Others and myself, we are all one Buddha. Let your malice be gone, to the last particle. Return to your original Buddha nature.[155]

On abira unken tara takanman kyūkyū nyo ritsuryō

NARRATOR: He chants a sacred spell. It is of unusual, surpassing sacredness. The sound of his voice reading the sutras, together with the sound of the winds on the river, echoes to the heavens gratifyingly. Then—how strange—from among the sacred pines, the spirit of Semimaru's wife, like a shadow, manifests herself.

SEMIMARU'S WIFE: Drawn by the power of this sutra I attain Buddhahood just like Devadatta who committed the five sins[156] and like the eight-year-old dragon maiden. My re-

---

[151]Mahāsthāma, the Bodhisattva to the right of Amitābha. The guardian of Buddha wisdom.

[152]Rāgarāja, a ferocious-looking but loving and protective deity.

[153]Viviparous, oviparous, birth from moisture, birth by metamorphosis.

[154]The twenty-five abodes of living beings are the four evil worlds, the four continents of the world of men, the six heavens of the world of desire, the seven heavens of the world of form, and the four heavens of the formless world. Iwano, *Japanese-English Buddhist Dictionary*, p. 217.

[155]He is here, again, directly addressing the spirit of Semimaru's dead wife.

[156]Devadatta was an evil cousin and a rival of Shakyamuni. His five sins were: (1) destroying the harmony of the religious community; (2) stoning Shakyamuni and causing him to bleed; (3) causing a

sentment has been dispelled, and now I shall become a Buddha of the five wisdoms.[157]

NARRATOR: Even her voice as she speaks is sweet, and she manifests herself as Nyoi Kannon,[158] gives off light and vanishes. Shone on by this glimmering light, Semimaru's eyes suddenly open. "What!" he says, and the lords and followers, high and low, all rejoice excitedly. Then they give prayers of thanks to the priest, and the prince and his lady return to court.

Their descendants prosper. The country flourishes with everlasting luck and prosperity. For countless tens of thousand generations their line continues on.

---

wild elephant to be set loose to trample Shakyamuni; (4) killing a nun; (5) attempting to poison Shakyamuni. Despite these sins, even he is seen as capable of attaining Buddhahood.

[157] Esoteric Buddhism distinguishes five types of wisdom characteristic of an enlightened being. See Iwano, *Japanese-English Buddhist Dictionary*, pp. 77–78.

[158] Also called Nyoirin Kannon, one of six representations of Kannon, she is a six-armed Buddha holding, among other implements, the gem of satisfaction and the wheel of the law.

Note: For all books in the series "Nihon koten bungaku tai-kei," published by Iwanami Shoten, the series title in the following entries is abbreviated as NKBT.

Amano Fumio. "Semimaru no tanjō," *Kokubungaku zasshi,* January, 1977, pp. 52–65.

Araki Shigeru. "Chūsei makki no bungaku," Iwanami kōza nihon bungaku shi, Vol. VI. Tokyo, Iwanami Shoten, 1959.

Beal, Samuel, *Buddhist Records of the Western World.* 2 vols. London, Kegan Paul, Trench, Trübner and Co., Ltd., 1906.

Brandon, James R. *Kabuki.* Cambridge, Mass., Harvard University Press, 1975.

Brower, Robert H., and Earl Miner. *Japanese Court Poetry.* Stanford, Calif., Stanford University Press, 1961.

Butler, Kenneth Dean. "The Textual Evolution of the *Heike Monogatari,*" *Harvard Journal of Asian Studies,* XXVI, 1966, 5–51.

[Shinshaku sōzu] *Chikamatsu kessaku zenshū.* Mizutani Futō, ed. 5 vols. Tokyo, Waseda Daigaku Shuppanbu, 1910.

Chikamatsu Monzaemonshū. Kawamata Keiichi, ed. Nihon bungaku sōsho, series 2, Vol. XI. Tokyo, Nihon Bungaku Sōsho Kankōkai, 1928.

Chikamatsu zenshū. Fujii Otoo, ed. 12 vols. Osaka, Osaka Asahi Shinbunsha, 1925–28.

Daijimmei jiten, 10 vols. Tokyo, Heibonsha, 1953–55.

Dunn, Charles J. *The Early Japanese Puppet Drama.* London, Luzac and Co., Ltd., 1966.

Fuboku wakashō. Nakatsukasa Eijirō, ed. [Kochū] kokka taikei, Vol. XXII. Tokyo, Kokumin Toshō, 1931.

Fūshi kaden in *Karonshū nōgakuronshū,* Hisamatsu Sen'ichi and Nishio Minoru, eds. NKBT, Vol. LXV. Tokyo, Iwanami Shoten, 1961.

Gempei seisuiki. Ikebe Yoshikata, ed. Kokubun sōsho, 3d. ed.; Vol. VIII. Tokyo, Hakubunkan, 1918.

Genji monogatari. Yamagishi Tokuhei, ed. NKBT, Vol. XV, Tokyo, Iwanami Shoten, 1959.

Gikeiki. Okami Masao, ed. NKBT, Vol. XXXVII. Tokyo, Iwanami Shoten, 1959.

Gōdanshō in *Gunsho ruijū*. Hanawa Hokiichi, comp. Vol. XVII. Tokyo, Keizai Zasshi-sha, 1904.

Golay, Jacqueline, "Pathos and Farce: Zatō Plays of the Kyōgen Repertoire," *Monumenta Nipponica*, Summer, 1973, pp. 139–49.

Gosenwakashū. Nakatsukasa Eijirō, ed. [Kochū] kokka taikei, Vol. III. Tokyo, Kokumin Toshō, 1927.

Goshūiwakashu. Nakatsukasa Eijirō, ed. [Kochū] kokka taikei Vol. III. Tokyo, Kokumin Toshō, 1927.

Gōtō Tanji. *Senki monogatari no kenkyū*. Tokyo, Chikuha Shoten, 1936.

Hagiwara Sakutarō. *Hagiwara Sakutarō zenshū*, Vol. III. Tokyo, Shinchōsha, 1959.

Hayashiya Tatsusaburō. *Chūsei geinōshi no kenkyū*. Tokyo, Iwanami Shoten, 1960.

—— *Kodai kokka no kaitai*. Tokyo, Tokyo Daigaku Shuppankai, 1955.

Hayashiya Tatsusaburō et al. "Semimaru o megutte," *Kanze*, May, 1962, pp. 23–29.

Heike monogatari. Takagi Ichinosuke et al., eds. NKBT, Vols. XXXII–XXXIII. Tokyo, Iwanami Shoten, 1960.

Hekianshō in *Gunsho ruijū*. Hanawa Hokiichi, comp. Vol. X. Tokyo, Keizai Zasshi-sha, 1904.

Hiramatsuke kyūzōbon Heike monogatari. Yamanouchi Junzō and Kimura Akira, eds. Kobe, Koten Kankōkai, 1965.

Hoff, Frank, and Willi Flindt. "The Life Structure of Noh," *Concerned Theatre Japan*, Spring, 1973, pp. 209–56.

Hōjōki, Tsurezuregusa. Nishio Minoru, ed. NKBT, Vol. XXX. Tokyo, Iwanami Shoten, 1957.

Hori Ichirō. *Waga kuni minkan shinkōshi no kenkyū*. 2 vols. Tokyo, Sōgensha, 1955.

Ise monogatari. Ōtsu Yūichi and Tsukishima Yū, eds. NKBT, Vol. IX. Tokyo, Iwanami Shoten, 1957.

Iwano Masao. *Japanese-English Buddhist Dictionary*. Tokyo, Daitō Shuppansha, 1965.

Iwasaki Takeo. "Sekkyō *Karukaya* to kinki no sekai," *Bungaku*, January, 1972, pp. 54–65.

Jinja taikan. Tokyo, Nihon Dempo Tsūshinsha, 1940.

Kadokawa Gen'yoshi. "Katarimono to Jishin mōsō," *Kokubungaku kaishàku to kanshō*, August, 1967, pp. 110–13.

Kanai Kiyomitsu. *Nō no kenkyū*. Tokyo, Ōfūsha, 1969.

Bibliography

Kanginshū in *Chūsei kinsei kayōshū*. Shinma Shin'ichi, ed. NKBT, Vol. XLIV. Tokyo, Iwanami Shoten, 1961.

Keene, Donald. *Anthology of Japanese Literature*. New York, Grove Press, 1955.

—— *Bunraku*. Tokyo, Kodansha International, 1965.

—— "The Hippolytus Triangle, East and West," in *Yearbook of Comparative and General Literature*, No. 11 (supplement), 1962, pp. 162–71.

—— *Twenty Plays of the Nō Theatre*. New York, Columbia University Press, 1970.

Kikkawa Eishi. *Nihon ongaku no rekishi*. Osaka, Sōgensha, 1967.

Kikuchi Ryōichi. "Shōdō bungei," *Iwanami kōza Nihon bungakushi*, Vol. IV. Tokyo, Iwanami Shoten, 1958.

Kishi Shōzō. *Shintōshū*. Tokyo, Heibonsha, 1967.

Kohon setsuwashū sōsakuin. Yamauchi Yōichirō, ed. Tokyo, Kazama Shobō, 1969.

Kojiki. Kurano Kenji and Takeda Yūkichi, eds. NKBT, Vol. I. Tokyo, Iwanami Shoten, 1958.

Kokinwakashū. Saeki Umetomo ed. NKBT, Vol. VIII. Tokyo, Iwanami Shoten, 1958.

Kokushō sōmokuroku, Vol. V. Tokyo, Iwanami Shoten, 1967.

Kondō Yoshi. "Heike biwa izen," *Bungaku*, Vol. XXIX, no. 10, 1961, pp. 69–80.

Konishi Jin'ichi. "New Approaches to the Study of the Nō Drama," *Bulletin of Tokyo Kyōiku University Literature Department*, March, 1960.

Konjaku monogatari. Yamada Yoshio *et al.*, eds. NKBT, Vols. XXII–XXVI. Tokyo, Iwanami Shoten, 1959–63.

Kōsai Tsutomu. "Semimaru—sakusha to honsetsu," *Kanze*, May, 1962, pp. 20–22.

Kusabe Tsuneichi. "*Sanshō dayū* ni tsuite," *Bungaku*, January, 1954, pp. 65–78.

Legge, James. *The Chinese Classics* I. Hong Kong, Hong Kong University Press, 1960.

—— *The Works of Mencius*. New York, Dover Publications, Inc., 1970.

McCullough, Helen Craig. *Tales of Ise*, Stanford Calif., Stanford University Press, 1968.

—— *Yoshitsune*. Stanford, Calif., Stanford University Press, 1966.

Makura no soshi, Murasaki Shikibu nikki. Ikeda Kikan *et al.*, eds. NKBT, Vol. XIX. Tokyo, Iwanami Shoten, 1965.

Man'yōshū. Takagi Ichinosuke *et al.*, eds. NKBT, Vols. IV–VII. Tokyo, Iwanami Shoten, 1957–62.

Matsunaga, Alicia. *The Buddhist Philosophy of Assimilation.* Tokyo and Rutland, Vt., Charles E. Tuttle Co., 1969.

Miyake Noboru. "Utaikata kōza *Semimaru,*" *Kanze,* May, 1962, pp. 34–37.

Miyoshi Kiyoyuki. "Iken jūni kajō" in *Gunsho ruijū.* Hanawa Hokiichi, comp. Vol. XVII. Tokyo, Keizai Zasshi-sha, 1904.

Mochizuki Shinkō. *Bukkyō daijiten.* Tsukamoto Zenryū, ed. 6 vols. Tokyo, Sekai Seiten Kankōkai, 1954.

Morris, Ivan. *The Life of an Amorous Woman.* New York, New Directions, 1963.

—— *The Pillow Book of Sei Shōnagon* 2 vols. New York, Columbia University Press, 1967.

Mumyōshō in *Karonshū nōgakuronshū.* Hisamatsu Sen'ichi and Nishio Minoru, eds. NKBT, Vol. LXV. Tokyo, Iwanami Shoten, 1961.

Muroki Yatarō. *Katarimono (mai, sekkyō, kojōruri) no kenkyū.* Tokyo, Kazama Shobō, 1970.

—— "Sekkyō kenkyū no tenbō," *Bungaku,* September, 1974, pp. 33–43.

—— "Sekkyō to Semimaru," *Kanazawa daigaku kyōikugakubu kiyō,* No. 12, 1964, pp. 157–68.

Mushakoji Minoru. *Heike monogatari to biwa hōshi.* Tokyo, Awaji Shoten Shinsha, 1957.

Nakayama Tarō. *Nihon mōjinshi.* Tokyo, Seikōkan Shuppanbu, 1945.

Nogami Toyoichirō, *Nōgaku zensho,* Vol. I. Tokyo, Sōgensha, 1952.

Nose Asaji. *Nōgaku genryū kō.* Tokyo, Iwanami Shoten, 1955.

O'Neill, P. G. *Early Nō Drama.* London, Lund Humphries, 1958.

Origuchi Shinobu. *Origuchi Shinobu zenshū,* Vol. X. Tokyo, Chūōkōron-sha, 1956.

Rankyoku kusemai yōshū. Takano Tatsuyuki ed. Nihon kayō shūsei, Vol. V. Tokyo, Tōkyōdō, 1960.

Reischauer, Edwin O. *Ennin's Travels in T'ang China.* New York, Ronald Press, 1955.

Ruijū kokushi in *Kokushi taikei,* Vol. V. Kuroita Katsumi, ed. Tokyo, Yoshikawa Kōbunkan, 1933.

Sadler, Arthur L. "Heike Monogatari," *Transactions of the Asia Society of Japan,* Vol. XLVI, No. 2, 1918; Vol. XLIX, No. 1, 1921.

Bibliography

Sanari Kentarō, ed. *Yōkyoku taikan.* rev. ed.; 7 vols. Tokyo, Meiji Shoin, 1964.

Sandai jitsuroku in [Kōtei hyōchū] *Rikkokushi,* Vol. IX. Saeki Ariyoshi, ed. Tokyo, Asahi Shimbunsha, 1931.

Sandō in *Karonshū nōgakuronshū.* Hisamatsu Sen'ichi and Nishio Monoru, eds., NKBT, LXV. Tokyo, Iwanami Shoten, 1961.

Sarugaku dangi in *Karonshū nōgakuronshū.* Hisamatsu Sen'ichi and Nishio Minoru, eds., NKBT, Vol. LXV. Tokyo, Iwanami Shoten, 1961.

Seishi kakei daijiten. Ōta Akira, comp. 3 vols. Tokyo, Seishi kakei daijiten kankōkai, 1934–36.

Senzaishū. Nakatsukasa Eijirō, ed. [Kochū] kokka taikei, Vol. IV. Tokyo, Kokumin Toshō, 1926.

Shinkokinwakashū. Hisamatsu Sen'ichi *et al.,* eds. NKBT, Vol. XXVIII. Tokyo, Iwanami Shoten, 1958.

Shokukokinwakashū. Nakatsukasa Eijirō, ed. [Kochū] kokka taikei, Vol. V. Tokyo, Kokumin Toshō, 1928.

Shugyokushū. Nakatsukasa Eijirō, ed. [Kochū] kokka taikei, Vol. X. Tokyo, Kokumin Toshō, 1928.

Shūiwakashū. Nakatsukasa Eijirō, ed. [Kochū] kokka taikei, Vol. III. Tokyo, Kokumin Toshō, 1926.

Soothill, William Edward, and Lewis Hodous. *A Dictionary of Chinese Buddhist Terms.* London, Kegan Paul, Trench, Trübner and Co., Ltd., 1937.

Suwa Haruo. "Chikamatsu to Ōmi kuni Takakannon Kinshōji," *Kinsei bungei,* November, 1962, pp. 45–55.

Takizawa Bakin. *Enseki zasshi,* Nihon zuihitsu taisei, series 2, Vol. I. Tokyo, Nihon Zuihitsu Taisei Kankōkai, 1929.

Tanabe Hisao. *Nihon no gakki.* Tokyo, Sōshisha Shuppan Kabushiki Kaisha, 1964.

—— *Nihon ongakushi.* Tokyo, Tokyo Denki Daigaku Shuppanbu, 1963.

Tanaka Makoto. "Osaka monogurui," in *Yōkyoku Kyōgen.* Nishio Minoru *et al.,* eds. Kokugo kokubungaku kenkyūshi taisei, Vol. VIII. Tokyo, Sanshōdō, 1961, pp. 253–58.

Tanizaki Jun'ichirō. *Tanizaki Jun'ichirō - zenshū,* Vol. XVI. Tokyo, Chūōkōron-sha, 1968.

Tashiro Keiichirō. "Yōkyoku *Semimaru* ni tsuite," *Hikaku bungaku kenkyū,* No. 23, March, 1973, pp. 116–40 and No. 24, September, 1973, pp. 43–56.

Teele, Roy E. "The Structure of the Japanese Noh Play," in *Chinese and Japanese Music-Dramas.* J. I. Crump and William P. Malm, eds. Michigan Papers in Chinese Studies, No. 19. Ann Arbor, Mich., Center for Chinese Studies, University of Michigan, 1975.

Tōkan kikō. Sasaki Nobutsuna *et al.,* eds. Nihon koten zensho, rev. ed., Vol. LXIV. Tokyo, Asahi Shinbunsha, 1956.

Tomikura Tokujirō. "Akashi Kakuichi o megutte," *Kokugo kokubun,* October, 1952, pp. 37–46.

—— "Biwa hōshira no yakuwari," *Kokubungaku kaishaku to kanshō,* November, 1960, pp. 13–25.

Toshiyori zuinō. Sasaki Nobutsuna, ed. Nihon kagaku taikei, Vol. I, Tokyo, Kazama Shobō, 1957.

Tōzai zuihitsu in *Ujishūi monogatari.* Fujii Otoō, ed., Yūhōdō bunko, Series 2, Vol. VII. Tokyo, Yūhōdō Shoten, 1914.

Umehara Takeshi. *Jigoku no shisō.* Tokyo, Chūōkōron-sha, 1967.

Wakan roeishū, Ryōjin hishō. Kawaguchi Hisao and Shida Nobuyoshi, eds. NKBT, Vol. LXXIII. Tokyo, Iwanami Shoten, 1965.

Waley, Arthur. *The Nō Plays of Japan.* New York, Grove Press, 1957.

Watson, Burton. *Records of the Grand Historian of China.* New York. Columbia University Press, 1961.

Yamagami, Izumo. "Koto no katarigoto no keifu," *Bungaku,* August 1962, pp. 79–93.

Yashiro Kazuo. *Sakai no kamigami no monogatari.* Tokyo, Shindoku Shosha, 1971.

Yashirobon Heike monogatari. Kichō koten seki sōkan No. 9. Tokyo, Kadokawa Shoten, 1973.

Yasuda, Kenneth K. "The Structure of *Hagoromo,* a Nō Play," *Harvard Journal of Asian Studies,* Vol. XXXIII, 1973, pp. 5–89.

Yokoyama Shigeru. *Sekkyō shōhon shū.* 3 vols. Tokyo. Kadokawa Shoten, 1968.

Yokoyama Tadashi. "Jōruri *Semimaro* to *Semimaru,*" in *Kinsei engeki ronsō.* Osaka, Seibundō, 1976.

—— "Onna Semimaru," *Jōruri zasshi,* June, 1943, pp. 35–38.

Yoshikawa Rikichi. "Semimaru setsuwa no genryū to Heianchō jidai no zokugaku riyō ni tsuite," *Kyoto teikoku daigaku kokubungakkai kinen rombunshū.* Kyoto, Kyoto Daigaku Shuppanbu, 1911.

Yotsugi monogatari in *Zoku gunsho ruijū,* Vol. XXXII, Part 2. Tokyo, Zoku Gunsho Ruijū Kanseikai, 1926.

Bibliography

Yūda Yoshio. "Chikamatsu nenpyō," *Kokubungaku kaishaku to kanshō,* January, 1957, pp. 70–77.

Yūda Yoshio and Torigoe Bunzō. *Kamigata kyōgen hon.* Tokyo, Koten Bunko, 1963.

"Zeami no Nō—4." Panel discussion in *Kanze,* September, 1963, pp. 52–59.

INDEX

Index

Index

Studies in Oriental Culture

Translations from the Oriental Classics

Companions to Asian Studies

Approaches to Asian Civilization, ed. Wm. Theodore de Bary and Ainslie T. Embree · 1964

The Classic Chinese Novel: A Critical Introduction, by C. T. Hsia. Also in paperback ed. · 1968

Chinese Lyricism: Shih Poetry from the Second to the Twelfth Century, tr. Burton Watson. Also in paperback ed. · 1971

A Syllabus of Indian Civilization, by Leonard A. Gordon and Barbara Stoler Miller · 1971

Twentieth-Century Chinese Stories, ed. C. T. Hsia and Joseph S. M. Lau. Also in paperback ed. · 1971

A Syllabus of Chinese Civilization, by J. Mason Gentzler, 2d ed. · 1972

A Syllabus of Japanese Civilization, by H. Paul Varley, 2d ed. · 1972

An Introduction to Chinese Civilization, ed. John Meskill, with the assistance of J. Mason Gentzler · 1973

An Introduction to Japanese Civilization, ed. Arthur E. Tiedemann · 1974

A Guide to Oriental Classics, ed. Wm. Theodore de Bary and Ainslie T. Embree, 2d ed. Also in paperback ed. · 1975

Introduction to Oriental Civilizations

Wm. Theodore de Bary, *Editor*

Sources of Japanese Tradition	1958	Paperback ed., 2 vols.	1964
Sources of Indian Tradition	1958	Paperback ed., 2 vols.	1964
Sources of Chinese Tradition	1960	Paperback ed., 2 vols.	1964